Power of Money

Power of Money

Editor
Debarati Roy

Vij Books India Pvt. Ltd.
New Delhi (India)

Published by

Vij Books India Pvt Ltd
(Publishers, Distributors & Importers)
2/19 (Second Floor), Ansari Road, Darya Ganj
New Delhi - 110002
Phones: 91-11-43596460, 47340674
Fax: 91-11-47340674
web: www.vijbooks.com
e-mail : vijbooks@rediffmail.com

Copyright © 2011, Publisher

ISBN: 978-93-81411-16-2

All rights reserved. No part of this publication may be reproduced, utilized in any form or by any means, electronic or mechanical, including photocopying, recording or by any information storage or retrieval system, without permission in writing from the publisher.

Contents

Preface *vii*

1. **Introduction** 1

   Money and its Significance • Money Supply • Types of Money • Monetary Policy • Wealth and Exchange

2. **Historical Backdrop** 19

   Barter and Gift • Emergence of Money • Commodity Money • Standardised Coinage • Trade Bills of Exchange • Tallies • Goldsmith Bankers • Demand Deposits • Banknotes • Representative Money • Fiat Money • Statistical Verification • Money and Prices • Paper Money • The Greenbacks • Purchasing Power of Money

3. **Money and Practical Life** 125

   Social Development and Money • A World without Money • Money: Greediness or Generosity? • Attraction for Giving • Interest Rate • Freedom of not Receiving

4. **Money and Economic Development** 153

   Economy and Role of Money • New Role of Money in Admissions • Role of Money in Development • Money and Internet

(vi)

5. Gift Economy   **195**

The Backdrop • The Characteristics • Social Structures • Gift Economies • Social Theories • Religious Views

6. Money and Politics   **205**

One Possible Reason • Political Reform and Soft Money • Political Power through Money • Money Buying Political Power

7. Electronic Money   **219**

Electronic Money Systems • Centralised Systems • Decentralised Systems • Off-line Anonymous Systems • Hard vs Soft Electronic Currencies • Future Progression • Various Issues

8. Cash and Credit Finance   **225**

The Qualities • Most Exchangeable Commodity • Socialist Idea • Paper Money • Growth of Cash • Usury, an Evil? • Different Theories • Category of Capital

9. Purchasing Power   **259**

Monetary Systems and Purchasing Power • Gold Exchange Standard • Deposit Currency and Purchasing Power • Proportioned Deposit Currency • Disturbance of Equation and of Purchasing Power • Completion of the Credit Cycle • Making Purchasing Power More Stable • Bimetallism • Proposed Solution • Tabular Standard

Bibliography   301

Index   307

Preface

Money is power and it rules the roost all over. In the beginning of the social interaction, between human beings, the barter system worked quite well. The barter system was basically a trade arrangement and required that two or more parties had a mutual desire to trade and had goods that the other one wanted to acquire. In the small and primitive cultures of pre-historic times, this was often enough. The only commodities that anyone had any interest in, were food, clothing and weapons. If one person had a weapon, and the other had some food, a deal could easily be arranged. But, the barter system could not last forever.

It was because of the ability of the human mind to understand symbols and to assign value to them that we were able to develop a means of moving past the barter system. Money became the means by which civilization and socialisation took place. Now, when a person wished to do something beyond the production of the basics, such as a work of art, he did not have to wait for someone willing to trade the food, he desired for his art. He could trade the art for money, and trade the money for the food. Money became the middle-man that allowed diversification and growth.

Money also needed to be a unit of account. This means that it must have a set value that could be assigned to a product or a service to determine, where it stood in the overall economic picture. If one made a piece of art, one needed to be able to set a money value on it, and that same money value needed to be accepted by a food merchant. One must also be able to store the money at value. This means that the money and its value had to be durable and relatively unchanging. This means that one did not have to go and buy any number of items, as soon as one sold the art piece. One could save his or her money, and accumulate it for use at another time. This was the beginning of the idea of wealth. Money has been called the root of all evils, but it is also the root of all growth.

Money matters everywhere in society, and it threatens to crowd out democracy. A rich person can purchase a finer house, a nicer car, better food, more effective schools and more courteous services. Then, why should his money not purchase more political influence? This paradox is the profound radicalism of the democratic idea. And on all fronts, it is threatened by the resurgent power of money.

Here is a book on, 'Power of Money', as a subject. This is an endeavour — probably, first in the area — which covers the entire subject in one cover. This research-based study is bound to attract serious attention from all those, who have economic concerns in any manner. The undersigned would feel honoured, if this modest work succeeds in stirring the calm waters and awaken the economic circles, at least to some extent.

We are indebted to all the scholars, authors and compilers, whose valuable contributions, we have benefited from, while preparing this book. We are also thankful to the publishers and website operators, whose works, we have referred to, during the compilation of this book. And last but not the least, the undersigned expresses his whole hearted gratitude to all his associates, who extended their full cooperation in shaping and finalising this book.

Enlightening remarks and serious advisory notes are sincerely solicited and heartly welcome.

— ***Editor***

1

Introduction

Money is perhaps, the most significant entity in any society and economy. Money is any object or record that is generally accepted as payment for goods and services and repayment of debts in a given country or socio-economic context. The main functions of money are distinguished as: a medium of exchange; a unit of account; a store of value; and, occasionally in the past, a standard of deferred payment. Any kind of object or secure verifiable record that fulfils these functions can serve as money.

Money originated as commodity money, but nearly all contemporary money systems are based on fiat money. Fiat money is without intrinsic use value as a physical commodity, and derives its value by being declared by a government to be legal tender; that is, it must be accepted as a form of payment within the boundaries of the country, for "all debts, public and private".

The money supply of a country consists of currency (banknotes and coins) and bank money (the balance held in checking accounts and savings accounts). Bank money usually forms by far the largest part of the money supply.

Money and its Significance

Money plays an important role in people's lives. Some may deny it and say it is not important while yet another say it is. Whatever the case may be the fact is money cannot be ignored.

There's a popular saying money can't buy you good health. In the current scenario good health care costs money. The pills that you consume, the healthy food stuff, medical check ups, even exercising at a gym in the proper outfits comes with a price tag attached. Hence, this phrase is not applicable to the present situation. Another famous saying is money can't buy love. All women crave for security and stability that is provided by wealth. No woman would willingly choose to be poor.

They might be ok initially but eventually they strive to make money and prove a point to all concerned. Most women have a sixth sense when it comes to money matters. They are not greedy but just look for someone who can provide for them and the children to come. However, money is not the be all. It is just a stepping stone, a tool towards the final goal. It provides us with comfort, helps us eat three square meals a day and sleep in peace.

It helps make life simpler with various gadgets and equipments designed for the purpose of making things easier. It is not true that more money means a lavish lifestyle, these days money is required even for a normal lifestyle. There are all types of individuals in this society.

The stinking rich who were handed things on a platter and received credit cards and inheritances as gifts rather than the usual toys or hugs also exist in this world. These people end up believing money can buy anything and everything. It is important not to let money rule you and make you take bad decisions that interfere with your everyday life. Friendships even marriages may break due to the interference of money.

Do not let money rule your life or make it a competition to see who earns more. If you are in a relatively convenient financial position you could consider helping those less fortunate than you

Introduction

are. Donate old clothes, books, food items if possible even money. This can make a huge difference to those peoples life and leave you feeling richer.

History

The use of barter-like methods may date back to at least 100,000 years ago, though there is no evidence of a society or economy that relied primarily on barter. Instead, non-monetary societies operated largely along the principles of gift economics. When barter did occur, it was usually between either complete strangers or potential enemies.

Many cultures around the world eventually developed the use of commodity money. The shekel was originally a unit of weight, and referred to a specific weight of barley, which was used as currency. The first usage of the term came from Mesopotamia circa 3000 BC. Societies in the Americas, Asia, Africa and Australia used shell money – often, the shells of the money cowry (*Cypraea moneta L.* or *C. annulus L.*). According to Herodotus, the Lydians were the first people to introduce the use of gold and silver coins. It is thought by modern scholars that these first stamped coins were minted around 650–600 BC.

The system of commodity money eventually evolved into a system of representative money. This occurred because gold and silver merchants or banks would issue receipts to their depositors – redeemable for the commodity money deposited. Eventually, these receipts became generally accepted as a means of payment and were used as money. Paper money or banknotes were first used in China during the Song Dynasty. These banknotes, known as "jiaozi", evolved from promissory notes that had been used since the 7th century. However, they did not displace commodity money, and were used alongside coins.

Banknotes were first issued in Europe by Stockholms Banco in 1661, and were again also used alongside coins. The gold standard, a monetary system where the medium of exchange are paper notes that are convertible into preset, fixed quantities of gold, replaced the use of gold coins as currency in the 17th-19th centuries in Europe. These gold standard notes were made legal tender, and redemption into gold coins was discouraged. By the beginning of the 20th century almost all countries had adopted the gold standard, backing their legal tender notes with fixed amounts of gold.

After World War II, at the Bretton Woods Conference, most countries adopted fiat currencies that were fixed to the US dollar. The US dollar was in turn fixed to gold. In 1971 the US government suspended the convertibility of the US dollar to gold. After this many countries de-pegged their currencies from the US dollar, and most of the world's currencies became unbacked by anything except the governments' fiat of legal tender and the ability to convert the money into goods via payment.

Etymology

The word "money" is believed to originate from a temple of Hera, located on Capitoline, one of Rome's seven hills. In the ancient world Hera was often associated with money. The temple of Juno Moneta at Rome was the place where the mint of Ancient Rome was located.

The name "Juno" may derive from the Etruscan goddess Uni (which means "the one", "unique", "unit", "union", "united") and "Moneta" either from the Latin word "monere" (remind, warn, or instruct) or the Greek word "moneres" (alone, unique). In the Western world, a prevalent term for coin-money has been *specie*, stemming from Latin *in specie*, meaning 'in kind'.

Functions

In the past, money was generally considered to have the following four main functions, which are summed up in a rhyme found in older economics textbooks: "Money is a matter of functions four, a medium, a measure, a standard, a store." That is, money functions as a medium of exchange, a unit of account, a standard of deferred payment, and a store of value. However, modern textbooks now list only three functions, that of medium of exchange, unit of account, and store of value, not considering a standard of deferred payment as a distinguished function, but rather subsuming it in the others.

There have been many historical disputes regarding the combination of money's functions, some arguing that they need more separation and that a single unit is insufficient to deal with them all. One of these arguments is that the role of money as a medium of exchange is in conflict with its role as a store of value: its role as a store of value requires holding it without spending, whereas its role as a medium of exchange requires it to circulate. Others argue that storing of value is just deferral of the exchange, but does not diminish the fact that money is a medium of exchange that can be transported both across space and time. The term 'financial capital' is a more general and inclusive term for all liquid instruments, whether or not they are a uniformly recognised tender.

Medium of Exchange

When money is used to intermediate the exchange of goods and services, it is performing a function as a *medium of exchange*. It thereby avoids the inefficiencies of a barter system, such as the 'double coincidence of wants' problem.

Unit of Account

A *unit of account* is a standard numerical unit of measurement of the market value of goods, services, and other transactions. Also known as a "measure" or "standard" of relative worth and deferred payment, a unit of account is a necessary prerequisite for the formulation of commercial agreements that involve debt. To function as a 'unit of account', whatever is being used as money must be:

- Divisible into smaller units without loss of value; precious metals can be coined from bars, or melted down into bars again.
- *Fungible:* That is, one unit or piece must be perceived as equivalent to any other, which is why diamonds, works of art or real estate are not suitable as money.

- A specific weight, or measure, or size to be verifiably countable. For instance, coins are often milled with a reeded edge, so that any removal of material from the coin (lowering its commodity value) will be easy to detect.

Store Value

To act as a *store of value*, a money must be able to be reliably saved, stored, and retrieved – and be predictably usable as a medium of exchange when it is retrieved. The value of the money must also remain stable over time. Some have argued that inflation, by reducing the value of money, diminishes the ability of the money to function as a store of value.

Standard of Deferred Payment

While *standard of deferred payment* is distinguished by some texts, particularly older ones, other texts subsume this under other functions. A "standard of deferred payment" is an accepted way to settle a debt – a unit in which debts are denominated, and the status of money as legal tender, in those jurisdictions which have this concept, states that it may function for the discharge of debts. When debts are denominated in money, the real value of debts may change due to inflation and deflation, and for sovereign and international debts via debasement and devaluation.

Money Supply

In economics, money is a broad term that refers to any financial instrument that can fulfil the functions of money (detailed above). These financial instruments together are collectively referred to as the money supply of an economy. In other words, the money supply is the amount of financial instruments within a specific economy available for purchasing goods or services.

Since the money supply consists of various financial instruments (usually currency, demand deposits and various other types of deposits), the amount of money in an economy is measured by adding together these financial instruments creating a *monetary aggregate*.

Introduction

Modern monetary theory distinguishes among different ways to measure the money supply, reflected in different types of monetary aggregates, using a categorisation system that focuses on the liquidity of the financial instrument used as money. The most commonly used monetary aggregates (or types of money) are conventionally designated M1, M2 and M3.

These are successively larger aggregate categories: M1 is currency (coins and bills) plus demand deposits (such as checking accounts); M2 is M1 plus savings accounts and time deposits under $100,000; and M3 is M2 plus larger time deposits and similar institutional accounts. M1 includes only the most liquid financial instruments, and M3 relatively illiquid instruments.

Another measure of money, M0, is also used; unlike the other measures, it does not represent actual purchasing power by firms and households in the economy. M0 is base money, or the amount of money actually issued by the central bank of a country. It is measured as currency plus deposits of banks and other institutions at the central bank. M0 is also the only money that can satisfy the reserve requirements of commercial banks.

Market Liquidity

Market liquidity describes how easily an item can be traded for another item, or into the common currency within an economy. Money is the most liquid asset because it is universally recognised and accepted as the common currency. In this way, money gives consumers the freedom to trade goods and services easily without having to barter. Liquid financial instruments are easily tradable and have low transaction costs. There should be no (or minimal) spread between the prices to buy and sell the instrument being used as money.

Types of Money

Currently, most modern monetary systems are based on fiat money. However, for most of history, almost all money was commodity money, such as gold and silver coins. As economies developed, commodity money was eventually replaced by representative money, such as the gold standard, as traders found the physical transportation of gold and silver burdensome. Fiat currencies gradually took over in the last hundred years, especially since the breakup of the Bretton Woods system in the early 1970s.

Commodity Money

Many items have been used as commodity money such as naturally scarce precious metals, conch shells, barley, beads, etc., as well as many other things that are thought of as having value. Commodity money value comes from the commodity out of which it is made.

The commodity itself constitutes the money, and the money is the commodity. Examples of commodities that have been used as mediums of exchange include gold, silver, copper, rice, salt, peppercorns, large stones, decorated belts, shells, alcohol, cigarettes, cannabis, candy, etc. These items were sometimes used in a metric of perceived value in conjunction to one another, in various commodity valuation or Price System economies.

Use of commodity money is similar to barter, but a commodity money provides a simple and automatic unit of account for the commodity which is being used as money. Although some gold coins such as the Krugerrand are considered legal tender, there is no record of their face value on either side of the coin. The rationale for this is that emphasis is laid on their direct link to the prevailing value of their fine gold content. American Eagles are imprinted with their gold content and legal tender face value.

Representative Money

In 1875 economist William Stanley Jevons described what he called "representative money," i.e., money that consists of token coins, or other physical tokens such as certificates, that can be reliably exchanged for a fixed quantity of a commodity such as gold or silver. The value of representative money stands in direct and fixed relation to the commodity that backs it, while not itself being composed of that commodity.

Fiat Money

Fiat money or fiat currency is money whose value is not derived from any intrinsic value or guarantee that it can be converted into a valuable commodity (such as gold). Instead, it has value only by government order (fiat). Usually, the government declares the fiat currency (typically notes and coins from a central bank, such as the Federal Reserve System in the US) to be legal tender, making it unlawful not to accept the fiat currency as a means of repayment for all debts, public and private.

Some bullion coins such as the Australian Gold Nugget and American Eagle are legal tender, however, they trade based on the market price of the metal content as a commodity, rather than their legal tender face value (which is usually only a small fraction of their bullion value).

Fiat money, if physically represented in the form of currency (paper or coins) can be accidentally damaged or destroyed. However, fiat money has an advantage over representative or commodity money, in that the same laws that created the money can also define rules for its replacement in case of damage or destruction. For example, the US government will replace mutilated Federal Reserve notes (US fiat money) if at least half of the physical note can be reconstructed, or if it can be otherwise proven to have been destroyed. By contrast, commodity money which has been lost or destroyed cannot be recovered.

Currency

Currency refers to physical objects generally accepted as a medium of exchange. These are usually the coins and banknotes of a particular government, which comprise the physical aspects of a nation's money supply. The other part of a nation's money supply consists of bank deposits (sometimes called deposit money), ownership of which can be transferred by means of cheques, debit cards, or other forms of money transfer. Deposit money and currency are money in the sense that both are acceptable as a means of payment.

Money in the form of currency has predominated throughout most of history. Usually (gold or silver) coins of intrinsic value (commodity money) have been the norm.

However, nearly all contemporary money systems are based on fiat money – modern currency has value only by government order (fiat). Usually, the government declares the fiat currency (typically notes and coins issued by the central bank) to be legal tender, making it unlawful to not accept the fiat currency as a means of repayment for all debts, public and private.

Commercial, Bank Money

Commercial bank money or demand deposits are claims against financial institutions that can be used for the purchase of goods and services. A demand deposit account is an account from which funds can be withdrawn at any time by check or cash withdrawal without giving the bank or financial institution any prior notice.

Banks have the legal obligation to return funds held in demand deposits immediately upon demand (or 'at call'). Demand deposit withdrawals can be performed in person, via checks or bank drafts, using automatic teller machines (ATMs), or through online banking.

Commercial bank money is created through fractional-reserve banking, the banking practice where banks keep only a *fraction* of their deposits in reserve (as cash and other highly liquid assets) and lend out the remainder, while maintaining the simultaneous obligation to redeem all these deposits upon demand. Commercial bank money differs from commodity and fiat money in two ways, firstly it is non-physical, as its existence is only reflected in the account ledgers of banks and other financial institutions, and secondly, there is some element of risk that the claim will not be fulfilled if the financial institution becomes insolvent.

The process of fractional-reserve banking has a cumulative effect of money creation by commercial banks, as it expands money supply (cash and demand deposits) beyond what it would otherwise be. Because of the prevalence of fractional reserve banking, the broad money supply of most countries is a multiple larger than the amount of base money created by the country's central bank. That multiple (called the money multiplier) is determined by the reserve requirement or other financial ratio requirements imposed by financial regulators.

The money supply of a country is usually held to be the total amount of currency in circulation plus the total amount of checking and savings deposits in the commercial banks in the country. In modern economies, relatively little of the money supply is in physical currency. For example, in December 2010 in the US, of the $8853.4 billion in broad money supply (M2), only $915.7 billion (about 10%) consisted of physical coins and paper money.

Monetary Policy

When gold and silver are used as money, the money supply can grow only if the supply of these metals is increased by mining. This rate of increase will accelerate during periods of gold rushes and discoveries, such as when Columbus discovered the new world and brought back gold and silver to Spain, or when gold was discovered in California in 1848.

This causes inflation, as the value of gold goes down. However, if the rate of gold mining cannot keep up with the growth of the economy, gold becomes relatively more valuable, and prices (denominated in gold) will drop, causing deflation. Deflation was the more typical situation for over a century when gold and paper money backed by gold were used as money in the 18th and 19th centuries.

Modern day monetary systems are based on fiat money and are no longer tied to the value of gold. The control of the amount of money in the economy is known as monetary policy. Monetary policy is the process by which a government, central bank, or monetary authority manages the money supply to achieve specific goals. Usually the goal of monetary policy is to accommodate economic growth in an environment of stable prices. For example, it is clearly stated in the Federal Reserve Act that the Board of Governors and the Federal Open Market Committee should seek "to promote effectively the goals of maximum employment, stable prices, and moderate long-term interest rates."

A failed monetary policy can have significant detrimental effects on an economy and the society that depends on it. These include hyperinflation, stagflation, recession, high unemployment, shortages of imported goods, inability to export goods, and even total monetary collapse and the adoption of a much less efficient barter economy. This happened in Russia, for instance, after the fall of the Soviet Union.

Governments and central banks have taken both regulatory and free market approaches to monetary policy. Some of the tools used to control the money supply include:

- changing the interest rate at which the central bank loans money to (or borrows money from) the commercial banks
- currency purchases or sales
- increasing or lowering government borrowing
- increasing or lowering government spending
- manipulation of exchange rates
- raising or lowering bank reserve requirements
- regulation or prohibition of private currencies
- taxation or tax breaks on imports or exports of capital into a country

In the US, the Federal Reserve is responsible for controlling the money supply, while in the Euro area the respective institution is the European Central Bank. Other central banks with significant impact on global finances are the Bank of Japan, People's Bank of China and the Bank of England.

For many years much of monetary policy was influenced by an economic theory known as monetarism. Monetarism is an economic theory which argues that management of the money

Introduction 13

supply should be the primary means of regulating economic activity. The stability of the demand for money prior to the 1980s was a key finding of Milton Friedman and Anna Schwartz supported by the work of David Laidler, and many others. The nature of the demand for money changed during the 1980s owing to technical, institutional, and legal factors and the influence of monetarism has since decreased.

Wealth and Exchange

In order to make clear the relation which the topic treated in this book bears to the general subject of economics, some primary definitions are necessary.

In the first place, economics itself may be defined as the science of wealth, and wealth may be defined as material objects owned by human beings. Of wealth, therefore, there are two essential attributes: materiality and appropriation.

For it is not all material things that are included under wealth, but only such as have been appropriated. Wealth does not include the sun, moon, and other heavenly bodies, nor even all parts of the surface of this planet, but only such parts as have been appropriated to the use of mankind. It is, then, appropriated parts of the earth's surface and the appropriated objects upon it which constitute wealth.

For convenience, wealth may be classified under three heads: real estate, commodities, and human beings. Real estate includes the surface of the earth and the other wealth attached thereto - improvements such as buildings, fences, drains, railways, street improvements, and so on. Commodities include all movable wealth (except man himself), whether raw materials or finished products.

There is one particular variety of commodity - a certain finished product - which is of especial importance in the subject of which this book treats; namely, money. Any commodity to be called 'money' must be generally acceptable in exchange, and any commodity generally acceptable in exchange should be called money. The best example of a money commodity is found today in gold coins.

Of all wealth, man himself is a species. Like his horses or his cattle, he is himself a material object, and like them, he is owned; for if slave, he is owned by another, and if free, by himself. But though human beings may be considered as wealth, human qualities, such as skill, intelligence, and inventiveness, are not wealth. Just as the hardness of steel is not wealth, but merely a quality of one particular kind of wealth, - hard steel, - so the skill of a workman is not wealth, but merely a quality of another particular kind of wealth-skilled workman. Similarly, intelligence is not wealth, but an intelligent man is wealth.

Since materiality is one of the two essential attributes of wealth, any article of wealth may be measured in physical units. Land is measured-in acres; coal, in tons; milk, in quarts; and wheat, in bushels. Therefore, for estimating the quantities of different articles of wealth, all the various physical units of measurement may be employed: linear measure, square measure, cubic measure, and measure by weight.

Whenever any species of wealth is measured in its physical units, a first step is taken towards the measurement of that mysterious magnitude called 'value.' Sometimes value is looked upon as a psychical and sometimes as a physical phenomenon. But, although the determination of value always involves a psychical process - judgement - yet the terms in which the results are expressed and measured are physical. It is desirable, for the sake of clearness, to lead up to the concept of value by means of three preliminary concepts; namely, transfer, exchange, and price.

A transfer of wealth is a change in its ownership. An exchange consists of two mutual and voluntary transfers, each in consideration of the other. When a certain quantity of one kind of wealth is exchanged for a certain quantity of another kind, we may divide one of the two quantities by the other, and obtain the price of the latter. For instance, if two dollars of gold are exchanged for three bushels of wheat, the price of the wheat in gold is two thirds of a dollar per bushel; and the price of the gold in wheat is one and a half bushels per dollar. It is to be noticed that these are ratios of two physical quantities, the units for measuring which are quite different from each other.

One commodity is measured in bushels, or units of volume of wheat, the other in dollars, or units of weight of gold. In general, a price of any species of wealth is merely the ratio of two physical quantities, in whatever way each may originally be measured.

This brings us, at last, to the concept of value. The value of any item of wealth is its price multiplied by its quantity. Thus, if half a dollar per bushel is the price of wheat, the value of a hundred bushels of wheat is fifty dollars.

Exchangeable Goods

Hitherto we have confined our discussion to some of the consequences of the first prerequisite of wealth - that it must be material. We turn now to the second prerequisite, namely, that it must be owned. To own wealth is simply to have the right to benefit by it that is, the right to enjoy its services or benefits.

Thus the owner of a loaf of bread has the right to benefit by it by eating it, by selling it, or by otherwise disposing of it. The man who owns a house has the right to benefit by enjoying its shelter, by selling it, or by renting it. This right, the right to or in the benefits of wealth-or more briefly, the right to or in the wealth itself - is called a "property right" or simply property.'

If things were always owned in fee simple, i.e. if there were no division of ownership,-no partnership rights, no shares, and no stock companies, - there would be little practical need to distinguish property from wealth; and as a matter of fact, in the rough popular usage, any article of wealth, and especially real estate, is often inaccurately called a 'piece of property' But the ownership of wealth is frequently divided; and this fact necessitates a careful distinction between the thing owned and the rights of the owners. Thus, a railroad is wealth. Its shares and bonded debt are rights to this wealth.

Each owner of shares or bonds has the right to a fractional part of the benefits from the railway. The total of these rights comprises the complete ownership of, or property in, the railway, Like wealth, property rights also may be measured; but in units of a different character.

The units of property are not physical, but consist of abstract rights to the benefits of wealth. If a man has twenty-five shares in a certain railway company, the measurement of his property is twenty-five units just as truly as though he had twenty-five bushels of wheat. What he has is twenty-five rights of a specific sort.

There exist various units of property for measuring property, as there are various units of wealth for measuring wealth; and to property may be applied precisely the same concepts of transfer, exchange, price, and value which are applied to wealth.

Besides the distinction between wealth and property rights, another distinction should here be noted. This is the distinction between property rights and certificates of those rights. The former are the rights to use wealth, the latter are merely the written evidence of those rights.

Thus, the right to receive dividends from a railroad is property, but the written paper evidencing that right is a stock certificate. The right to a railway trip is a property right, the ticket evidencing that right is a certificate of property. The promise of a bank is a property right; the bank note on which that promise is engraved is a certificate of property.

Any property right which is generally acceptable in exchange may be called 'money.' Its printed evidence is also called money. Hence there arise three meanings of the term money, viz. its meaning in the sense of wealth; its meaning in the sense of property; and its meaning in the sense of written evidence. From the standpoint of economic analysis the property sense is the most important.

What we have been speaking of as property is the right to the services, uses, or benefits of wealth. By benefits of wealth is meant the desirable events which occur by means of wealth. Like wealth and property, benefits also may be measured, but in units of a still different character. Benefits are reckoned either 'by time' — as the services of a gardener or of a dwelling house; or 'by the piece' — as the use of a plow or a telephone. And just as the concepts of transfer, exchange, price, and value apply to wealth and property, so do they apply to benefits.

The uses (benefits) of wealth, with which we have been dealing, should be distinguished from the utility of wealth. The one means desirable events, the other, the desirability of those events. The one is usually outside of the mind, the other always inside. Whenever we speak of rights to benefits, the benefits referred to are future benefits. The owner of a house owns the right to use it from the present instant onward. Its past use has perished and is no longer subject to ownership.

The term 'goods' will be used in this book simply as a convenient collective term to include wealth, property, and benefits. The transfer, exchange, price, and value of goods take on innumerable forms. Under price alone, as thus fully applied to goods; fall rent, wages, rates of interest, prices in terms of money, and prices in terms of other goods. But we shall be chiefly concerned in this book with prices of goods in terms of money.

Circulation of Money against Goods

Little has yet been said as to the relation of wealth, property and benefits to time, A certain quantity of goods, may be either a quantity existing at a particular instant of time, or a quantity produced, consumed, transported, or exchanged during a period of time. The first quantity is a stock; or fund, of goods; the second is a flow, or stream, of goods.

The amount of wheat in a flour mill on any definite date is a stock of wheat, while the monthly or weekly amounts which come in or go out constitute a flow of wheat. The amount of mined coal existing in the United States at any given moment is a stock of mined coal; the weekly amount mined is a flow of coal.

There are many applications of this distinction; for instance, to capital and income. A stock of goods, whether wealth or property, existing at an instant of time is called capital. A flow of benefits from such capital during a period of time is called 'income'. Income, therefore, is one important kind of economic flow. Besides income, economic flows are of three chief classes, representing respectively changes of condition (such as production or consumption), changes of position (such as transportation, exportation, and importation), and changes of ownership, which we have already called 'transfers.'

Trade is a flow of transfers. Whether foreign or domestic, it is simply the exchange of a stream of transferred rights in goods for an equivalent stream of transferred money or money substitutes. The second of these two streams is called the 'circulation' of money. The equation between the two is called the 'equation of exchange'; and it is this equation that constitutes the subject matter of the present book.

2

Historical Backdrop

Barter and Gift

There is no evidence of a society or economy that relied primarily on barter. Instead, non-monetary societies operated largely along the principles of gift economics. When barter did in fact occur, it was usually between either complete strangers or would-be enemies.

With barter, an individual possessing a material object of value, such as a measure of grain, could directly exchange that object for another object perceived to have equivalent value, such as a small animal, a clay pot or a tool.

The capacity to carry out transactions is severely limited since it depends on a coincidence of wants. The seller of food grain has to find a buyer who wants to buy grain and who also could offer in return something the seller wants to buy. There is no common medium of exchange into which both seller and buyer could convert their tradable commodities. There is no standard which could be applied to measure the relative value of various goods and services.

In a gift economy, valuable goods and services are regularly given without any explicit agreement for immediate or future rewards (i.e. there is no formal *quid pro quo*). Ideally, simultaneous or recurring giving serves to circulate and redistribute valuables within the community.

There are various social theories concerning gift economies. Some consider the gifts to be a form of reciprocal altruism. Another interpretation is that social status is awarded in return for the 'gifts'. Consider for example, the sharing of food in some hunter-gatherer societies, where food-sharing is a safeguard against the failure of any individual's daily foraging. This custom may reflect altruism, it may be a form of informal insurance, or may bring with it social status or other benefits.

Emergence of Money

In the absence of a medium of exchange, non-monetary societies operated largely along the principles of gift economics. The Mesopotamian civilization developed a large scale economy based on commodity money. The Babylonians and their neighbouring city states later developed the earliest system of economics as we think of it today, in terms of rules on debt, legal contracts and law codes relating to business practices and private property. Money was not only an emergence, it was a necessity.

The Code of Hammurabi, the best preserved ancient law code, was created ca. 1760 BC (middle chronology) in ancient Babylon. It was enacted by the sixth Babylonian King, Hammurabi. Earlier collections of laws include the code of Ur-Nammu, King of Ur (ca. 2050 BC), the Code of Eshnunna (ca. 1930 BC) and the code of Lipit-Ishtar of Isin (ca. 1870 BC). These law codes formalised the role of money in civil society. They set amounts of interest on debt... fines for 'wrong doing'... and compensation in money for various infractions of formalised law.

Historical Backdrop

The Shekel referred to an ancient unit of weight and currency. The first usage of the term came from Mesopotamia circa 3000 BC. and referred to a specific mass of barley which related other values in a metric such as silver, bronze, copper, etc. A barley/shekel was originally both a unit of currency and a unit of weight, just as the British Pound was originally a unit denominating a one pound mass of silver.

Commodity Money

Bartering has several problems, most notably that it requires a 'coincidence of wants'. For example, if a wheat farmer needs what a fruit farmer produces, a direct swap is impossible as seasonal fruit would spoil before the grain harvest. A solution is to trade fruit for wheat indirectly through a third, "intermediate", commodity: the fruit is exchanged for the intermediate commodity when the fruit ripens.

If this *intermediate commodity* doesn't perish and is reliably in demand throughout the year (e.g. copper, gold, or wine) then it can be exchanged for wheat after the harvest. The function of the intermediate commodity as a store-of-value can be standardised into a widespread commodity money, reducing the coincidence of wants problem. By overcoming the limitations of simple barter, a commodity money makes the market in all other commodities more liquid.

Many cultures around the world eventually developed the use of commodity money. Ancient China, Africa, and India used cowry shells. Trade in Japan's feudal system was based on the koku – a unit of rice. The shekel was an ancient unit of weight and currency. The first usage of the term came from Mesopotamia circa 3000 BC and referred to a specific weight of barley, which related other values in a metric such as silver, bronze, copper, etc. A barley/shekel was originally both a unit of currency and a unit of weight.

Where ever trade is common, barter systems usually lead quite rapidly to several key goods being imbued with monetary properties. In the early British colony of New South Wales, rum emerged quite soon after settlement as the most monetary of goods. When a nation is without a currency it commonly adopts a foreign currency. In prisons where conventional money is prohibited, it is quite common for cigarettes to take on a monetary quality, and throughout history, gold has taken on this unofficial monetary function.

Standardised Coinage

From early times, metals, where available, have usually been favoured for use as proto-money over such commodities as cattle, cowry shells, or salt, because they are at once durable, portable, and easily divisible. The use of gold as proto-money has been traced back to the fourth millennium BC when the Egyptians used gold bars of a set weight as a medium of exchange, as had been done earlier in Mesopotamia with silver bars.

The first known ruler who officially set standards of weight and money was Pheidon. The first stamped money (having the mark of some authority in the form of a picture or words) can be seen in the 'Bibliothèque Nationale' of Paris. It is an electrum stater of a turtle coin, coined at Aegina Island. This remarkable coin dates about 700 BC. Electrum coins were also introduced about 650 BC in Lydia.

Coinage was widely adopted across Ionia and mainland Greece during the 6th century BC, eventually leading to the Athenian Empire's 5th century BC, dominance of the region through their export of silver coinage, mined in southern Attica at Laurium and Thorikos. A major silver vein discovery at Laurium in 483 BC led to the huge expansion of the Athenian military fleet. Competing coinage standards at the time were maintained by Mytilene and Phokaia using coins of Electrum; Aegina used silver.

It was the discovery of the touchstone which led the way for metal-based commodity money and coinage. Any soft metal can be tested for purity on a touchstone, allowing one to quickly calculate the total content of a particular metal in a lump. Gold

Historical Backdrop

is a soft metal, which is also hard to come by, dense, and storable. As a result, monetary gold spread very quickly from Asia Minor, where it first gained wide usage, to the entire world.

Using such a system still required several steps and mathematical calculation. The touchstone allows one to estimate the amount of gold in an alloy, which is then multiplied by the weight to find the amount of gold alone in a lump. To make this process easier, the concept of standard coinage was introduced. Coins were pre-weighed and pre-alloyed, so as long as the manufacturer was aware of the origin of the coin, no use of the touchstone was required.

Coins were typically minted by governments in a carefully protected process, and then stamped with an emblem that guaranteed the weight and value of the metal. It was, however, extremely common for governments to assert that the value of such money lay in its emblem and thus to subsequently reduce the value of the currency by lowering the content of valuable metal.

Although gold and silver were commonly used to mint coins, other metals could be used. For instance, Ancient Sparta minted coins from iron to discourage its citizens from engaging in foreign trade. In the early seventeenth century Sweden lacked more precious metal and so produced "plate money", which were large slabs of copper approximately 50 cm or more in length and width, appropriately stamped with indications of their value.

Metal based coins had the advantage of carrying their value within the coins themselves — on the other hand, they induced manipulations: the clipping of coins in the attempt to get and recycle the precious metal. A greater problem was the simultaneous co-existence of gold, silver and copper coins in Europe.

English and Spanish traders valued gold coins more than silver coins, as many of their neighbours did, with the effect that the English gold-based guinea coin began to rise against the English silver based crown in the 1670s and 1680s. Consequently, silver was ultimately pulled out of England for dubious amounts of gold coming into the country at a rate no other European nation would share. The effect was worsened with Asian traders not sharing the European appreciation of gold altogether — gold left Asia and silver left Europe in quantities European observers like Isaac Newton, Master of the Royal Mint observed with unease.

Stability came into the system with national Banks guaranteeing to change money into gold at a promised rate; it did, however, not come easily. The Bank of England risked a national financial catastrophe in the 1730s when customers demanded their money be changed into gold in a moment of crisis.

Eventually London's merchants saved the bank and the nation with financial guarantees. Another step in the evolution of money was the change from a coin being a unit of weight to being a unit of value a distinction could be made between its commodity value and its *specie* value. The difference is these values is seigniorage.

Trade Bills of Exchange

Bills of exchange became prevalent with the expansion of European trade towards the end of the Middle Ages. A flourishing Italian wholesale trade in cloth, woollen clothing, wine, tin and other commodities was heavily dependent on credit for its rapid expansion. Goods were supplied to a buyer against a bill of exchange, which constituted the buyer's promise to make payment at some specified future date.

Provided that the buyer was reputable or the bill was endorsed by a credible guarantor, the seller could then present the bill to a merchant banker and redeem it in money at a discounted value before it actually became due.

These bills could also be used as a form of payment by the seller to make additional purchases from his own suppliers. Thus, the bills – an early form of credit – became both a medium of exchange and a medium for storage of value. Like the loans made by the Egyptian grain banks, this trade credit became a significant source for the creation of new money. In England, bills of exchange became an important form of credit and money during last quarter

Historical Backdrop 25

of the 18th century and the first quarter of the 19th century before banknotes, checks and cash credit lines were widely available.

Tallies

The acceptance of symbolic forms of money opened up vast new realms for human creativity. A symbol could be used to represent something of value that was available in physical storage somewhere else in space, such as grain in the warehouse. It could also be used to represent something of value that would be available later in time, such as a promissory note or bill of exchange, a document ordering someone to pay a certain sum of money to another on a specific date or when certain conditions have been fulfilled.

In the 12th Century, the English monarchy introduced an early version of the bill of exchange in the form of a notched piece of wood known as a tally stick. Tallies originally came into use at a time when paper was rare and costly, but their use persisted until the early 19th Century, even after paper forms of money had become prevalent.

The notches were used to denote various amounts of taxes payable to the crown. Initially tallies were simply used as a form of receipt to the tax payer at the time of rendering his dues. As the revenue department became more efficient, they began issuing tallies to denote a promise of the tax assessee to make future tax payments at specified times during the year. Each tally consisted of a matching pair – one stick was given to the assessee at the time of assessment representing the amount of taxes to be paid later and the other held by the Treasury representing the amount of taxes be collected at a future date.

The Treasury discovered that these tallies could also be used to create money. When the crown had exhausted its current resources, it could use the tally receipts representing future tax payments due to the crown as a form of payment to its own creditors, who in turn could either collect the tax revenue directly from those assessed or use the same tally to pay their own taxes to the government. The tallies could also be sold to other parties in exchange for gold or silver coin at a discount reflecting the length of time remaining until the taxes was due for payment.

Thus, the tallies became an accepted medium of exchange for some types of transactions and an accepted medium for store of value. Like the girobanks before it, the Treasury soon realised that it could also issue tallies that were not backed by any specific assessment of taxes. By doing so, the Treasury created new money that was backed by public trust and confidence in the monarchy rather than by specific revenue receipts.

Goldsmith Bankers

Goldsmiths in England had been craftsmen, bullion merchants, money changers and money lenders since the 16th century. But they were not the first to act as financial intermediates; in the early 17th century, the scriveners were the first to keep deposits for the express purpose of relending them. Merchants and traders had amassed huge hoards of gold and entrusted their wealth to the Royal Mint for storage. In 1640 King Charles I seized the private gold stored in the mint as a forced loan (which was to be paid back over time).

Thereafter merchants preferred to store their gold with the goldsmiths of London, who possessed private vaults, and charged a fee for that service. In exchange for each deposit of precious metal, the goldsmiths issued receipts certifying the quantity and purity of the metal they held as a bailee (i.e. in trust). These receipts could not be assigned (only the original depositor could collect the stored goods).

Gradually the goldsmiths took over the function of the scriveners of relending on behalf of a depositor and also developed modern banking practices; promissory notes were issued for money deposited which by custom and/or law was a loan to the goldsmith, i.e. the depositor expressly allowed the goldsmith to use the money for any purpose including advances to his customers.

Historical Backdrop

The goldsmith charged no fee, or even paid interest on these deposits. Since the promissory notes were payable on demand, and the advances (loans) to the goldsmith's customers were repayable over a longer time period, this was an early from of fractional reserve banking.

The promissory notes developed into an assignable instrument, which could circulate as a safe and convenient form of money backed by the goldsmith's promise to pay. Hence goldsmiths could advance loans in the form of gold money, or in the form of promissory notes, or in the form of checking accounts.

Gold deposits were relatively stable, often remaining with the goldsmith for years on end, so there was little risk of default so long as public trust in the goldsmith's integrity and financial soundness was maintained. Thus, the goldsmiths of London became the forerunners of British banking and prominent creators of new money based on credit.

Demand Deposits

The primary business of the early merchant banks was promotion of trade. The new class of commercial banks made accepting deposits and issuing loans their principal activity. They lend the money they received on deposit. They created additional money in the form of new bank notes.

The money they created was partially backed by gold, silver or other assets and partially backed only by public trust in the institutions that created it.

Demand deposits are funds that are deposited in bank accounts and are available for withdrawal at the discretion of the depositor. The withdrawal of funds from the account does not require contacting or making any type of prior arrangements with the bank or credit union.

As long as the account balance is sufficient to cover the amount of the withdrawal, and the withdrawal takes place in accordance with procedures set in place by the financial institution, the funds may be withdrawn on demand.

Banknotes

The history of money and banking are inseparably interlinked. The issuance of paper money was initiated by commercial banks. Inspired by the success of the London goldsmiths, some of which became the forerunners of great English banks, banks began issuing paper notes quite properly termed 'banknotes' which circulated in the same way that government issued currency circulates today.

In England this practice continued up to 1694. Scottish banks continued issuing notes until 1850. In USA, this practice continued through the 19th Century, where at one time there were more than 5000 different types of bank notes issued by various commercial banks in America. Only the notes issued by the largest, most creditworthy banks were widely accepted. The script of smaller, lesser known institutions circulated locally. Farther from home it was only accepted at a discounted rate, if it was accepted at all. The proliferation of types of money went hand in hand with a multiplication in the number of financial institutions.

These banknotes were a form of representative money which could be converted into gold or silver by application at the bank. Since banks issued notes far in excess of the gold and silver they kept on deposit, sudden loss of public confidence in a bank could precipitate mass redemption of banknotes and result in *bankruptcy*.

The use of bank notes issued by private commercial banks as legal tender has gradually been replaced by the issuance of bank notes authorised and controlled by national governments. The Bank of England was granted sole rights to issue banknotes in England after 1694. In the USA, the Federal Reserve Bank was granted similar rights after its establishment in 1913. Until recently, these government-authorised currencies were forms of representative money, since they were partially backed by gold or silver and were theoretically convertible into gold or silver.

Gold-backed Banknotes

The term gold standard is often erroneously thought to refer to a currency where notes were fully backed by and redeemable

Historical Backdrop

in an equivalent amount of gold. The British pound was the strongest, most stable currency of the 19th Century and often considered the closest equivalent to pure gold, yet at the height of the gold standard there was only sufficient gold in the British treasury to redeem a small fraction of the currency then in circulation. In 1880, US government gold stock was equivalent in value to only 16 per cent of currency and demand deposits in commercial banks. By 1970, it was about 0.5 per cent.

The gold standard was only a system for exchange of value between national currencies, never an agreement to redeem all paper notes for gold. The classic gold standard prevailed during the period 1880 and 1913 when a core of leading trading nations agreed to adhere to a fixed gold price and continuous convertibility for their currencies. Gold was used to settle accounts between these nations. With the outbreak of World War I, Britain was forced to abandon the gold standard even for their international transactions. Other nations quickly followed suit. After a brief attempt to revive the gold standard during the 1920s, it was finally abandoned by Britain and other leading nations during the Great Depression.

Prior to the abolition of the gold standard, the following words were printed on the face of every US dollar: "I promise to pay the bearer on demand, the sum of one dollar" followed by the signature of the US Secretary of the Treasury. Other denominations carried similar pledges proportionate to the face value of each note. The currencies of other nations bore similar promises too. In earlier times this promise signified that a bearer could redeem currency notes for their equivalent value in gold or silver. The US adopted a silver standard in 1785, meaning that the value of the US dollar represented a certain equivalent weight in silver and could be redeemed in silver coins. But even at its inception, the US Government was not required to maintain silver reserves sufficient to redeem all the notes that it issued. Through much of the 20th Century until 1971, the US dollar was 'backed' by gold, but from 1934 only foreign holders of the notes could exchange them for metal.

Representative Money

Representative money refers to money that consists of a token or certificate made of paper. The use of the various types of money including representative money, tracks the course of money from the past to the present. Token money may be called "representative money" in the sense that, say, a piece of paper might 'represent' or be a claim on a commodity also. Gold certificates or Silver certificates are a type of representative money which were used in the United States as currency until 1933.

The term 'representative money' has been used in the past "to signify that a certain amount of bullion was stored in a Treasury while the equivalent paper in circulation" represented the bullion. Representative money differs from commodity money which is actually made of some physical commodity. In his *Treatise on Money*, (1930:7) Keynes distinguished between commodity money and representative money, dividing the latter into "fiat money" and "managed money."

Fiat Money

As discussed earlier, Fiat money refers to money that is not backed by reserves of another commodity. The money itself is given value by government *fiat* (Latin for "let it be done") or decree, enforcing *legal tender laws*, previously known as "forced tender", whereby debtors are legally relieved of the debt if they pay it in the government's money. By law, the refusal of a legal tender (offering) extinguishes the debt in the same way acceptance does. At times in history (e.g. Rome under Diocletian, and post-revolutionary France during the collapse of the assignats) the refusal of legal tender money in favour of some other form of payment was punished with the death penalty.

Governments through history have often switched to forms of fiat money in times of need such as war, sometimes by suspending the service they provided of exchanging their money for gold, and other times by simply printing the money that they needed. When governments produce money more rapidly than economic growth, the money supply overtakes economic value. Therefore, the excess money eventually dilutes the market value of all money issued. This is called inflation. In 1971 the United States finally switched to fiat money indefinitely. At this point in time many of the economically developed countries' currencies were fixed to the US dollar, and so this single step meant that much of the western world's currencies became fiat money based.

Following the Gulf War the president of Iraq, Saddam Hussein, repealed the existing Iraqi fiat currency and replaced it with a new currency. Despite having no backing by a commodity and with no central authority mandating its use or defending its value, the old currency continued to circulate within the politically isolated Kurdish regions of Iraq. It became known as the "Swiss dinar". This currency remained relatively strong and stable for over a decade. It was formally replaced following the Iraq War.

From Feudal Status to Cash Nexus

The difference between the feudal and the industrial systems of society is in the main the difference in the nature of the dependence of the bulk of the people. In the feudal system the masses were bound to the soil, which was owned by a comparatively small number of feudal lords. The mass of the people was divided into freemen, villeins, and serfs. All these were dependent upon the land for their subsistence, and owed varying amounts of service to their feudal lords.

The loosening of the feudal bond is allied to the gradual infiltration of cash payments into the social organism. This process was of slow but insistent growth. The feudal servant's obligation to pay his dues in labour or in kind was gradually dissolved, and, instead, he had to pay a money rent. Concurrently it became possible for the masses to free themselves from direct bondage to the soil, but in so doing they became increasingly dependent upon the necessity of earning a wage. So marked has that dependence become that it has had applied to it the picturesque term "wage-slavery", not wholly without foundation. Undoubtedly for the great mass of people today the prime feature of economic life is the necessity of earning a wage, just as in the feudal system the prime necessity was to obtain the use of land from the feudal lord.

The study of the emergence of the cash nexus is an important preliminary to a correct grasp of economic problems. Money has existed in all societies in which any kind of trade as distinct from primitive barter was carried on. In early societies a money transaction was a rare event, the hunting or agricultural pursuits of the community being the real basis of communal life.

Thus in African tribes we find cowry shells used as money; among the American Indians, skins of animals. In more highly organised societies the dominant form rapidly became some metal or other, until it was more or less replaced by paper currency.

The use of metal as currency goes far back into the agricultural era. Etymology shows that prior to the use of metal the exchange of commodities was made upon the basis of their worth in live stock. With the development of society and the increase of the use of metals the latter replaced cattle as the money instrument, and at different stages iron, copper, silver, and finally gold were adopted as cash. The Greeks, Phoenicians, and Romans all developed a considerable amount of commerce which was conducted upon a cash basis.

Under the Roman regime the process went a step further, and led to the introduction of the credit nexus in the form of the bill of exchange. The decay of the Roman Empire under the successive onslaughts of the semi-barbarian tribes arrested the growth of commerce, and produced an interval of unsettlement which later gave way to a period of stability under the form of the feudal system.

The precarious conditions of the time led men to seek security by attaching themselves to a strong military leader, whose protection they obtained in return for service. That system developed on the Continent to a higher degree than in England, whose insular position afforded it a certain amount of protection. But the invasion of the Continental tribes, the Angles and Saxons and later the

Danes, helped to stimulate the feudal system of land tenure, and the great conquest by William of Normandy gave the system its dominating character.

Feudalism, however, was at no time entirely free from an overlayer of commerce conducted upon a cash basis. The feudal lords had a direct interest in encouraging a certain degree of trade. They needed, to uphold their position, a high degree of craftsmanship in the manufacture of weapons and armour. They required the merchant to supply them with fine apparel.

The technical skill of Europe was insufficient for their highest requirements, and they sought their weapons and their textiles from Damascus and other Asiatic cities. Such commerce was, however, but a superficial manifestation of feudal life. The great mass of the people was to all intents and purposes self-supporting, and the exchange of commodities, with its concomitant use of money, rarely entered into their lives.

The typical illustration of feudal life is to be found in the feudal villages scattered far and wide over the countryside, not in the rare towns which rose up where the craftsmen congregated or where the caravan routes made convenient merchant centres.

The feudal village consisted of a few houses clustered along the village street near the manor of the feudal lord. The villagers held their land in servile tenure from the latter, and in return for their holdings had to work for the lord of the manor for a fixed number of days per week throughout the year, and for a fixed period during special seasons such as ploughing, and harvesting. They were unable to leave the village without first obtaining their lord's permission. They were classed generally as villeins, and were subdivided into virgaters or cottars in accordance with the size of their holdings.

A virgater was a holder of some thirty acres, a cottar had some five acres only. In addition to the labour rents, they were compelled also to give other rents in kind, such as corn or honey. Above them in the social scale was a small body of freemen, who were on the whole exempt from labour dues, but who were still under the obligation to pay rents in kind. At the other end of the scale were the few bondmen or serfs, who held no land and were wholly dependent upon the feudal lord.

The land of the village was divided into permanent pasture, waste, wood, and arable. The pasture was used in common by the lord and the tenants. The wood provided them with timber and fuel. The waste land fed the swine. The arable land was worked on the open-field system.

The fields were divided into strips some eleven to twenty-two yards wide. These strips were divided among the lord and the tenants, and each man's holding was scattered in this way over the whole of the manor lands, no two adjacent strips belonging to the same man.

Each village had two or three such fields. In a three-field village, one field would lie fallow each year, while, of the other two, one would be put under barley or oats, the other under wheat or rye. In addition to his strips in the open field the lord had also some enclosed fields near his manorial hall. His holding in both strips and enclosed fields was called the demesne.

The feudal lord, particularly after the Conquest, held several possessions in various parts of the country, and it was his custom to place his lands under the control of the bailiff. To plough the demesne, the tenants combined their oxen into teams of eight, and also to some extent made use of this practice in ploughing their own holdings, although individual ploughing was probably more common.

The villagers lived almost entirely upon their own produce. They possessed their few oxen and swine, raised upon the common pasture and waste land. They got their timber and their fuel from the wood. They prepared their own leather and wool. Each village was practically a self-contained unit, except for a few commodities such as iron, other metals, and salt. Sugar was unknown, and its place was taken by honey. In the early days of the system the King was merely a superior feudal lord and lived upon the produce of his lands, like his vassals.

Historical Backdrop 35

Such a system, primitive as it was, might appear to have the elements of permanency in it. A change, however, was destined to intrude very gradually and to end by converting the feudal system into the modern industrial one. The impetus to change came in the first place, not from the striving of the tenants, but from the needs of the feudal lords.

While it would appear that the tenant's position in such a system was by no means an enviable one, there does not appear to have been any noticeable discontent. True, the tenants were at the lord's mercy and, when he abused his power, their power of redress was practically nil. But the affairs of the community were controlled rather by traditional regulation than by despotic power. The tenant had certain claims by reason of his class position. His duties to his lord were prescribed by usage; he was by nature conservative, and showed no desire to upset the social structure.

The feudal lord's needs were not so easily satisfied as those of his tenants. He owed his position to his prowess as a fighter. He needed good weapons, good armour, good horses. His prestige necessitated better clothing than the village could provide. He had duties to his overlord. Upon occasion, he had to accompany the latter to battle and bring with him a body of fighters. While he could support his retainers at home upon the produce of his lands, the system failed when he took the field.

The provisioning of even a small army could be better effected by the purchase of necessaries than by forcible extortion. Even in times of peace, the fact that he possessed several fiefs at long distances from one another made it to his interest to introduce a more convenient system than that of labour and produce rents. He was more detached from the primitive product of his own lands than were his tenants, and he was acquiring a growing attachment to the products of commerce.

What held true of the feudal lord held true to a greater extent of his overlord, the King. The King had a still greater state to keep up. He had a larger retinue to clothe. He had Continental possessions which, by intermarriages, in course of time came to include the best provinces of France. He had to support an army and to be able to provision it. It was easier to buy food wherever convenient than to transport it from his own domains. To do that he stood in need of money.

The decline of feudalism is the history of the commutation of labour and produce dues into money rents. This process is naturally earliest in evidence in relation to the larger domains. Up to the reign of Henry I. (1100-35), the produce of the royal manors used to be sent direct so the King's court, but the 'method of marketing them close at hand and sending the money received to the King was much more convenient for all parties. The larger estates followed on the same lines. The Church adopted the practice.

Early Church history affords records of detailed arrangements for provisioning monasteries direct from manorial produce. This was later replaced by the commercial method of sale and purchase. On the smaller demesnes the enterprising bailiff could better satisfy his ambitious lord by letting land out for a money rent instead of for labour and produce dues.

When, however, the relations between feudal lord and tenant were direct, natural conservatism prevented the change from developing, except at a very slow rate. The infiltration of the cash nexus throughout society was not destined to be direct from feudal lord to tenant. It was rather from feudal lord to merchant, from merchant to craftsmaster, and from craftsmaster to journeyman. It led to a growing increase in the town population and a growing interdependence between town and countryside. Produce rents were not practicable for town dwellings, and were early supplanted by money rents.

The growth of the towns gave the countryside a profitable market for its produce. It made the tenant's produce and labour a source of gain, and gave him an incentive to produce for sale instead of for subsistence. Thereby it increased the tendency towards holding land on lease in return for money rent. The old system of tenure was, however, very persistent, and remained until the commercial system had superseded the agricultural.

The merchant emerges in economic history at first as a trader dependent upon and subservient to the feudal lord. He traded in a small way with the inmates of the feudal castle. The growth of the religious orders enabled him to attach himself to some high Church dignitary. As the need for the merchant became greater, towns sprang up in the neighbourhood of the large castles and monasteries. The merchants were general traders. They dealt in the native products, which comprised wool, rough cloth, leather, and food, and also imported products, such as finer cloths, silks, furs, arms, spices, and wines.

The feudal lords were jealous of their position and were not inclined to give the merchants any special privileges. The advent of the Crusades, however, gave the merchants an opportunity which they were not slow to seize. The feudal lords stood in urgent need of money in order to equip themselves for their pious ventures. For a certain fixed sum the merchants were allowed to purchase their charter of freedom. The granting of the charter was followed by their organisation into a gild merchant, which gave them sufficient solidarity to defend their purchased privileges. The gild merchant secured for its members the sole right to trade in their town.

It is not surprising to find that the development of the English towns was to a large extent copied from towns on the Continent, nor that throughout the whole of the Middle Ages the commercial development of the Continent was generally ahead of that of this island. The causes which operated at home in the direction of fostering the growth of commerce operated to a greater degree abroad. The interests of the Continental feudal lords were wider, their quarrels were more frequent, their need for money to maintain armed forces was greater.

Their dependence upon the merchant was therefore more marked, and the Continental merchant was in a better position to obtain a privileged position. Hence the Continental towns assumed a commercial importance at an earlier date.

In England those towns more happily situated for Continental trade made the greatest progress, and it is in them that the gild merchant was first incorporated. Thus the merchants in London and the Cinque Ports at-an early date obtained trading privileges, though they appear never to have troubled about the actual formation of a gild merchant. The first gild merchant was formed about AD 1100, and the number increased rapidly until the height of their development was reached in about AD 1300.

The rise of the merchant brought with it the creation of the craftsman. The more skilful manual worker of the village found it to his advantage to free himself from the land, with its labour and produce dues, and sell the products of his craft to the merchant or to his fellow-villagers. The further penetration of the cash nexus into the social organism led to the formation of another industrial stratum. Specialised crafts developed quickly in various towns, and very soon after the formation of gilds merchant we find craft gilds springing up.

Before the actual separation of craft gilds from gilds merchant, the latter included craftsmen among their members, but regulations were introduced to limit the craftsmen's activities. No craftsman could sell his wares outside his own town, which meant very largely that he was obliged to sell to a merchant. To become a merchant he must first give up his craft and sell his tools.

The attempt on the part of the upper stratum to protect itself from the newer and lower stratum is one which we shall see repeated by the craftsman against the journeyman. The first evidence of a craft gild is in 1130, and is in the cloth industry, the weavers having then organised in London, Lincoln, and Oxford. Shortly afterwards fullers and cloth finishers, goldsmiths and butchers, formed themselves into gilds in various towns, and the movement continued to gather strength until about 1350. It maintained its vigour for about a century till 1450, and then slowly declined.

In the early days of the craftsman it was comparatively easy to obtain the necessary skill, and the outfit required to set up in

Historical Backdrop 39

industry was not expensive. The market was very circumscribed, being usually limited to the town itself and the surrounding rural district. Inter-urban commerce was carried on by the merchants. The profits made by the craftsmen, although not great, were sufficiently attractive to cause an inflow of new members. Competition began to make itself felt, and when the craftsmen found their profits being undercut by the growing competition they organised themselves upon restrictive and protective lines.

The increasing specialisation of craft led to the development of sufficient technical skill to justify the introduction of the apprenticeship system, the first evidence of which is in 1260. This system was soon used to restrict the numbers of those entering a craft. An attempt to meet this evil was made by legislation, and in 1531 an Act was passed fixing the maximum fee for apprenticeship. As early as the fourteenth century, however, certain craft gilds had made regulations to limit their numbers, to restrict output, and to inflate prices. The lure of the more profitable cash commerce was seducing the peasant from the soil, and in 1406 an Act was passed to prevent men whose incomes were less than £1 per annum from apprenticing their children in the towns.

Steps were also taken by the more influential members of the gilds to get the control into their own hands. They fixed the hours of the gild meetings at difficult times, and ordained the wearing of costly liveries. The term of apprenticeship was lengthened to seven years, the number of apprentices were limited, and every endeavour was made to render the gild practically a hereditary monopoly. Even at the end of his term the apprentice was no longer certain of becoming a craftsman.

In order to qualify, he was obliged to produce a masterpiece. This masterpiece was first instituted as a test of skill, but later degenerated into a means of exclusion. The work required was of such a character as to necessitate much expense, with the object of keeping out the poorer class of worker. The result was that the apprentices who could not qualify as craftsmen slowly became a new class of journeymen, condemned to work for, I wage for the wealthy members of the craft. The journeymen in time became so numerous that they formed themselves into associations. They are the forerunners of the wage-earning class, the ancestors of the modern proletariat. Their attempts at organisation for protection were not to the liking of the municipalities, which were controlled by the gilds merchant and the craft gilds.

The earliest evidence of this development is in London, where in 1303 the cordwainer journeymen were refused permission to make ordinances for themselves. From that time onward the growth of the journeyman class was very rapid, and the different associations which rapidly sprang up afford evidence of the extent to which the division of labour and the specialisation of craft had progressed.

In the latter half of the fourteenth and during the fifteenth century, journeymen associations were formed of saddlers, cordwainers, tailors, blacksmiths, carpenters, drapers, and ironmongers. In the sixteenth century, founders, fishmongers, clothworkers, and armourers were added to the list.

Three strongly characterised industrial and trading classes-the merchant, the craftsmaster, and the journeyman-had developed therefore out of the feudal system of lords and tenants. The apprentices did not form a distinct class, as their function was to develop at first into craftsmasters, but later increasingly into journeymen. Whence did these classes trace their source? Not from the feudal lords, since it is only comparatively late in the day that we find the cadets of noble families, the Dc La Poles of Hull and others, embarking upon industry. The recruits of industrialism were drawn from the tenant classes, from the freemen, the villeins, and the serfs. The Act of 1406 refusing apprenticeship to sons of men whose income was less than £1 per annum shows that a trade career had offered an avenue of escape from the soil even to the poorer grades of tenant.

The infiltration of the cash nexus into feudal society had up to this period, on the whole, connoted an increase of freedom and economic well-being. Counter-currents were not wanting, it is true, and the flow from fixed status to freedom was by no means

Historical Backdrop 41

devoid of them. Those currents will be found to grow in force later on until the promised freedom will turn to an economic pressure akin to thraldom. This trend will, however, not develop until the cash nexus shall have yielded to the credit or finance nexus. The tenants, then, freed themselves from the soil and migrated to the towns.

The resultant growth of the towns in size and in power is a feature of the period from the thirteenth to the fifteenth centuries. Civic authority passed from the hands of the gilds merchant to those of the craft gilds, not without a fluctuating struggle. Civic rights were secured by a charter of incorporation. These charters were given by the Kings grudgingly, as they were held to be an alienation of royal powers.

But the King's necessity or his ambition proved the road to civic freedom. Henry II., for instance, snatched at the crown of Sicily for his son in 1255, and found himself embroiled in an expensive foreign policy. To this fact may be traced the grant of many borough charters:-Norwich, Nottingham, Northampton, Lincoln, and Lynn in 1255; eight further ones in the following year. But the gild authorities used their powers, not only to secure their freedom, but artificially to protect their industry.

They introduced regulations to control prices, hours of labour, influx of apprentices and journeymen. The passing of power from the gilds merchant to the craft gilds freed the merchant from his dominating urban interests, and his search for gain led him to develop new avenues of production. Open-field cultivation was slowly giving way to enclosed-field cultivation; arable land was being turned into pasture, and the wool clipped from the sheep was supplying the material for England's great staple industry.

The woollen industry was one of the oldest in England, already well developed in the twelfth century. It then declined, but regained prominence in Edward III.'s reign (1327-77) partly owing to the encouragement given to Flemish weavers to settle in England. The decrease of arable meant at first the depopulation of the countryside, and the growth of sheep farming (1500-50) led to many bitter complaints. Legislation endeavoured to check it, with indifferent success. Poor Law measures to relieve distress were framed, at first on a voluntary basis (1531), afterwards to be made compulsory (1563). After many years, however, the sheep runs were to deal a hard blow at the towns, those protected corporations which seemed so secure in their privileges.

The struggle between the towns and the countryside is connected with the rise of the clothiers-the merchants who specialised in the staple industry of the country. The clothier is regarded as the forerunner of the modern capitalist, but can better be looked upon as the primitive financier.

In the early days of the merchant class the inequality of fortune was not greatly pronounced. The gilds merchant had some of the aspects of communism. An early privilege of the gild member was that of sharing in any bargains made by a fellow-gildsman.

This privilege was modified later on, but would certainly tend to equalisation of profits. It was only on the decline of the gilds merchant that evidence of huge fortunes in the merchant class comes to hand. In 1363 a London vintner was of sufficient prestige to feast four Kings, while in 1460 William Canynges, a clothier of Bristol, entertained Edward IV.

In 1339 Thomas Blanket of Bristol is cited as employing in his own house weavers and other workmen. He was a capitalist, with- the industry under his personal control. In the sixteenth century Jack of Newbury (John Winchcombe) had the reputation of being the greatest clothier England had yet known. He owned 200 looms within a single room. William Stumpe of Malmesbury is stated to have employed 2,000 men.

The attempts to restrict cloth manufacture to corporate towns and to keep up craft prices unduly, drove the industry into the market towns and to the countryside. The clothier ceased to be a direct manufacturer and tended to become a middleman, who bought the cloth from the small country weavers and disposed of it. To do this he required greater financial resources than had hitherto been necessary. His operations were limited, not by the size of his factories, but by his cash resources. He is the forbear of the modern financier.

The corporate towns did not submit without a struggle, but in the end artificial exclusiveness yielded to economic forces. Norwich declined in the early part of the sixteenth century. It sank from second to sixth city in the kingdom. Contemporary records show similar declines in other woollen towns and prosperity in non-corporate towns and villages. During the reigns of Edward VI, and Mary several Acts were passed to protect the corporate towns, but, though they retarded the decline, they could not arrest it entirely. Alva's persecutions in the Netherlands had more effect.

From 1564 onward they drove to this country Dutch, Flemish, and Walloon clothworkers, whose skill was greater than that of the native workers. Their arrival unsettled the cloth industry for a time. Norwich seized upon the opportunity to restore its shattered fortunes, and obtained permission for some of the immigrants to settle there. In a short time the town's prosperity was restored and its revenue doubled. Colchester enjoyed similar good fortune. On the whole, however, the corporate towns lost their privileged position, and a new type of town came into prominence. This is particularly noticeable in the West Riding of Yorkshire. York and Beverley declined, while Wakefield, Bradford, Halifax, and Leeds flourished.

In London the greater volume of commerce gave a somewhat different aspect to the economic development than in the corporate towns. In the latter the craft gild maintained its hold until threatened by the successful competition of the market town and the countryside.

In London greater specialisation took place in the craft gild itself, and gave birth to the powerful livery companies. The livery was at first a sign of fraternity. Later it became the sign of wealth and exclusiveness. Those of the craft who could afford to wear the livery associated themselves to acquire power and to exclude the poorer members. They then followed the custom of the times, and sheltered their privileges behind Royal Charters.

The Taylors Company (later known as the Merchant Taylors) first came into evidence in 1267, but only obtained its Charter in 1326. The Grocers followed in 1345, and the Mercers in 1347. Later still the Vintners, Drapers, Fishmongers, Goldsmiths, Skinners, Haberdashers, Salters, Ironmongers, and Clothworkers obtained similar privileges.

The members of these companies usurped the place of the old craftsmasters. They hired the journeymen to work for them for a wage, and established the permanent wage-earning class. The journeymen's prospects of setting up as masters dwindled, though it was still open to the more successful to do so.

It is interesting to form a parallel between the infiltration of the cash nexus into the social organism as a whole and into the more limited organism of craft industry. We have seen, in the former case, the original dues in service and in kind give place to cash payments, and so bring into existence the industrial groups of the crafts. In craft industry itself the relation between master and apprentice remained for a long time largely on a non-cash basis.

The apprentice gave his labour, and in return received instruction, food, and lodging. The earlier journeymen continued to lodge with the masters, receiving only a small wage until they could establish themselves in trade. As the period of journeymanship lengthened, and journeymen took to marriage before they were established independently, they lived away from their master's house, and the food and lodging was commuted into a higher wage. The advent of the clothier and the livery companies accelerated the process until the wage basis superseded the service basis.

The livery companie's were not long secure in their privileges, and soon began to feel pressure from a new source. The aggregation of cash resources, the expansion of trade, the greater enterprise of the people, led to the growth of international trade. Formerly this had been largely in the hands of foreigners, but now English merchants established connections abroad. These merchants

Historical Backdrop

appear to have been very largely self-made men, and, as such, were eyed askance by a writer of the sixteenth century, who complained that "the breeding of so many merchants in London, risen out of poor men's sons, hath been a marvellous destruction to the whole realm."

As they grew in prosperity and influence, the oversea merchants followed the customary procedure of association and incorporation. They had to meet the opposition of the clothiers and the livery companies, but in the end they gained the coveted position. The London Company of Merchant Adventurers was incorporated in 1407, and similar companies were formed in the provinces. A century and a half later the still greater aggregation of cash resources and the stimulus of maritime adventure was destined to bring into existence the great incorporated trading companies, such as the Levant (1581) and the East India Company (1600).

The fluidity imparted by the cash nexus, which slowly but surely was breaking down artificial and traditional restrictions in industry, was necessarily yet slower in its operation in the basic occupation of agriculture, partly because tradition and custom were more deeply seated, partly because the less conservative type was being lured into industry, and partly because the inherent characteristics of agriculture lend themselves less to rapid change. Such a change, was, however, manifesting itself. The open-field system of cultivation was essentially non-progressive.

The individual's holding was scattered in strips among the holding of the rest of the tenants. It profited little to root out weeds when they could spread again from an adjoining strip. The interlocking of services was a distinct handicap. The tenant with progressive ideas was tied both, as to his time and his methods by the hidebound custom of his cotenants.

The growth of commutation gave him a slowly widening avenue of freedom. He redeemed his control over his own time by a small money payment. The sale of his produce in the market towns increased his cash resources. He could buy out the holdings of his backward neighbour. He could consolidate several adjoining strips into a workable plot, which he could hedge round. Hence arose the fields that are a characteristic of modern England. His capacity for improvement was limited, it is true. Usually the lord was anxious for commutation, but the tenant's means were limited.

One great factor suddenly came to his aid. The Black Death (1348-49) depopulated the countryside. It destroyed almost one-half of the population. In doing so, it doubled the cash resources of the remainder. Commutation fees naturally tended to adjust themselves to the altered value of money, but were slow in doing so. The experience of 1914-20 has shown us that an alteration in the value of money will reflect itself in wages and prices of commodities sooner than in the rate paid for services.

Doctors', lawyers', school fees are controlled by social custom as well as by competition. Similar influences prevailed with regard to commutation fees. The peasants could obtain enhanced prices for their produce in the towns, and could purchase their freedom. If it were denied, they could leave their holdings and go elsewhere to work as agricultural labourers.

The wages of the latter class rose rapidly. The feudal lords were in a quandary; either they had to allow commutation at the old rates or risk losing their tenants. They yielded to the needs of their situation. Later on they invoked the aid of the law, and by unworthy artifices tried to cancel the commutations. This led to the celebrated Peasants' Revolt of 1381, when the peasants avenged themselves upon the lawyers for conniving at the malpractices of the feudal lords. Economically the peasants won. In spite of reactionary legislation which followed the suppression of the rebellion, villeinage had received the fatal blow. The landlords dared not demand services from their tenants.

The growth of enclosed cultivation was accelerated The next century was to see a trend towards sheep-rearing which temporarily dispensed with the services of the labourer and depopulated the countryside. It caused stagnation in agriculture for some centuries, but brought recompense in the development of rural weaving. Service and labour dues were not destined to disappear entirely

Historical Backdrop

in certain localities until a much later date, but on the whole the cash nexus had prevailed.

One aspect of the transition still remains to be examined. We have traced the aggregation of cash resources in the hands of the crafts, the merchants, and the peasants. The greatest aggregation was, however, to be found elsewhere. It has been pointed out previously that the commutation proceeded chiefly from the needs of the Kings and the feudal lords to maintain troops. Sombart has pointed out the difficulty of accounting for the growth of large cash masses through trade alone. He traces it rather to the commissariat arrangements necessary for the conduct of wars and crusades.

There is more than plausibility in the suggestion. It accounts for the emergence of the financier abroad at an earlier date than in England. The financiers of the early English Kings were the Jews. Despite the hostility of the people, they succeeded in carrying on their business. This was possible only by enjoyment of the Royal favour. In 1290, however, Edward I, expelled them. We can be certain that this far-sighted monarch did not take such a step until he found he could dispense with their aid. Their place was taken by the financiers of Italy. Loans were obtained from Lucca (1276-92), and Florence (1294).

The corporate English towns on a smaller scale also became money-lenders to the King. In 1318 Edward II, borrowed from London, and in 1351 Edward III. raised a small loan from Hereford. That the usual recourse to forced taxation was not made in these cases shows that the towns were now powerful enough to withstand royal extortion. In 1345 Edward III. repudiated a large loan owing to Florence, and thereby caused a collapse of the Florentine banks. After that, recourse was had to Netherland financiers, and it is not until after 1400 that cash aggregations in England had become sufficiently large to enable the Kings to rely upon their own subjects for their needs.

Having followed the action of the drama in this great transition from one form of society to another, let us view the technique by which it was wrought. Coins existed in England since the visit of Pytheas, a Greek, 330 BC. Before the Roman conquest British Kings issued their own coinage, with, peculiarly enough, the inscription in Latin, as, e.g., "Cunobelinos Rex." During the Roman occupation commerce prospered and Roman coinage was introduced. After the Romans left the island (AD 400) trade disappeared and the nation relapsed. In the seventh century, however, the Kings of the Heptarchy issued their own coins.

Those of the kingdoms of Kent, Essex, and Mercia are known. In the eighth century the Norsemen settled in Scotland and Ireland and brought their coinage into use. Later on, indeed, it was to be through Scandinavia that the East sent to us the silver that formed the basis of our currency. In the time of Canute money had become customary to such an extent that heriots, the dues payable on succession to land and usually consisting of the best animals or similar payment in kind, had to some extent become commuted to a money due.

In the tenth century coin must have been still more familiar, as in AD 991 a money tax, the Danegeld, was instituted to buy out the Danes. After the Norman conquest the silver penny was the basic coin. In the reign of the Conqueror (1066-87) the silver penny weighed 22 grains troy. It steadily depreciated in weight, a depreciation which is held to have kept it fairly constant in value, as the price of commodities was falling. In the reign of Edward III. (1327-77) it weighed only 18 grains. In that of Edward IV. (1461-83), 12 grains. Mary (1553-58) reduced it still further to 8 grains, and Elizabeth in 1601 to 7 3/4 grains. This constant loss of weight is attributed to the practice of the money-changers in selecting the heavier coins for export.

The halfpenny and farthing were not coined until after 1200. Previously the needs for smaller change were met by dividing the penny into halves and quarters, an operation which was to find an interesting counterpart in Scotland six centuries later, when during the suspension of specie payment by the Government (1797-1823), the need for small change was met by tearing the £1 note in halves and quarters.

Historical Backdrop

Coinage was minted in every borough in the tenth century. The difficulty of securing uniformity was a real one. Henry I. (1100-35) had the right hand of all the moneyers in the kingdom cut off for debasing their issues. In 1300 an Act was passed to standardise the issue by insisting upon the "London touch", i.e., that all coins should be of the standard of those coined in London. Foreign trade brought into the kingdom a varying assortment of Continental coinage, and the trade of moneychanger was an important one.

Gold came into use but slowly. Henry III. (1216-72) introduced gold coinage imitated from the French and Italians, but the experiment was premature. Edward III. repeated it with greater success by coining the gold noble. The pound sterling itself shows a foreign influence, the word sterling being a corruption of easterling, the name applied to the foreigners from the Hanse towns. Gold and silver issued by the Royal Mints were equally the legal tender until 1670, when silver only was made legal tender till 1717, though no ratio was fixed between the two metals. From 1717 to 1816 gold and silver were again nominally legal tender at one guinea = twenty-one shillings, but in actual practice the gold coin was the real standard one, and this practice was legalised by the 1816 Act which made silver legal tender up to forty shillings.

The coinage was at first very crude, the impression being made by a blow from a hammer. Such coins easily lent themselves to clipping, sweating, and filing. It was only at a comparatively late date (1663) that the mill and press were introduced at the Mint. It appears remarkable that such a slender mechanism should have been the agent in breaking up one form of society and fostering another. Yet cash money acted as a solvent upon the rigid feudal organism, slowly dissolving its crust and setting free industrial layers which in turn tended to crystallise out.

The solvent, however, penetrated still deeper and set free fresh layers, so that the partially crystallised layers broke down under pressure from above and below, until the whole of the organism promised to become fluid and each molecule in it endowed with equal freedom of movement. That process was not to be completed.

The organism was later to develop symptoms of increasing rigidity. The differentiation between the classes was to become once more increasingly definite until modern society is threatened with a return to the primeval caste system. The study of this process will, however, take us out of the time of the cash nexus into the modern era of financialism.

From Cash Nexus to Credit Restriction

It is a long journey from the Middle Ages to the time when a group of powerful financiers is destined to throw the sinister shadow of an unseen despotism across the world. The first stage of historical development, a stage so fraught with industrial progress that the latter part of it has aptly been termed "the industrial revolution." Its financial aspect is characterised by the conflict between the powerful and privileged Bank of England and the small "six-partner" banks, ending in the extinction of the latter.

In the earlier days of finance its centre was in Italy and the Netherlands. The Bank of Venice was founded about 1400, that of Genoa 1407, Amsterdam in 1609, then followed Hamburg and Rotterdam. The Bank of England was not founded until 1694, at a time when English enterprise was already making itself felt over the known world.

The world's financial centre quickly passed from the Continent to England. The pride of place remained unchallenged until recently, when a regrouping of financial interests round New York has given serious cause for reflection. In studying English banking we are indirectly studying that of the world. All countries have conformed more or less to the English system, and the effects of that system are to be felt throughout the world's industrial organism.

The genesis of banking was in the craft of the gold smiths. We have already seen that the variety of foreign coin in England had rendered the trade of money-changer an important one. The money changer merged into the goldsmith. In the fifteenth century the English goldsmith could compare favourably with his fellow another countries. A Venetian, writing at the end of the fifteenth century, stated: "In one single street, named the Strand, leading

Historical Backdrop

to St. Paul's, there are fifty-two goldsmiths' shops, so rich and full of silver vessels, great and small, that in all the shops in Milan, Rome, Venice, and Florence put together, I do not think there would be found so many of the magnificence that are to be seen in London."

The aggregation of cash resources in the hands of the London merchants has been mentioned. The need for some safe place for storing money until it should be required for commerce made itself felt. The natural place to suggest itself was the city's stronghold, the Tower of London. But the merchants reckoned not upon the perfidy of princes. In 1640 Charles I seized £130,000 of merchants' deposits. True he restored it, using it as a lever for a forced loan of £40,000, but the merchants had learnt their lesson. They preferred to keep their treasures in their own possession or in charge of their cashiers. Here again, however, there were pitfalls.

During the Civil War which shortly ensued (1642) cashiers shared the prevailing custom of going to fight with the armies, and were not always averse to taking some of their master's treasures with them. The merchants found they could trust their cashiers as little as their King. The only class that inspired sufficient confidence was the goldsmiths, and the practice developed of depositing money with them.

To this practice is traceable the origin of both the cheque and the bank-note. The merchant, when he had large payments to make, would at first withdraw his money. Later on he hit upon the expedient of giving an order upon the goldsmiths to pay over the sum to the creditor.

The economy in the case where both debtor and creditor deposited with the same goldsmith is obvious. The merchant's order upon the goldsmiths to pay is the origin of the modern cheque. The goldsmiths gave receipts for all deposits placed with them, and soon the goldsmiths' receipts were used instead of merchants' orders to pay. Their circulating power was better. The goldsmiths were trusted, and their notes were freely accepted. They were the foundation of the modern bank-note. Nor was their popularity short-lived. Even after the foundation of the Bank of England they were in common use. The triumph of the goldsmith's note over the merchant's order to pay was a purely economic one. It supplies a historical corrective to the modern view that the cheque has supplanted the bank-note because it is a better instrument, the truth being that the cheque only survives because the issue of notes has been everywhere restricted.

During Cromwell's protectorate (1649-60) there was perfect security in the land. The Jews were allowed to return, though the legislation against them was not specifically withdrawn. The goldsmiths prospered exceedingly and the people trusted them. They began to be referred to as bankers. In the reign of Charles II. (1660-85) their lot was not so happy. Charles II was a spendthrift; he kept a standing army and a large fleet. He indulged in inconclusive wars with the Dutch. All this cost money. Charles got as much as he could from his good cousin, Louis XIV of France, and when that proved insufficient he borrowed.

Naturally enough he borrowed from the wealthy goldsmiths. Having done so, he took the shortest way out of the difficulty, that of refusing to pay back. In 1672 he suspended payment out of the Exchequer for twelve months. At that time he owed the goldsmiths £1,300,000, which represented the deposits of the merchants. Some ten thousand persons were ruined by this gracious princely act. Later he promised to repay, but negotiations were protracted, and it was only in 1705, in the reign of William and Mary, that the goldsmiths began to recover a small portion of the debt. Charles's action helped to settle the fate of the Stuart dynasty. It alienated the merchants.

Charles indeed lived and died a King, but his brother James had a short reign of three years, when the country dismissed him and called William of Orange to the throne. William responded to the call, and became King of England in 1688. He saw the need of binding the commercial interest to his cause. The goldsmiths' prestige had suffered a blow by the acts of the Stuarts, but the need for banking facilities was urgent. In 1694 the Bank of England was founded.

Historical Backdrop　　　　　　　　　　　　　　　　　| 53 |

The commonly accepted view of the Bank of England is that it is a paternal institution carefully watching over the financial good of the people and using its monopoly for their welfare. This view is unhistorical. The Bank of England was from its inception a privileged monopoly, jealous of its supposed rights as all monopolies are, short-sighted and deaf to the demands of progress. Its monopoly in the first case consisted in the fact that it was the sole bank to obtain an Act authorising its foundation.

When in 1696 the King promoted the foundation of the Land Bank, the Bank of England seriously set to work to protect itself. The Land Bank was a fiasco. It was formed on an absurd principle, that money could be lent on land to a greater amount than the land was worth. Only £7,100 was subscribed to the issue, of which the King contributed £5,000.

The Bank of England was founded with financial resources of £1,200,000, individual subscriptions being limited to £20,000. The entire sum was lent to the Government at 8 per cent, interest, plus a charge of £4,000 for management of the debt. The Bank therefore had an income of £100,000, but no cash resources save what it could obtain from deposits. The notes it issued bore interest at the rate of 2d. per diem per £100 (= 3 per cent.). This practice ceased in 1709.

The convertibility of these notes in the earlier days could only be secured by the directors themselves finding the cash for redemption when necessary. The failure of the Land Bank was used as a lever by the directors to increase their capital by another £1,001,171, and to obtain a real monopoly by the legislative provision that no other corporation in the nature of a bank should be established by Act of Parliament. The Bank of England was allowed to increase its note issue from the original £1,200,000 to the amount of its subscribed capital, but the notes must be payable on demand. This precluded the use of the 'option' clause, which was to play such an important part in Scotch banking later on.

The provision against the formation of other banks under Act of Parliament did not shield the Bank of England from competition.

The Company of Mine Adventurers, a fraudulent creation, constituted itself a note-issuing bank. Once more the Bank of England stirred itself in the defence of its monopoly. The Act of 1709 made it unlawful "for any body politic or any corporation whatsoever united or to be united in covenants or partnerships exceeding the number of six persons, in that part of Great Britain called England, to borrow, owe or take up any sum or sums of money on their bills or notes payable on demand or at any less time than six months." A similar restriction was subsequently to be made in Ireland, within a radius of sixty-five miles from Dublin, in favour of the Bank of Ireland, but fortunately Scotland never suffered from this form of legal tyranny.

The 'six-partner' restriction obtained for over a century, during a period which was to inaugurate the greatest industrial revolution the world has ever known. It is of the utmost importance to bear this in mind in considering the failure of the industrial revolution to realise the hopes which it called into being. Even in 1826, when the Bank of England consented to abandon this form of monopoly, it only did so in favour of an equally vicious one, that no bank of issue should be founded within sixty-five miles of London. With assured control of the world's financial centre it could eye with equanimity the competition of its provincial rivals.

The first Bank of England notes issued were for large amounts, not less than .£20. They were secured, be it observed, not upon tangible assets, but upon debt, the debt due by the Government to the Bank. The security of one form of paper upon another form of paper would appear to common sense somewhat illusory, and has been violently challenged. MacLeod says: "Each loan to Government was attended with an augmentation of currency to an equal amount. Now to a certain extent this plan might be attended with no evil consequences, but it is perfectly clear that its principle is utterly vicious. There is nothing so wild or absurd in John Law's Theory of Money as this. His scheme of basing a paper currency upon land is sober sense compared to it. If for every debt the Government incurs, an equal amount of money is to be created, why here we have a philosopher's stone at once.

What is the long-sought El Dorado compared to this ? Even there the gold required to be picked up and fashioned into coin."

"Granting that to a small extent this may be done without any practical mischief, yet, as a general principle, what can be more palpably absurd ?" MacLeod's question has gone unanswered. Its legacy remains for the present generation. Neither Governments nor Government-controlled banks have mended their ways. The Bank of France has notes in circulation to the amount of francs 37,100,000,000 secured as to francs 24,900,000,000 on advances to the State. England has a Treasury note issue of over £M300 secured only as to £M28 ½ in gold, £M19½ in Bank of England notes, and the rest representing Government debt. The practical mischief is being done. The currency has depreciated with respect to almost the only convertible gold currency left, that of the American dollar. Upon the ability of the nations to redeem their huge debts is staked the economic prosperity or disaster of their peoples.

Let us trace the onward sweep of the industrial revolution. In 1698 Savery invented his primitive engine for clearing watch from mines, showing that deep mining was already in hand. In 1705 Newcomen improved upon Savery's invention. In 1709 ironworks were founded at Coalbrookdale. In 1719 silk spinning was introduced by Sir Thomas Lombe. In 1733 Kay's flying shuttle increased the rate of weaving. These were but some of the forerunners of the still greater volume of industrial expansion in the latter half of the century.

The cash nexus had proved insufficient for the needs of industry. The additional aid of the Bank of England note could not satisfy the demands for currency. Banks commenced to spring up in the provinces. Small tottering institutions they were, doomed to inadequate resources by the 'six-partner' restriction. Still, they were all that could be had, and with their help England struggled forward. In 1750 twelve such banks had already been founded, each with its own note issue. In 1750 also, James Watt experimented with the power of steam. In 1755 ironworks were started at

Merthyr Tydvil. In 1759 the Bank of England supplemented the unwieldy £20 note by £15 and £10 notes.

The year 1600 had seen the formation of the first joint-stock company, the East India Company. Previous companies were simply merchant gilds incorporated to exploit a territorial monopoly, but with no joint liability. The growth of joint-stock companies was a characteristic of the seventeenth century. New lands were everywhere coming into the economic ken. Speculation in such ventures grew warmer and warmer, and finally boiled over in the great South Sea Bubble (1720).

That episode is too well known to need description. The Bank of England had a narrow escape. Parliament passed the Bubble Act to regulate the increase of joint-stock companies. The largest commercial enterprises, however, now involved such cash requirements that individuals could rarely undertake them. Hence Parliament had to sanction the incorporation of joint stock companies to an increasing extent. The dealing in shares of such companies became a separate branch of industry, and in 1759 the London Stock Exchange was founded.

Meanwhile the cotton industry was slowly progressing. In 1760 the export of cotton was only twentieth that of the woollen industry. But the former industry had one great advantage. The woollen industry was choked with Government regulations. Its younger rival's freedom of development was comparatively untrammelled. In 1764 Hargreaves invented the spinning jenny, in 1769 Arkwright the water frame, in 1779 Crompton the mule, in 1785 Cartwright the power loom.

Lancaster began to prosper. It attracted men of enterprise. Brindley, that untaught genius, built his first canal in 1761 between Worsley and Manchester; he followed this up, in 1766, with the one between Manchester and Liverpool. Soon his celebrated navigators, or 'navvies', were at work over England. Watt in 1769 patented his steam-engine. England was forging ahead. The growth of national wealth attracted the attention of the social "student. In 1776 Adam Smith wrote his Wealth of Nations.

Historical Backdrop

What was the Bank of England doing to promote the growing industry? It was keeping at least one eye upon its monopoly. It obtained a renewal of its charter in 1742 by an Act which reiterated the 'six-partner' restriction for all other banks. In 1764 it paid £110,000 for another renewal. In 1781 it lent £M2 to the Government for a further extension, and in 1800 £M3 in a similar bargain. It patriotically came forward to assist the Government in its wars, but economic history is silent as to its endeavours to help industry.

The community turned for financial support to those flimsy partnerships of 6 persons which the law allowed. Their number increased enormously. From 12 in 1750 they had risen in 1795 to no less than 400, and in 1810 to 721. Simple arithmetic will show that the whole financial transactions of the nation, apart from the Bank of England, rested upon the shoulders of less than 4,400 persons. Hastily springing up in response to an urgent need, many of these small partnerships lacked both financial and business stability and perished almost as soon as formed. Others rose in their stead. Some of their directors were unscrupulous, some were incompetent, some lacked substance.

In those cases the banks failed. Sudden and uncalled-for runs could be stopped by the use of the 'option clause' or 'post-dated' note, which steadily increased in use, but this safeguard was forbidden in 1765. More democratic than the Bank of England, the provincial banks abandoned the high value notes for notes of small amounts, in accordance with the pressing needs of the time. Undoubtedly they overdid it, but they were feeling their way in the midst of financial obscurity.

The paternal State, knowing the needs of commerce better than commerce itself, prohibited notes of less than £1 in England in 1775, and improved upon this in 1777 by increasing the minimum value to £5. During the currency restriction period of 1797-1823 small notes were again allowed, but were a second time prohibited.

It is a significant fact that the main industrial revolution was accomplished outside London. No great invention or enterprise appears to have had its birth in the metropolitan city. The Bank of England did not deliberately choke progress, but it lacked the incentive to enterprise that free competition alone can give. The area of its commerce is not clearly indicated, but it is a fair assumption, from the fact that in 1826 the Bank of England suffered the 'six-partnership' restriction to be withdrawn in favour of a monopoly of note issue within sixty-five miles of the capital, that that radius was the extent of its effective influence.

No small upstart private bank could compete at too close a range with the powerful corporation. The better known of the private banks, at any rate, were further afield. The area within the sixty-five miles radius became industrially the least developed in England.

The home counties dropped back into the agricultural stage. The metropolis itself sank from a city of industry to one of merchants and middlemen. It now lives on largely as a parasitic growth upon the industry of the rest of the country.

In the Middle Ages London and the towns near it had their industries. Spitalfields had its silk trade; Guildford was known in the fourteenth century for its cloth. The Weald of Sussex had its ironworks: in 1740 there were still ten furnaces at work, with an output of 1,400 tons per annum, but the industry was already a declining one. Yet the other agricultural counties in England prospered under their provincial banks.

Defoe, in his Tour, tells of the cloth industry of Bradford in Wiltshire and of Frome, the serge of Devises, the dyed cloths of Stroud, the industries of Trow-bridge and Taunton. That belt of country, fifty miles by twenty, from Cirencester in the north to Sherborne in the south, from Witney in the east to Bristol in the west, was, according to him, "a rich enclosed country, full of rivers and towns, and infinitely populous, insomuch that some of the market towns are equal to cities in bigness and superior to many in number of people."

This flourishing district included, in addition to its rivers, other assets, such as Wood's Bank in Gloucester, founded 1716, originally

Historical Backdrop

a candle shop, the Bristol Old Bank (1750), Gillet's Bank at Witney, Stuckey's Bank in Somerset. Lincolnshire possessed Smith's Bank at Lincoln, and Garlit's Bank at Boston, and its agricultural machinery might claim with some right to be the best in the world. "By 1800," Toynbee says, "the manufacture of silk hosiery had centred in Derby, that of woollen hosiery in Leicester, though Nottingham had not yet absorbed the cotton hosiery. But at the beginning of the century there were still many looms round London and in other parts of the South of England. In 1750 London had 1,000 frames, Surrey 350."

In 1779 the iron bridge was constructed at Coalbrookdale. In 1783 Bell introduced calico printing. In 1785 Watt's engine was applied at Popplewick in Nottinghamshire to cotton mills. In 1790 the first iron vessel was built. In the same year Symington made his first attempt with the steamtug, and was successful some twelve years later. Wakened out of the torpor of controlling regulation by the strides of the cotton industry, the woollen manufacturers bestirred themselves.

In 1800 they adapted cotton machinery to their own business. In 1808 Heathcoat produced his lace-making machine, and in 1813 Blackett's 'Puffing Billy' marked another step in progress, while in the same year Bell's Comet appeared on the Clyde. Stephenson was heard of in 1814. Pit-props were first used in 1795, and the invention of the Davy lamp (1815) shows that mining was reaching deeper levels, where explosive gases were to be met with.

In 1814 the first woollen mill was established at Stanningley near Leeds, the event marking the decline of weaving at home. Roads underwent improvement, Macadam introducing his system in 1815. In 1825 the first railway was laid between Stockton and Darlington, to be followed in 1830 by that between Liverpool and Manchester.

The rise of industry was accompanied by an advance in agriculture. The common field system had lingered on. Enclosures had been made sporadically in the previous centuries, but in 1750 the old communal method of husbandry still checked progress over the greater portion of the arable land. According to Toynbee, "though these common fields contained the best soil in the kingdom, they exhibited the most wretched cultivation." Arthur Young states: "Never were more miserable crops seen than all the spring ones in the common fields, absolutely beneath contempt. The trend towards enclosed cultivation was noticeable in Norfolk in the first half of the eighteenth century".

The enclosures were economic in origin and made without Parliamentary aid. The result was that Norfolk developed an improved type of husbandry, which made the name of this county so famous in the farming world. Stock-breeding attracted attention. From 1760 to 1785 Bakewell reared his celebrated 'Leicester' breed of sheep. At the same time the brothers Culley produced the Shorthorn or Durham breed of cattle.

Tull's system of husbandry, which he practised in Berkshire in 1701, died with him, and war not revived again until shortly before 1770. The supremacy of enclosed lands over common fields became so obvious that from 1774 onwards Bills were introduced into Parliament to enforce enclosure.§ The first General Enclosure Act was passed in 1801, and others followed. But legislation accomplished with great injustice what the economic trend had effected smoothly elsewhere. The labourers were dispossessed with scant regard to their rights, and bitter indignation was aroused.

The action of the private banks in the promotion of agriculture is worthy of notice. The anonymous author of The Utility of Country Banks Considered, writing in 1802, and speaking of the Gainsborough district, says: "Sandy heaths and marshy bogs have been converted into fertile fields, and several extensive enclosures have been undertaken, to the great advantage of the country and the profit of individuals, which improvements have been greatly promoted by the banks of that thriving town." Again he narrates: "I had an opportunity of observing the improvements which have taken place within a very few years in one of the most barren and desolate parts of England, I mean the Wolds of Yorkshire, whose bleak mountains, which hardly furnished a blade of grass to a few famished sheep, are now waving fields of corn. The crops of oats and barley were, this last harvest, immense. . . . Improvements like these are objects of national importance, and it is my opinion that they never could have been effected without the aid derived from the country banks. The Bank of England would not have advanced the sums necessary."

Let us turn for a moment from these glorious triumphs of economic history, won by enterprise and competitive banking, to international relations. France had been under a powerfully centralised monarchy. Militarily it had had a period of glory. Louis le Grand Soleil gained victories by his marshals over all his enemies, but towards the end of his reign the tide turned, and when his sun set he left an impoverished and hungry people. Economically they were still in the stage of craft industry. The two succeeding reigns saw matters go from bad to worse.

The royal expenses grew while the people became poorer. In 1789 the great Revolution broke out. How hateful craft restrictions must have become is shown by the fact that one of the earliest acts of the Revolution was to abolish the gilds (1791). The rise of Napoleon is not essentially a matter of economic interest, but his war with England was fated vitally to affect the world's financial future. He had to fight the world's great financial power, and he fought it with the same weapon. He had no State Bank when the conflict began, but he soon learnt the need for it. Doubtless he found that private banks preferred the innocent gains of commerce to the destructive profits of war. In 1800 he established the Bank of France. In 1803 he bestowed upon it the privilege of note issue in Paris and other cities where it had branches. In 1848 it acquired an exclusive privilege in this respect.

The war between England and France was waged between an industrial country and a military genius. England won rather by its factories than by the small but dauntless armies that it despatched to fight the Corsican. The Continental nations were vanquished with surprising ease, but England supplied the sinews of war for them to fight again. The manpower of France was sapped by years of campaign while the industrial resources of England grew.

From the financial point of view, the war was one between two States supported by their privileged banks up to the pitch of almost ruining their respective nations. The position in England was that there was one bank only with ample cash resources, the other 400 being stunted in this respect by an absurd restriction.

Such scanty cash resources as they could command were drained from them, not for the arts of peace, but for the devilries of war. The Government began to call upon the country's cash resources. In 1793 a loan of £M6 1/4 was issued. Between 1793 and 1801 loans to £M314½ were issued, of which £202,372,000 was raised. The withdrawal of cash resources was a hard blow to the country banks.

The weakest went to the wall. In November, 1793, in one month alone, out of the 400 banks, 100 failed, while 200 others were severely shaken. The drain of gold was first felt at Newcastle, where the banks stopped payment. The shareholders had adequate resources to meet all demands upon them, but the Government had filched their gold and denied them the protection of the 'option' clause or post-dated note.

The internal strain upon gold was followed by an external one. In 1795 England made its first foreign loan to Germany, £4,600,000; in 1797, a second one of £1,620,000. Up to 1801 £M15 was raised for the benefit of our Allies, of which more than £M9 was paid in cash. Again the provincial banks succumbed to the withdrawal of their cash resources. The crisis of 1797 originated, according to both Baring and Tooke, in the latter half of 1795. In 1793 nearly £M3 was exported in cash for loans and other purposes, in 1794 in 1795 £M11. Even the Bank of England with its larger resources found it necessary to protest emphatically. In December, 1794, it declared it could no longer assist the Treasury. Pitt replied by obtaining a fresh advance of £M2.

Again the crisis began at Newcastle, the concentric drain of gold towards London naturally making itself first felt at the most distant point. The panic swept through the country, and threatened to destroy the Bank of England itself. The latter's cash resources dropped to £1,272,000. There was no alternative but to suspend cash payments. On May 3, 1797, the Bank Restriction Act was passed, forbidding the Bank to make any payments in cash to any creditors or to use cash for any payments except to the Army and Navy or in pursuance of an order from the Privy Council. This Act remained in force till 1823.

The industry of the country was threatened with ruin. The country banks had to restrict and call in their advances, and their clients were obliged to cover themselves by forced sales of securities, factories, and goods at immense sacrifices. To what was the disaster due? To the instability of the provincial banks, says the complacent school of orthodox economy. Not at all. To the short-sightedness of Government.

The war may have been a historical necessity, but Government restrictions had prevented a financial system being established on sufficiently strong foundation to stand the shock. The privileged Bank of England supinely handed over the nation's cash resources for export to Continental Allies, and industry received the worst set-back it had known since the inauguration of the industrial revolution.

The country banks never recovered their prestige. Staunch supporters they found in plenty to plead their cause, but: the trend of history was against them. Not economic history, be it remarked, but political history. Militarism was rampant, and privileged interests waxed under its shadow. With the decline of the country banks we see the beginnings of that movement of unrest among the workers which in the long run so strangely upset the philosophic tenets of the Manchester school.

The industrial revolution had not been accomplished without an immense amount of economic disturbance. The depopulation of the countryside of the first half of the fifteenth century had given place to a prosperous population, combining the still primitive agricultural methods with weaving at home. The improvement in agriculture in the latter half of the eighteenth century was localised and slow in spreading.

The growth of the factory system struck a blow at the countrysides method of livelihood. It displaced the domestic weaving industry. At the same time it offered to labourers good wages in the towns. It offered the most enterprising men chances of rising on the flowing tide to the position of large employers. They gladly availed themselves of the opportunities, and flocked to the new factory centres. While the provincial banks were allowed to carry on their beneficent work, complaints were scarcely to be heard except from the agricultural labourer, whose attachment to the soil left him an industrial derelict.

When the provincial banks succumbed to the State's folly, the vista changed. No longer could factories be erected to absorb the growing army of industrial workers. Expansion did not cease at once, but it lost velocity. The stress of lessening employment and worsened prospects provoked cries of complaint from the worker, which steadily grew in volume.

In 1802 the State interfered, taking the first step in regulating factory industry by protecting pauper labour. In 1831 the insistent appeals of the humanitarians further prevailed over the Manchester theories. It was a question of fact against doctrine. Protective legislation was extended to children. In 1844 it was further extended to women. Manchesterism fought with wonderful eloquence, but Manchesterism lost. The disillusioned workers became conscious that the system was not working to their advantage. Machines assumed the guise of evil spirits to be exorcised at all costs.

Antagonism to the introduction of machinery was nothing new. The gilds had always resisted it. Now, however, the antagonism took a violent form. In 1812 the Luddites started their machinery-breaking campaign. Industrial expansion was threatened from many sides. The vitality imparted by the provincial banks had been impaired, the credit of the country was swaddled by legislation,

Historical Backdrop

the cash resources were sapped by foreign loans, the worker was disappointed and defiant. The country struggled on. The Napoleonic wars were finished in 1815, leaving the nation crippled and prostrate, but recovery was not long in manifesting itself. The cessation of the cash drain enabled the provincial banks to flourish again. In 1821 cash payments could be resumed, though not Legally restored until 1823. Elasticity in credit developed once more. Manchesterism was at the height of its triumph. In 1823 Huskisson initiated his Free Trade policy.

The Napoleonic wars over, England returned to the financing of overseas enterprise. From 1822 to 1825 millions of pounds were invested in South American republics. England, freed from restrictions as regards cash payments, was again prospering. Tooke states that industry and commerce were never so flourishing as between 1821 and 1824.

The harvests in 1822, 1823, and 1824 were exceptionally good. A new speculation mania took place. It was the South Sea Bubble again. Companies were founded to the number of 624, with financial resources of £M372. Then came the crash. The Bank of England's reserve cash dwindled in 1824 from £M13½ to £M11½. In April, 1825, it had sunk to £6,650,000. Who was to blame?

Andreades emphatically puts the blame on the Bank, but the Bank itself was bound by restrictive legislation. It raised its rate to 5 per cent., the limit fixed by the Usury laws. The remedy was not sufficient, its reserves sank lower and lower, and in December, 1825, were only £1,260,890.

The drainage of cash resources to South America continued. Cash disappeared, though the Mint worked day and night. Stocks had to be sold at a ridiculous figure.

Once more the flimsy provincial banks, with no method of protection and with their restricted cash resources, quailed before the storm. Thirty-six of them failed. The Bank of England put into circulation 600,000 £1 notes, gave new advances of £400,000, and the crisis passed.

In spite of the aid of the £1 note in the 1825 crisis, notes under £5 were again prohibited in 1826, as the growing note issues of the provincial banks excited the jealousy of the Bank of England. At the same time the need for a more stable form of provincial bank was at last recognised, and the Bank of England reluctantly allowed the withdrawal of the six-partner limit in exchange for a monopoly of all note issue within sixty-five miles of London.

The legislators were even so ill-advised as to propose to extend the prohibition of notes under £5 to Scotland. They were startled at the apposition the proposal provoked. A whole nation rose in indignation. Sir Walter Scott, the great novelist, championed the popular cause. Rebellion was in the air and the Union was in danger. The advantages or disadvantages of the small note were a matter of intellectual discussion to English statesmen. To the Scotch people, who had risen to industrial triumphs by its aid, it was a matter of vital importance.

The advantage of the £i note over the £5 was demonstrated by the inflow of Scotch notes into England, so the circulation of these was prohibited in the latter country in 1828. The Act of 1826 allowed the formation of joint-stock banks in the provinces, with right of note issue.

It did not prevent the formation of similar institutions in London without such a right. So great was the need of financial accommodation that banks at once sprung up, availing themselves, in the absence of notes, of the method of cheque payments. The Bank of England, selfish to the end, could not tolerate the competition. It used all its influence with the Government, but it lost. The matter was referred to a Committee.

The Act of 1833 was the result. It made Bank of England notes legal tender, and exempted the Bank from the Usury laws in respect of bills of not more than three months, a valuable lesson from the 1825 crash. It did something more in reaffirming the legality of the joint-stock banks. The effect was remarkable. In the years 1835-36, upwards of one hundred new banks sprang up in England and Wales. Among them were the London and

Historical Backdrop

Westminster and the London Joint-Stock Bank. In 1839 the Union Bank and the London and County Bank were founded. These joint-stock banks were those very stable institutions which the country had yearned for during a century of expansion and warfare.

The slender six-partner banks handed over to them their task. All the big banks in England today were founded after 1833. Those founded before then have been swallowed up or crowded out. The Bank of England fought for its monopoly with an energy worthy of a better cause. The joint-stock banks, led by men like Gilbart, met power by ruse until in the end the Government was forced to intervene (1844.).

The lessening of the Bank of England's monopoly by the Act of 1833 was followed by three years of great prosperity. The competition of the new joint-stock banks lowered the rate of interest. Commerce and agriculture prospered.

The harvests of 1834, 1835, and 1836 were exceptionally abundant. Foreign countries raised loans in London to the extent of £M20. Railway, mining, canal, and banking companies were floated to the amount of £M135. The first shock came from America. President Jackson resolved not to renew the charter of the United States National Bank. This caused a panic, and the American houses sold all sorts of securities to the English banks.

The Bank of England alone advanced £M6. Then the harvest failed in 1838. England had to import cereals to the value of £M10 and export gold to do so. The Bank of Belgium failed at the end of 1838; the Bank of France protected itself by calling upon London for gold. Again the management of the Bank of England was at fault.

In spite of the demands upon it, it reduced its rate of interest from 5 to $3\frac{1}{2}$ per cent, in November, 1838. When the failure of the Bank of Belgium gave it an unmistakable warning it thought fit to send another £M1 to America. In May, 1839, it realised its situation, and raised its rate of interest to 5 per cent. Its reserve had then fallen to just over £M4. In July it sank to less than £M3, and the Bank of England was faced with bankruptcy. It tried to sell securities, but there were no buyers. In desperation it had recourse to the Bank of France.

Through the mediation of the Baring Brothers technical difficulties were overcome, and a loan of £M2 was arranged. The Bank had saved itself from its own folly, but at a cost to the community. Sixty-three other banks were dragged into failure, of which twenty-seven had separate note issues.

The crisis of 1839 profoundly agitated the public mind. England was the world's financial centre, and was without protection against demands upon its cash resources from abroad. The only protective device which had suggested itself to the bankers, the option clause or post-dated note, had been prohibited by the legislators. The interest aroused in the question is shown in the extraordinary number of pamphlets published at this period. Gradually the conflicting theories ranged themselves round two main principles: the Banking Principle and the Currency Principle.

The chief exponent of the Banking Principle was Tooke. The principle affirmed that the note issue should be unrestricted by the State as to quantity-that the community would protect itself against over-issue. Its adherents were not averse to State control of quality-i.e., protective measures against issue by worthless firms. In this they were false to themselves. The obvious remedy against bad notes was by promoting the competition of sound institutions which was how coming into play as a result of the Act of 1833.

The Currency Principle was most ably represented by S. J. Loyd (afterwards Lord Overstone). His school maintained the extraordinary principle that note issue was quite a distinct function from all other banking business, and that note circulation should be forced to correspond with the variations in bullion or cash reserves.

The argument was ably conducted on both sides. The Currency Principle won. The cynic may attribute its triumph, not to superiority of argument, but to the fact that its adherents (including the Bank

Historical Backdrop

of England) represented a greater weight of interest than its opponents. But the Currency Principle did not score a complete triumph. The absurdity of trying to apply it in its absolute terms was too apparent. Even Lord Overstone compromised. According to him the issue of notes should be confided to a bank exclusively established for this object. "The importance of a rigid adherence to this principle cannot be over-estimated; and if it be incompatible with the mixed functions of the Bank of England, it seems to become a serious question whether it is not better to separate altogether the business of banking from that of regulating the currency, rather than suffer so essential a rule to be in any degree compromised."

The impossibility of such an act was too great even for Overstone to urge it. Torrens hit upon a compromise. Instead of having a separate bank of issue, the Bank of England was to be divided into two departments. This was a veritable judgement of Solomon. The proposal was incorporated in the Act of 1844.

The Currency Principle failed in another point. It alleged that note issue should be based upon bullion. But the country's commerce was being carried on by a note issue not entirely covered by bullion. To reduce it to the necessary amount would be to court disaster. To allow it to expand would be to allow a repetition of the 1839 panic.

The solution was obvious. It must be fixed as it stood. Whatever the future needs of commerce, however great the expansion in industry, howsoever pressing the demands of finance, the uncovered note issue of the country must remain at the then level. This was also secured by the Act of 1844. The provisions were simple. The note issue of provincial banks was not to exceed the mean of the twelve weeks preceding April 27, 1844. All banks ceasing to redeem their notes on demand were to lose their right of issue.

No private banks could amalgamate and issue notes if the amalgamation resulted in an association of more than six persons. The notes of private banks were not to be legal tender. The intention of the Act was to eliminate the private issues. It has succeeded. When it was passed there were 207 private banks and 72 joint-stock banks of issue in England, with a circulation of £8,631,647. They have all disappeared. The note issue has been transferred to the Bank of England.

The Bank Charter Act of 1844 was the crowning piece of financial legislation. Every other nation has copied it. True, none have accepted it in all its rigidity. The Federal Banks of America and the Reichs-bank of Germany have a greater degree of flexibility, which has been an important factor in enabling these nations to overtake their rival. In the main, however, the views of Overstone and Torrens have prevailed. From 1844 onward we have to face the melancholy spectacle of economic society gradually losing its fluidity. Rigidity he comes increasingly pronounced in the social organism.

The working masses are born to a life of toil from which there is no reasonable prospect of escape. At the other end arises a small body of international financiers, whose workings are nebulous but effective. The presence of a subtle tyranny is felt, while its details are not yet properly focused. Freedom of contract gives way to a growing extent to the grip of status.

The individual cannot advance by his own efforts, so he bands with his fellows to escape from penury. The titanic efforts of organised Labour occupy the universal stage. There are no indications that the intestine struggles of society will lead to progress. On the contrary, there is every evidence that the fate awaiting the world is that of economic disruption.

Who passed the Bank Charter Act of 1844? None other than Manchesterism's greatest statesman, Robert Peel. The greatest deed of legislative interference in individual liberty came from the very man who is held to be its apostle. The history of Manchesterism coincides with an increasing interference with private banking, and Peel's Act was the crowning feat.

Retribution was speedy. Manchesterism succumbed to the assaults upon it, nor could all the eloquence of John Bright save it. The great Factory Act of 1847 showed the extent of its defeat, and the farther Acts of 1850, 1864, and 1874 bear testimony to its decline. The Anti-Corn Law League (1838-46) gave England its policy of limited Free Trade, but Cobden (1804-65) was not long in his honoured grave before the Free Trade doctrine was violently assailed. Its supporters are a dwindling number, and the return to Protection is an increasing possibility.

From Credit Restriction towards Financial Thraldom

Facts will be less easily controlled and trends must be examined the outcome of which is a matter of conjecture. We shall find that the suppression of the banks of issue has been followed by the emergence, in turn, of the limited liability company, the financial trust, and the financial pool. The financial system has not yet reached its full development, but some of its manifestations are so perturbing that we may well pause and ask whither that system is tending.

Peel's Act was applied in 1845 to Scotland and to Ireland. It soon caused a panic. Its sponsors alleged that the panic was in spite of the Act, but even they were forced to admit that they were disconcerted by its operation.

The panic occurred in 1847. The harvests in 1842, 1843, and 1844 were exceptionally good. Commerce was flourishing and speculation rife. In 1845 the Irish potato crop failed. In 1846 the failure was worse. Gold had to be exported to purchase cereals. The Bank's reserve fell from £M15 in December, 1846, to £M2½ in April, 1847.

The bank rate was raised to 5 per cent., but the panic continued. Between August and October bankruptcies involving £M15 took place. The Bank's reserve rose to £M8, only to fall again in October to £M3½. The rate was raised to 5½ per cent, in October, and advances were refused on public securities and Exchequer Bonds. Consols fell from 84½ to 77 3/4. The Royal Bank of Liverpool failed, and many other banks followed suit.

The Government authorised the suspension of the Act. The effect was magical. The mere knowledge that accommodation could be secured stopped the run. The Act had done nothing that its promoters had expected. The relation between note issue and bullion reserve had not been maintained. In August, 1846, the note issue was £M20 and the bullion £M16. In April, 1847, the note issue was still £M20, while the bullion had sunk to £M10. Baring was quite unable to explain the extraordinary phenomenon. Peel himself was obliged to acknowledge the wisdom of suspending the Act. It had neither prevented speculation nor a financial crisis.

The joint-stock banks now began to challenge the Bank of England in importance. The wings of the banks of issue had been clipped by Peel's Act. Their power to expand their credit facilities was rigidly curtailed. Enterprise had to turn elsewhere for accommodation, and it turned to the joint-stock banks. These had an advantage over the provincial banks in that they were not limited by the six-partner restriction. They could increase their financial resources by issue of new stock. It is true that they lacked the enterprise-the skill in meeting their customers' requirements that the note-issuing banker had always shown.

This has been attributed to the fact that the dealings between banks of issue and their clients were of a personal and intimate nature, and that this aspect of banking was bound to disappear when the small banks were replaced by the Targer ones. Such a view is erroneous. It was not a question of size which determined the private banker's methods.

His interest was to issue as safely as possible as many notes as he could, and he was only limited by his clients' power to build up industry. His activity was naturally directed into seeking out men of sound business ability and assisting to establish them in their business or to extend its scope.

The joint-stock banks were forbidden to issue notes. They had to find a substitute. Economists say that the cheque was a substitute and that its development rendered the note unnecessary. We have seen that cheque payment was a more primitive form of transaction than note payment, and had disappeared in economic evolution before a better system. Now that the law had suppressed the better

Historical Backdrop

form, the lower form again came into use. The cheque, rightly considered, is not a form of credit at all; it is simply a method of payment. A cheque drawn by anyone against his deposit at a bank does not represent a credit.

The deposit itself represents a credit from the individual to the bank. Such credit is useless to industry until the bank puts it at the disposal of producers. This is done by an overdraft, not by an actual loan of gold, but by giving: the producer a call upon a certain quantity of gold.

The difference between note credit and overdraft credit is of the utmost importance. To ignore it is to vitiate the whole science of economy. It can be summed up in a phrase. The cheque is centripetal, the note is centrifugal.

In other words, the tendency of the note, in normal times of industry, is to circulate further and further from its point of issue, to penetrate through all the industrial layers, from the biggest producer to the meanest wage-earner. The tendency of the cheque is in the reverse direction. Its trend is to be presented for payment or cancellation through the clearing house as soon as possible. Economic history affirms this.

The notes of the private bank were more popular even than coin. They vitalised the community. They gave the manufacturer the wherewithal to pay wages until he had marketed his goods. On the other hand, the cheque has never permeated the economic organism. Its use is confined to the upper strata only. It rarely enters into the lives of the workers, and is never used for wages. Comparison is obscured by the fact that until the recent war practically the only notes in England were those of the privileged Bank of England.

These notes in their cumbrous units (£5) were unwanted by the large mass of the people,. Compared with them the greater elasticity of the cheque was a boon. Neither cheque nor Bank of England note, however, could hold its own for long under open competition with the notes of an ordinary bank. The difference in character between the note and overdraft system of credit has led to one important result. The bank-note by its circulating ability replaces gold and relieves the strain upon the bank's resources. The overdraft has no circulating ability except that which can be obtained by the agency of a clearing house.

The effect is that the overdraft system means a much greater strain upon the cash reserve. This had to be met by increasing the cash reserves, not only by getting the shareholders to put up a larger sum total with which to start the bank, but also by encouraging the community to increase its gold deposits. To this difference is largely due the growth of the deposit system.

The practice of paying interest on deposits in England is comparatively a new one. The Bank of England still refuses to do so, but the Bank of England has practically ceased to be a people's bank at all, if indeed it ever deserved that title. It is today simply the bank for the bankers and the State. The joint-stock banks, to protect the overdraft system, were obliged to attract big deposits, and have therefore offered interest on deposit accounts since their formation in 1833.

Curiously enough the joint-stock banks advertise the huge amounts of deposits that they owe as a sign of their stability. It is to some extent an index of the confidence that the public has in them, but reflection will show that these deposits are in reality a huge liability which could not be met at any given moment.

The holders of deposit accounts with the Big Five banks have claims on these institutions for some £M1, 500 which they have deposited from time to time. This immense Sum is not covered by the cash reserve. The joint-stock banks have ceased to hold their own reserves, and have banked in their turn with the Bank of England. That institution has now the only effective reserve in the kingdom, some £M128½. A similar tendency has operated in other countries. The Bank of Belgium has the sole cash reserve of Belgium, the Bank of France that of France, and the German Reichsbank that of Germany.

The upholders of the present centripetal system of banking maintain that the concentration of reserves in one national store

Historical Backdrop

is a good thing. It must be pointed out, however, that economy is not a national but a world science, and that a nation's political boundaries do not correspond to a community's economic ones. The influence that has produced a centralised store of gold in the State bank is not economical but political in origin. It is the result of legal restrictions of note issue.

The centripetal trend has not yet run its full course, and to obtain a clear judgement as to what it really means its further development must be visualised. The cash resources of each country have been concentrated in one national store. The next step will be for these national stores to concentrate in their turn. There is a manifest tendency for them to do so, and unfortunately for England's claim to financial greatness there is no evidence that England will be the venue of that concentration. On the contrary, America has, by virtue of recent events, obtained an undoubted major call upon the world's gold supply, and slowly but surely gold is gravitating thither.

One result is obvious. As the private individual had cause to regret that he did not get the same consideration from the centralised joint-stock banks that he was able to get from the old banks of issue, so already have the nations of Eastern Europe bitter reason to complain that their urgent need for credits receives no attention. They are threatened with the alternative, either of economic dissolution into primitive agricultural communities, trading only by barter, or of obtaining credits from American financial pools at a crushing rate of interest.

A second result of the centripetal system should be equally obvious, but has escaped notice. The centralisation of credit control that has been going on since the passing of Peel's Act, and kindred Acts in other countries, has had a reflex action upon the whole industrial organism. It has induced that strange phase of modern industry known as trustification. It will be shown that this perturbing result is due, not to an inherent vice of capitalism, as the Marxists believe, but to the unnatural vice of State-restricted finance.

The deposit system was responsible for the most acute financial panic the world has known, which occurred in 1857. The greatest blow was felt in the United States. The great gold discoveries in 1849 had led to a large increase in cash resources and had induced great prosperity.

Railway expansion took place on an unprecedented scale. Between 1849 and 1857 some 21,000 miles of railroad were laid, about seven-ninths of the total railway system of that country. To finance the growing industries banks multiplied from 745 in 1847 to 1,416 in 1857. The statesmen had taken a lesson from England, and had passed Acts imposing limitations upon note issue. So restricted was the note issue that it was less than the bullion reserve.

Recourse was of necessity made to the overdraft and deposit system. To attract deposits high rates of interest were offered to depositors. The effect was to withdraw the cash resources of the nation from circulation into the banks' strongrooms. The restriction imposed by legislation prevented the issue of notes to replace the cash so withdrawn. The result was a sudden demand for currency, with a consequent panic. In New York alone, out of the sixty-three banks only one did not suspend payment. Throughout the country there were over 5,000 failures, with total liabilities of more than $M294.

The repercussion reached England, still struggling under the effects of the Crimean War. The demand for gold from the United States led to restriction of cash resources here. The Western Bank and the City of Glasgow Bank failed. The reserve of the Bank of England dropped from £M10 to £500,000 on November 11, in spite of a bank rate of 10 per cent. Next day the cash reserve was £320,000, and the bank was within forty-eight hours of bankruptcy. Again Peel's Act was suspended. Notes to the amount of £M2 over the statutory limit were printed, but only £928,000 had been put in circulation before the community's thirst for circulating medium was appeased and the panic was over.

The overdraft system of financing industry was not long in showing its limitations. It was efficient only for short-dated credits of a few months. It was a useful method for established businesses, but it did not assist in promoting new enterprises. That function had largely been exercised by the old banks of issue, but Peel's Act had limited their powers. A way out had to be found, unless industrial development was to be stopped.

The remedy was supplied in the first place by joint-stock companies of unlimited liability, but this soon proved unsatisfactory. Industrial evolution was creating business responsibilities vaster than before, both in regard to magnitude and period. An example will show what is meant. If a man fashions a rough piece of wood into a sandal and fastens it to his foot by withies, he receives the benefit of his labour the same day. If a man erects small brick works and sells his product, he needs small cash resources in the first place, and obtains his return probably within a year. If, however, a joint-stock company builds a railway it requires large cash resources, and its profit will not accrue until some years later.

The collapse of the railway boom in 1845 showed the perils to which the investors with unlimited liability were exposed. In the event of failure they wereliable for the company's debts to the extent of the whole of their possessions. The principle of limited liability was no new one.

It had been evolved by the Romans, but could only be exercised under charter of corporation granted by the Senate, which rarely gave it to a trading company. In England the same restriction held. The Bank of England itself was from the outset a limited liability company. The Act of 1694 laid down that the Bank was not allowed to borrow or owe more than the amount of its capital, and if it did so the individual members became liable to the creditors in proportion to the amount of their stock.

The resistance to limited liability was very great on the part of the established firms, but in the end vested interests had to yield to economic pressure. By the Acts of 1855 and 1862, a certificate of incorporation with limited liability was to be had for the asking. New companies sprang up everywhere in answer to the demand, hitherto suppressed, for industrial expansion. In 1863 limited liability companies were financed to the amount of £M100, in 1864 £M156, in 1865 £M107. No less than 3,480 companies were launched between 1863 and 1866. But when the leeway had been made up, the flotations dropped to normal again. In 1866 the total financed was £M68, in 1867 £M29, and the £M100 mark was not passed again until 1872.

The limited liability system has continued to grow in volume. Not only does it preponderate as a method of establishing new businesses, but almost every large old-established business has conformed to the new method. In assessing its place in the economic structure, however, it should not be forgotten that the system did not come into prominence until the banks of issue had been doomed to extinction.

Those banks had shown themselves to be the credit medium between the men of enterprise and the community. Had they been allowed to increase their resources by the abolition of the six-partner restriction, there is no reason why they should not have developed pari passu with the industrial side of commerce. The canals of England were dug by the financial aid of private banks, and the railways could have been constructed in the same way. Short-sighted legislation alone presented an insuperable obstacle and caused the growth of the system of limited liability, the defects of which have never been lost sight of by the social student.

The joint-stock banks were sufficiently stable to stand the panic of 1857, and were rapidly challenging the position of the privileged Bank of England. Another crisis was at hand. It occurred in two phases-the first in 1864, the second and worse in 1866. The events leading up to the crisis were as follows: The American Civil War (1861-65) strained the resources of that country. To pay its way the Federal Government issued non-convertible notes (green-backs).

The suspension of cash payment led to a great efflux of gold. Cotton-growing in the South was seriously affected, with the result that Lancashire industry was almost paralysed. The influx of gold into England from America was to some extent counterbalanced by exports to the East. Gold to the amount of £M24 was sent to India between 1862 and 1866. Trade was expanding, the limited liability companies were being floated to an undue extent, endeavouring to reach their economic level, since legislation had delayed their growth. Centralisation of cash resources proceeded rapidly. Deposits which totalled £M63 in 1860 had reached £M91 in 1864. In addition, the banking firms were trying to meet the needs of the expanding industry. Note issue being barred, they had recourse to a system known as 'financing', i.e., issuing accommodation bills on a large scale, not upon actual production, but upon prospective results.

A company, instead of issuing shares direct to the public through the medium of a limited company, would deposit its stocks and bonds with a finance company, which on that security advanced the necessary credit resources.

This practice of 'financing' yielded big profits, and led to many private firms entering into the field. Among these was Overend, Gurney and Company. This firm had had conspicuous success in its earlier transactions, financing cotton operations in USA and railway operations in Great Britain. It enjoyed immense popularity, and in 1865 was transformed into a limited company.

In 1864 the first stringency occurred. The bank rate was forced up to 9 per cent. The crisis seemingly passed, with the liquidation of the smaller tradesmen. But it left a feeling that the practice of financing was a risky one, and the more prudent finance houses withdrew. Overend, Gurney and Company continued. An action brought by the Mid-Wales Railway led to a judgement on May 9, 1866, that financing was illegal.

Two days later the crash came. May 11 is known as Black Friday in financial history. Lombard Street was besieged by a mass of applicants for accommodation. The Bank of England's reserve fell from £M6 to £M3 in a day, in spite of a 10 per cent rate. The same day the Government wrote to the Bank suspending Peel's Act, and the panic subsided in due course. Again (as in 1847) it was not necessary for the Bank to issue in excess of the limit imposed by Peel.

The crisis further centralised the banking interests by crushing out the weaker banks and the finance companies. It also crushed out many an enterprising tradesman. The failures actually recorded amounted to over £M50, and investments of every description were affected.

The crisis had one other effect. It brought into evidence the fact that the Bank of England was no longer the big banking influence in the world. The suspension of Peel's Act was urged upon the Government by the joint-stock banks, only the Bank of England's representative on the deputation withholding his hand. The Government could not withstand their influence, neither could the Bank of England. One of the representatives of the joint-stock banks bluntly said to the Bank of England's representative: "I can draw a couple of cheques tomorrow morning which will shut you up at once."

Financial development has since taken a step further. The influence of the joint-stock banks is now secondary to that of the Morgan pool. A similar threat would never be repeated in all its bluntness, but no one can doubt the power that lurks behind the silence. After 1866 English finance entered into a period of comparative stability.

The limited companies expanded in all directions. South America, particularly the Argentine, was fast developing, and the development was largely financed from London. The result was to be a failure which involved the greatest house of the nineteenth century. At one time Baring's reputation surpassed that of all others. Its bills were held to be safer than Exchequer Bonds. The years 1888-9 were exceptionally prosperous. People sought a good investment for their savings, and the growing prosperity of Argentina attracted them. Flotations for financing industry in that country were controlled by Baring's. Speculation became rife. South Americans took advantage of the position to promote unsound ventures.

Then doubts arose. In the spring of 1890 Argentine securities fell in value. The Bank of England foresaw the coming pressure

Historical Backdrop 81

and raised its rate to 6 per cent. The City financiers strongly objected. The joint-stock banks sided with the financiers and kept their discount rate at 4½ per cent, only. Under this competition the Bank of England was forced to reduce its rate to 5 per cent, and still further to 4 per cent.

Baring's were underwriters for a big flotation for the Buenos Ayres Water Works Company, but the public were frightened, and the house was left with the bulk of the issue on its hands. On 8th November application was made to the Bank of England for aid. Investigation showed that the soundness of the holdings in Argentine securities was very doubtful, and the world soon learnt that Baring's had failed. People rushed to realise their securities, and Consols fell sharply.

The crisis was tided over by the action of the Bank of England, which started a guarantee fund to cover Baring's obligations. In a few days £M10 was promised. The bank rate had to be raised to 6 per cent, but the Bank of France relieved the position by loaning £M3 to the sister institution in England.

The crisis was not as painful as those which had preceded it. It seized upon popular imagination rather by the fall of a great reputation than by the suffering it caused to the community at large. It was the last big crisis in England, and henceforth, the financial world was to be dominated by events in America.

The fall of Baring's has been attributed by some to the accumulation of funds in the hands of financial trusts, an important feature of modern finance. A financial trust is a company that operates by purchasing shares in industrial companies. These trusts originated first of all in a desire for security on the part of the investor.

In the early days of joint-stock banking the best form of investment was held to be mortgage on land, which, in a country still largely agricultural, was easily saleable. With the growth of centripetal finance England became more and more dependent on foreign sources for her cereals. Agriculture declined. Land mortgage ceased to be a safe banking investment. The advent of the limited company, in answer to the economic need for long credits, which the overdraft system could not undertake, threw the risk attaching to such investments on to the public. That element of risk was always great, since the public had no opportunity of thoroughly testing the soundness of the many new issues. Certain financial companies arose, the object of which was to eliminate or reduce the risk factor.

The London Financial Society, founded in 1863, spread its holdings over the many railway companies. Its object was not to promote new industry but to profit by established industry. The growing unwillingness of finance to promote new industry is one of the signs of economic sclerosis which was already beginning to invade the English industrial system.

The panic of 1866 showed that the railway stocks were not easily saleable in a time of financial stringency. The investing public therefore turned its attention to other directions. In 1868 the Foreign and Colonial Government Fund was founded. Its object was to lessen risk by spreading its holdings over a number of Government stocks. A similar institution was the Government Stock Investment Company.

The higher dividends paid by commercial undertakings led to kindred companies being formed to deal in industrial stock. The Submarine Cables Trust was floated in 1871. This was a trust to deal in a specific form of enterprise, but it pursued the method of distributing its holdings. Attempts were made to form a bank share trust, but the banks protected themselves by refusing to allow their shares to be sold to such bodies.

In 1884 the Mercantile Investment and General Trust was formed on more general lines and following upon that there came an increasing number of similar formations up to 1890, when the Baring crash gave a temporary check to the new movement. The movement soon recovered, however, and today the Stock Exchange list shows financial trusts in every branch of industry. There are, among others; milling, rubber, railway, cotton, telegraph, estate, and general trusts.

Historical Backdrop

Although these trusts were formed originally to reduce the risk attaching to investment, that aspect of their activity has fallen into the background. When they first appeared the presumed safe investments were few and dear. Consols were high in price and small in yield. The growth of State and municipal finance has led to a multiplicity of such investments, and has effectively transferred the savings of the timid investor from productive enterprise to the unfathomed pool of public debt. Since 1890 the Trusts have catered not so much for safety as for dividends.

They have become underwriters for fresh flotations, usually not for new enterprises but for the extension of old enterprises. In Stock Exchange jargon they are known as the 'shops.' Their ability to obtain inside information and their control of cash resources makes them a powerful factor in the financial world. If a trust buys, the stock is held to be going into good hands, the news gets round, and a boom ensues. If a trust sells, it is held that the industry whose stock is unloaded is in a bad way, and depression follows.

It has been maintained that the financial trusts have introduced a stabilising element in the value of securities. They act as a kind of barometer, by the study of which one can gauge the industrial situation. It would be difficult to prove this. Since the advent of the financial trust, with its power of enhancing and depressing the values of stocks and shares, the wildest fluctuations in values have occurred, boom after boom has been engineered, and slump after slump has followed.

The small investor is without protection, as he is beginning to learn to his cost. He can only cease to rely on his own judgement and commit his slender resources to the care of the trust companies.

If the normal rate of interest be 5 per cent., and manipulation of the market enables share values to be enhanced or depressed to a greater amount, it is obvious that there will be a constant incentive to gain, not from production, but from manipulation. Experience shows that such market manipulation is an increasing aspect of the financial system.

The transit of the world's financial centre from England to America is not yet an acknowledged fact, but there are many indications that this has already taken place. At one time the most powerful financial influence in the world was wielded by the European Rothschilds, with the English branch at their head.

In the latter part of last century stories of fabulous wealth, accumulated in the hands of American financiers, eclipsed the legendary tales of bygone ages, the splendours of the 'richest East', and the envied fortunes of Europe's magnates. The names of Vanderbilt and Astor became household words, to wane in glory before the greater lustre of Carnegie and Rockefeller. These in turn are dimmed by the transcending brilliance of the Morgan family.

It is significant that while England was the undisputed centre of the world's finance, crises developed their greatest intensity in this country. France and Germany suffered only their secondary repercussions. Fluctuations in bank rates were less feverish there than in England. Latterly the greatest crises have been in America, while England has suffered prolonged periods of financial depression.

The English crisis of 1890, great as it appeared at the time, was dwarfed by its sequel, the American crisis of 1893. The first shock was felt at the point furthest from the centre. The distrust caused by the failures in Argentine caused a sale of holdings in Australia. The withdrawal of cash resources was followed by the failure of many Australian banks. The repercussion was felt in Germany, Austria, Italy, France, and even Turkey. It caused the closing of the mints in India and the shutting down of one-third of the silver mines of the world.

The growing distrust led to a refusal by European financiers to invest further in American industry. The interest on old investments was no longer reinvested in the country, but was transmitted to Europe. The result was an unquenchable drain of gold from the American banks. The enforced circulation of silver by the passage of the Sherman silver law further operated to drive

Historical Backdrop

out gold. The gold in the United States Treasury sank from $M326 in 1889 to $M171 in 1896. The result was that in the period June to August, 1893, no less than 141 banks suspended payment. The business failures in 1894 numbered over 15,000, and more than one railway system went into liquidation. Money rates jumped in one day from normal to 75 per cent. The crisis was due not to over-issue of notes, but to the deposit system and to State restrictions.

Financial history after the panic of 1893 is largely that of the financial pools. A financial pool is formed by the pooling by big financiers of the resources of the financial trusts and the industrial companies that they control, in furtherance of an agreed policy. The Standard Oil Company, in which John D. Rockefeller was the leading spirit, played an important part in controlling industry in America, until the mastery passed later to the Morgan interests. J. P. Morgan's interest in Standard Oil was at first a minor one, but apparently increased in course of time. It was, however, owing to his obtaining control of the banking system that he was able to become the world's dominating financier.

In February, 1895, he was associated with the London Rothschilds in a syndicate to supply 3,500,000 ounces of gold to the United States Treasury in return for Government bonds. The panic of 1893 had led to a constant outflow of gold, which had caused prolonged trade depression. Morgan allied himself with the gold-shipping firms in an attempt to stabilise the exchange price of the dollar so as to keep gold in the Treasury. The attempt failed in July, 1895. He nevertheless competed to buy a further issue of bonds for the same purpose, and his syndicate obtained $M38 of them out of an issue of $M100. In 1899 he was associated with the Standard Oil interests in the flotation of the Amalgamated Copper Company, the unsavoury story of which has been graphically described by the originator of the proposal.

In 1900 came the great fight between Morgan and Hill for the control of the Northern Pacific Railway. The price of the stock under constant buying rose from 43 3/4 in September, 1900, to 180 in May, 1901. It then became evident that a corner had been manipulated in the stock, which rose to 1,000! Operators were obliged to throw all other securities into the market to cover themselves, and prices slumped. The money rate rose to 75 per cent in one day, and the morning after the crisis it was back again at 3 per cent.

In 1901 Morgan floated the United States Steel Corporation, financed at no less than $M 1,400. As underwriters Morgan and Company appear to have made a profit of $M12½ on a sum of $M25. The unfortunate shareholders lost heavily, the $100 shares ultimately sinking to $10. The production of the United States Steel Corporation increased by only 40 per cent in the period 1901-13, while of its rivals, the Bethlehem Steel Company increased production by 3,779 per cent, and the Inland Steel Company by 1,495 per cent, in the same period.

In 1902 Morgan formed a syndicate to carry through the conversion of the United States Steel Corporation bonds. Apparently the result of this operation was to give the underwriting syndicate some SM7 as a reward for raising some $M13 2 for the Corporation. The deal was made the subject of an action at law, on the ground that it was a deliberate attempt to 'milk' the shareholders for the benefit of the underwriters, with whom many of the directors were associated. The directors won a complete legal victory, while grave reflections were cast upon the motives of the shareholder who challenged their action. There is, however, little doubt that the legal verdict was the reverse of the moral verdict.

The period 1902-07 was noticeable for a great money stringency in the United States. This was particularly evident in the autumn when the crop movements took place. The reserves of the New York banks fell below the legal limit in September, 1902, twice in 1905, four times in 1906. In 1905 the rate for call money touched 125 per cent.

The same period was remarkable for a growth in the State banks. The National banks, incorporated under the Federal laws, had proved insufficient for the country's needs and banks developed outside the ambit of those laws. They lacked certain of the privileges

Historical Backdrop 87

of the National banks, but they supplied a want. In 1900 their number was 9,519, in 1907 it reached 13,317. Their resources increased from $M5, 841 to $M11, 168, and their cash reserves from $M221 to $M392.

In 1907 occurred the most sensational panic America had ever known. The long period of depression had given place to a period of trade expansion, and from 1904 onwards speculation for a rise in prices took place.

The increasing trade led to a demand for cash for internal circulation. Gold was imported from Europe. In October to December, 1907, some $M124 was imported, yet the reserves of the New York banks declined by $M61. Some $M300 was absorbed in internal circulation. The crash came very suddenly. A financial pool had gambled in copper and had involved certain banks in its operations.

There was a collapse in the stock market. Buying power disappeared mysteriously. The shrinkage in values was no less than $M 5,000. The clearing-house banks refused to clear for the banks involved in the copper pool.

The position on the Stock Exchange became most critical. Its president, Mr. Thomas, called upon Morgan at 2.20 p.m. on October 24, and informed him that the Exchange must close unless money was forthcoming. The same afternoon Morgan summoned the presidents of the big New York banks, and pledged a fund of $M25 to relieve the situation.

The generally accepted view is that Morgan acted as a public benefactor in the matter. The more reasoned inference would appear to be that he had carefully manipulated a panic, and stepped in exactly at the moment when he could derive the maximum advantage. The sequel is interesting.

The Secretary of the United States Treasury, Mr. Cortelyou, hurried back to New York and insisted that the financial interests of the country should be united. The one man capable of assuming control was Morgan, and he dictated his own terms. Large deposits of public funds were transferred from the Treasury to the National banks, to the extent of $M35 in New York alone. With the aid of these and other resources Morgan proceeded to help the jeopardised banks, but only upon the condition that he should replace certain directors and managers by men of his own choice.

In addition, the circulating medium of the country was increased by the issue of certificates by the bank-clearing houses. These were issued to the amount of $M100 in New York, $M37 in Chicago, $M13 in Philadelphia, and to smaller amounts in other cities. The crisis passed as rapidly as it had developed, but it had done incalculable damage not only in America but elsewhere.

The English bank rate rose from 4½ to 5½ per cent, on October 31, to 6 per cent, on November 4, to 7 per cent, on November 7, the highest mark since 1873. In January, 1908, it fell again to 4 per cent. The result of the crisis was to make Morgan the supreme controller of the most powerful banking system in the world.

The crisis was not due to excessive note issues. It was due to that economic arch-folly, State interference in note circulation. The crisis passed as soon as the banks issued clearing-house certificates. This is affirmed by a celebrated modern economist, who yet, curiously enough, supports the heresy of State control of banking.

Morgan took advantage of his triumph in 1907 to secure the passage of the Aldrich-Vreeland law in 1908, and of the Federal Reserve Act of 1913, which placed the control of the banks of the United States under a board of seven people. This Act forced the National banks, and practically compelled the State banks and Trust companies, to place their ultimate reserves under the control of the above-mentioned Board.

The outflow of public expenditure during the Great War has somewhat obscured the working of the new system, but the general result is clear. The nations of the world are dependent

Historical Backdrop

upon America for credit, and American finance is controlled by the Morgan pool. As far as can be seen at present, America is itself in the throes of a credit stringency, and the hope that Europe cherishes of obtaining adequate aid upon reasonable terms from the United States would seem doomed to frustration.

The financial pool differs from the financial trust in one important respect. The trusts are definite organisations, registered under law. Their actions are, to some extent controllable.

The pools are merely shadowy groups of undefined personalities. They are created and dissipated at the arbitrary decision of financial magnates. They operate through their control of the resources of the banks and the financial trusts. They induce artificial inflation and artificial depression. They work their will upon the world's industrial needs. They transfer their activities from wheat to public debt, from public debt to oil, from oil to sugar, from sugar to railroad systems.

No market can withstand their influence. They enhance the gigantic fortunes of their members to transcendent dimensions. The determining influences of the world's destinies are within the control of a few men, who can be numbered almost on the fingers of the hand. Within this narrow circle the fight for supremacy goes on. Pools are broken and reformed as power fluctuates from one side to another.

Under their operations rich men have found their envied wealth crumble to nothing. The dominating pool at present is the Morgan pool. Financial control may pass from it to other and more forceful pools in future, but the tendency is centripetal and financial power becomes daily more concentrated.

The crowning point is not yet reached, but the end is in sight. That end is the control of the world's resources in the hands of a small group of financiers, a despotism more monstrous than the world has ever known.

Statistical Verification

Last Thousand Years

Since both the level of prices and the quantity of money in circulation cannot in practice be perfectly measured, and since the level of prices depends upon other factors besides the quantity of money, - viz. the quantity of circulating credit, the velocities of circulation of that credit and of money, and the volume of business, - it would be absurd to expect any exact correspondence between variations in the quantity of circulating money and variations in the price level; and it is likewise absurd to state, as some have stated, that the absence of exact statistical correspondence proves the absence of any influence of quantity of money on price level. Nevertheless, when the volume of money changes greatly and quickly, the effect on prices from this cause is usually so great as to make itself manifest.

The general trend of prices has usually been upward, as Figure 101 shows. According to the diagram prices are now about five times as high as a thousand years ago and are from two to three times as high as in the period between 1200 and 1500 AD. Beginning with the last-named date, or shortly after the discovery of America, prices have almost steadily risen.

The discovery of America was followed in 1519 by the invasion of Mexico under Cortez and, twenty years later, by Pizarro's conquest of Peru. From these conquests and the consequent development of New World mining of precious metals, dates the tremendous production of gold, and especially of silver, during the sixteenth century.

From the discovery of America until the after effects of its discovery began to be felt, or, to be exact, through the year 1544, the average annual output of gold was less than five million dollars, and of silver about the same. The rich mines of Potosi in Bolivia were discovered in 1546. Prom 1545 to 1560 the annual production of silver averaged eighteen millions, which was over fourfold the previous rate. The product of gold also increased, though slightly. The rates of production for both metals rose steadily (with slight interruption, 1811-1840) up to the present time.

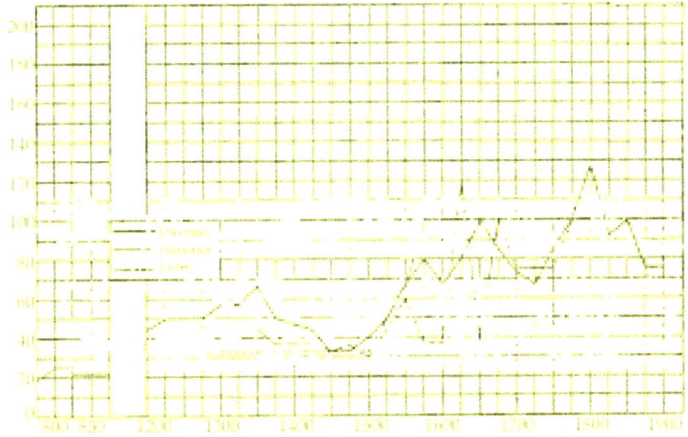

Figure

These new world mines began to pour their product into Europe: first into Spain, the chief owner of the mines, then, by trade, into the Netherlands and other parts of Europe, and then into the Orient - that great 'sink of silver.' Accordingly, as Cliffe Leslie has shown, prices rose first in Spain, then in the Netherlands, and then in other regions.

But, though the new supplies of the precious metals distributed themselves very gradually through Europe, and the rise of prices was consequently in some regions delayed, there can be no doubt that they rose or that the rise was great. The rise between the discovery of America and the beginning of the nineteenth century was several hundred per cent. This rise was simultaneous with an increase of the stock of the precious metals, because production outran consumption.

Although the total production of the precious metals continued to increase until 1810, the ratio of the yearly production to the existing stock became gradually less. Corresponding to this slackening of production, and presumably because of it, prices did not continue to rise at the same rapid rate as at first. Furthermore, with the development of trade with the East, more and more of the new supplies found their way thither. The most rapid rise occurred during the sixteenth century.

Last Four Centuries

The stock of money metals at any time in any country is evidently the difference between the total product and the sum of the consumption and the net export. Jacob has estimated roughly the stock in Europe at various dates. The following table compares the estimated metallic stocks in Europe with the estimated price levels:

Money and Prices

Estimated Product, Consumption, and Stock of Precious Metals in Europe, expressed in Millions of Dollars, and Price Levels with the enormous increase in the quantity of the precious metals, small wonder if prices have risen!

Date	Product and Export	Consumption	Stock	Prices
1500	670	290	170	35
1600	640	740	550	75
1700	4280	3880	1420	90
1800	13,000	8960	1850	100
1900			5890	125 (?)

There has been a general increase (1) in the stock of money metals, and (2) in the price level, and that the greatest increase of each was in the sixteenth century. We find also that the prices did not increase as fast as the quantity of money. This relative slowness on the part of prices was to be expected, because of the increased volume of business. This, we know, must have come with increased population and with progress in the arts - especially the arts of trade - and with development in transportation. As to changes in the velocity of circulation of money we know absolutely nothing.

Historical Backdrop

Nineteenth Century

During the last century the price movements have been more carefully recorded and show many ups and downs. The most complete statistics (those of Sauerbeck) are for England. They are represented in figure below. As is well known, English prices were inflated by the issue of irredeemable paper during the Napoleonic wars. This period of the paper standard extended from 1801 to 1820. But prices in paper were only slightly higher than prices in gold, and the chief price movements (except in a few years) were but slightly affected by the existence of a paper standard. The main periods of price movements in England since 1789 may be stated as follows:

Prices rose 1789-1809, stock increasing.

Prices fell 1809-1849, stock stationary.

Prices rose 1849-1873, stock increasing.

Prices fell 1873-1896, stock increasing slightly.

Prices rose 1896-present, stock increasing.

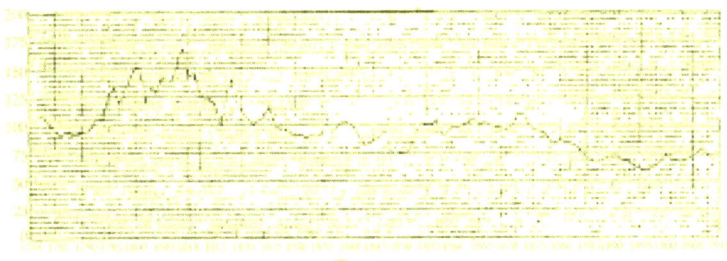

Figure

In each case is cited the movement in the stock of money metals in Europe as given in the table of Del Mar. The only period which does not, at first glance, agree with what we might expect if our theory of price levels in relation to money is correct, is the period 1873-1896. Of the other four periods, three are periods of rising prices and increasing stocks. The fourth is a period of a stationary stock; and since the volume of trade undoubtedly increased, a fall of prices was naturally to be expected.

The exceptional period 1873-1896 — a period of falling prices — is probably to be accounted for by the increasing volume of trade and the successive demonetisation of silver by various countries. The foregoing parallelism between monetary stocks and prices is somewhat remarkable in view of the incompleteness of the data.

In the table there are lacking, not only exact statistics as to the volume of trade and all statistics whatever of velocity of circulation, but also statistics of the volume of bank notes, government notes, and deposit currency. We know, however, that modern banking, which had scarcely developed at all before the French Revolution, developed rapidly throughout the nineteenth century. It is also known that banking and deposit currency developed more rapidly during the third period in the table (1849-1873) than during the fourth (1873-1896), which fact contributes somewhat to explain the contrast between the price movements of these two periods.

Price Movements

We may, therefore, summarise the course of price movements during the nineteenth century by the following probable statements:

- Between 1789 and 1809 prices rose rapidly, the index numbers of Jevons moving from 85 to 157 when prices are expressed in the gold standard, or 161 when expressed in paper. That is, prices practically doubled in twenty years. This rise was due to the increased stock of gold and silver, which in turn was due to their large production during this period as compared with the periods before and after. The production of silver was especially great. The Napoleonic wars with their destruction of wealth and interference with trade probably exercised some influence in the same direction.

- Between 1809 and 1849 prices fell. The fall was measured by Jevons as a fall from 157, gold (or 161, paper), to 64. That is, in forty years prices were reduced to less than half, or, to be more exact, to two fifths. This fall in prices was

Historical Backdrop

presumably due to the lull in the production of the precious metals, which prevented the aggregate stock from keeping pace with the volume of business. Indeed, the aggregate stock remained stationary while the volume of business increased. Even the development of bank currency was insufficient to offset the continued increase in the volume of business. It is interesting to observe that this period of falling prices was interrupted by a temporary rise after 1833, which Jevons was at a loss to account for, but which was apparently due to the inflow of Russian gold after the discoveries of gold in Siberia in 1830.

- Between 1849 and 1873 (although with two notable interruptions) prices rose. They rose, according to Jevons's figures supplemented by Sauerbeck's, from 64 to 86, and according to Sauerbeck's alone, from 74 to 111. That is, in 24 years prices increased, according to one calculation, by one third; according to another, by one half. This rise was presumably in consequence of the gold inflation following the famous California gold discoveries in 1849 and Australian discoveries in 1851 and 1852. The simultaneous rapid development of banking contributed to the same result in spite of the continued increase in trade.

- Between 1873 and 1896 prices fell This fall was presumably due to the slackening in the production of gold; to the adoption of the gold standard by nations previously on a silver basis, and the consequent withdrawal of gold by these new users from the old; to the arrest of the expansion of silver money consequent on the closure of mints to silver; to the slackening in the growth of banking; and to the ever present growth of trade.

During the long fall of prices from 1873 to 1896, country after country adopted the gold standard. We have already seen that Germany adopted the gold standard in 1871-1873, thus helping to render impossible the maintenance of bimetallism by the Latin Union. The Scandinavian monetary union adopted the gold standard in 1873.

Between that date and 1878 the countries of the Latin Union suspended the free coinage of silver and came practically to a gold basis. In the United States the legislation of 1873 signified that with resumption (which took place in 1879), the country would come to a gold basis, although no considerable amount of silver, except for small change, had been coined here for several decades previously. The Netherlands virtually adopted the gold standard in 1875-1876, Egypt in 1885, Austria in 1892, India in 1893, Chili in 1895, Venezuela and Costa Rica in 1896, Russia, Japan, and Peru in 1897, Ecuador in 1899, and Mexico in 1905. In fact, most countries of importance have now definitely adopted the gold standard.

The preceding figures apply only to gold countries. But in 1873 gold and silver countries, as it were, fell asunder. It is interesting, therefore, to enquire whether the movement of prices in gold countries was parallel or antithetical to that in silver countries. As might be expected, we find it antithetical. The demonetisation of silver in gold countries made a greater amount of that metal available for silver countries. Accordingly, we find that prices rose in India from 107 in 1873 to 140 in 1896, in Japan from 104 in 1873 to 133 in 1896,2 and in China from 100 in 1874 to 109 in 1893.1 These figures, although not as reliable and representative as the figures for gold countries, agree in indicating a rise of prices. The amount of rise is differently indicated, ranging roughly from 10 per cent to 35 per cent. The following table shows the contrast between the gold and silver countries as between 1873-1876 and 1890-1893, the last year being that of the closure of the Indian mint to silver.

Prices in Gold and Silver

	GOLD	SILVER
1873-1876	100	100
1890-1893	78	117

The gold prices fell a little more than 20 per cent and that silver prices rose a little less than 20 per cent.

If some way had been contrived by which gold and silver could have been kept together (say by world-wide bimetallism), prices would not have fallen so much in gold countries, or risen so much (if at all) in silver countries, but would probably have fallen in gold countries slightly - probably about 10 per cent up to 1890-1893 and more up to 1896. This is because the stocks of specie in silver countries were less than half those in gold countries (including those with the "limping standard" from leftover silver); so that had there been a transfer of a given amount of silver from the silver Orient to the gold Occident, this would have affected Oriental prices about twice as much as Occidental.

The transition of India from the silver to the gold side has left about nine tenths of the specie (gold and overvalued silver) in the gold column. In other words, the world is now practically on a gold basis. The result has been to make Indian prices move in sympathy with European prices, instead of in opposition.

- From 1896 to the present, prices have been rising because of the extraordinary rise in gold production and the consequent increase in money media of all kinds. The gold of South Africa combined with the gold from the rich mines of Cripple Creek and other parts of the Rocky Mountain Plateau, and reinforced by gold from the Klondike, caused, and is still causing, a repetition of the phenomenon of half a century ago.

That there has been a distinct rise in prices is evident from the figures of all index numbers. Those of The Economist, Sauerbeck, Dun, the Labour Bureau Reports, and Bradstreet are given here.

English Close of Dec.	Economist	Sauerbeck	American Dun	Labour Bureau	Bradstreet
1896 ..	1950	61	74	90	59
1897 ..	1890	62	72	90	61
1898 ..	1918	64	77	93	66
1899 ..	2145	68	85	102	72
1900 ..	2126	75	91	111	79
1901 ..	1948	70	91	109	76
1902 ..	2003	69	102	113	79
1903 ..	2197	69	99	114	79
1904 ..	2136	70	97	113	79
1905 ..	2342	72	98	116	81
1906 ..	2499	77	105	123	84
1907 ..	2310	80		130	89
1908 ..	2197	73		123	80
1909 ..	2373	74		127	85

The high points of 1900 and 1907, as compared with the low level of 1896, must be regarded as at least partly due to expansion of credit. The fairest comparison (to eliminate the effects of undue changes in credit) is perhaps that of the years 1896, 1903 and 1909. That the rise of prices has been world wide is evidenced not only by index numbers, which are only available for a limited number of countries, but by general impressions of consumers and by special reports and investigations.

Retrospect

It will be seen that the history of prices has in substance been the history of a race between the increase in media of exchange (M and M') and the increase in trade (T), while (we assume) the velocities of circulation were changing in a much less degree. Knowing little of the variations in the development of trade, we may tentatively assume a steady growth, and pay chief attention

Historical Backdrop

to the variations of circulating media. Sometimes the circulating media shot ahead of trade and then prices rose. This was undoubtedly the case in the periods numbered 1, 3, and 5 of the five periods just considered. Sometimes, on the other hand, circulating media lagged behind trade and then prices fell. This must have been the case in the periods numbered 2 and 4.

It is important to emphasise at this point a fact mentioned; namely, that the breakdown of bimetallism and the consequent division of the world into a gold section and a silver section have made each section more sensitive than before to fluctuations in the production of the precious metals. The present flood of gold can spread itself only over the gold section of the world, and not over the whole world as was virtually the case with the Californian gold immediately after 1849. At that time gold displaced silver in bimetallic France and sent it to the Orient. In this way the Orient afforded relief for bimetallic countries by draining off silver and making room for gold; and the bimetallic countries thereby afforded relief to gold countries also.

Since 1873, therefore, the gold reservoir of Europe and America has been separated from the silver reservoir of the East, with the consequence that the European and American reservoir level has been made more sensitive to either a scarcity or a superabundance of gold. The result has been to aggravate both the fall of prices from 1873 to 1896 and the present rise, although the later effect is mitigated by the previous extension of the gold standard.

The Outlook

The outlook for the future is apparently towards a continued rise of prices due to a continued increase in the gold supply. Today almost as much gold is produced every year as was produced in the whole of the 16th century. The most careful review of present gold-mining conditions shows that we may expect a continuance of gold inflation for a generation or more. "For at least thirty years we may count on an output of gold higher than, or at least comparable to, that of the last few years." This gold will come from the United States, Alaska, Mexico, the Transvaal, and other parts of Africa and Australia, and later from Colombia, Bolivia, Chili, the Ural Province, Siberia, and Korea. It must be remembered that it is the stock of gold and not the annual production which influences the price level; and that the stock will probably continue to increase for many years after the production has begun to decline, - as long, in fact, as production keeps above consumption.

A lake continues to rise long after the freshet which feeds it has reached its maximum. So the stock of gold will continue to increase long after the annual production of gold has stopped increasing. Whether or not prices will continue to rise depends on whether the increase in gold and the circulating media based on gold continues to exceed the growth of trade. It is the relation of gold to trade that chiefly affects prices. Even if the stock of gold should increase for many years, prices may not rise; for trade may increase still faster. If the annual additions of gold to the total stock remain constant and consequently the stock continually increases, the ratio between the constant annual addition and the increasing stock will evidently decrease, and the increase in stock will count for less and less in raising prices.

It is difficult to predict the future growth of trade and therefore impossible to say for how long gold expansion will keep ahead of trade expansion. That for many years, however, gold will outrun trade seems probable, for the reason that there is no immediate prospect of a reduction in the percentage growth of the gold stock, nor of an increase in the percentage growth of trade. Not only do mining engineers report untold workable deposits in outlying regions (for instance a full billion of dollars in one region of Colombia alone), but any long look ahead must reckon with possible and probable cheapening of gold extraction. The cyanide process has made low grade ores pay.

If one lets imagination run a little ahead of our times, we may expect similar improvements in the future whereby still lower grades may be worked or possibly the sea compelled to give up its gold. Like the surface of the continents, the waters of the sea contain many thousand times as much gold as all the gold thus far extracted in the whole history of the world. It is to be hoped

Historical Backdrop 101

that the knowledge of how to get this hidden treasure may not be secured. To whatever extent inventors and gold miners might be enriched thereby, scarcely a worse economic calamity can be imagined than the resulting depreciation. It may be, however, that only by such a calamity can the nations of the world be aroused to the necessity of getting rid of metallic standards altogether.

Paper Money

We have briefly summarised the history of price movements since the discovery of America and shown their relation to the stock of the precious metals. But, as we have emphasised, the precious metals do not include all forms of circulating media. Paper money and bank deposits have come during the nineteenth century to occupy very important places in currency systems.

We shall not attempt any complete review of the effects of paper money on prices. The best that can be done is to mention briefly the most striking cases of paper money inflation and contraction. These are all cases of irredeemable paper money. When paper money is redeemable, its possible increase is restricted by that fact and, what is more important, the effects of the increase are dissipated over so large an area as to have little perceptible effect on prices.

This dissipation takes place through the export of specie from the country in which the paper issues occur. Though the paper cannot be itself exported, it can displace gold or silver, which amounts to the same thing so far as spreading out the effect on prices is concerned. But when the paper is irredeemable, after specie has been expelled from circulation (whether by export, melting, or hoarding in anticipation of disaster) there is no such spreading-out effect. The effects on prices are then entirely local and therefore greatly magnified.

The consequence is that the most striking examples of price inflation are cases of irredeemable paper money. The rise of prices is often still further aggravated by the gradual substitution of other and better money or resort to barter, which further restricts the sphere in which the paper is used and within that sphere makes it the more redundant. Where the paper money is looked upon with disfavour, for whatever reason - whether because its promised redemption has been indefinitely postponed, or simply because of the bare fact that it is depreciating, or because of any other consideration-its sphere of use is restricted. Creditors and tradesmen avoid taking it if they can, by 'contracting out' in advance; by barter; by fixing a double set of prices, one in paper and the other in some other money; and by outright refusal.

In the end it may happen that the paper ceases to be used at all. In that case its value depreciates indefinitely and therefore prices (so far as still expressed in terms of paper) rise indefinitely. Whatever the situation, the equation of exchange continues to hold true though its significance becomes of less importance, because T, instead of comprising practically all trade, comes to mean only that disappearing portion of trade still transacted by means of paper money.

The value of irredeemable paper money is, therefore, extremely precarious. If once it starts depreciating - from whatever cause - it is likely to depreciate further, not simply because of the ever present temptation to further issue, but also because of a growing public sentiment against it which sooner or later restricts its use. In many cases the irredeemable paper money continues to be used with sufficient acceptability to give it a virtual monopoly as a medium of exchange.

Although theoretically irredeemable paper money may be the cheapest and most easily regulated form of currency, and although, in some cases, it has remained a stable currency for a considerable period, the lesson of history is emphatically that irredeemable paper money results in monetary manipulation, business distrust, a speculative condition of trade, and all the evils which flow from these conditions.

Paper Money in France

One of the early paper-money schemes was that of John Law, who established a bank of issue in France in 1716. Two years later

(December 4, 1718), the bank was taken over by the Crown. Soon shrewd traders were acquiring specie for notes and exporting the specie secretly, although exportation of specie was illegal. May 27, 1720, only four years after its establishment, the bank stopped payment of specie. By November of the very same year the paper had fallen to one tenth of its par value, and after this it became utterly worthless.

The case of the assignats of the French Revolution is classic. It was in December, 1789, that the first issue, four hundred million francs, was ordered, based ostensibly on the landed property of the nation. The notes were issued in April, 1790, and bore 3 per cent interest. According to the original plan, all of the assignats received in payment for land were to be burned. But original plans seem never to be carried out with respect to paper money. Instead, a hundred millions were reissued in the form of small notes. Prices began to rise.

In June of the year 1791, six hundred millions more were issued. Depreciation to the extent of 8 to 10 per cent immediately followed. Specie was rapidly disappearing. Another three hundred millions of francs were ordered in December, 1791. By February, the assignats were over 30 per cent below par. In April, 1792, came a decree for the issue of three hundred millions more, and in July for the same amount additional. Most prices were very high, but wages seem to have still remained at the level of 1788. By December 14 of 1792, thirty-four hundred million francs had been issued in assignats, of which six hundred millions had been burned, leaving twenty-eight hundred millions in circulation.

Laws were enacted to fix maximum prices, but were evaded. By 1796, forty-five billion francs had been issued, of which thirty-six billions were in circulation. In February of that year the gold louis, of 25 francs, was worth 7200 francs in assignats; and the assignats were worth 1/288 of par. A new kind of paper money, the mandate, was next issued, but soon fell to 5 per cent of its nominal value. In the end the twenty-five hundred million mandates and the thirty-six billion assignats were repudiated and became entirely worthless.

Paper Money in England

England's experience with irredeemable paper money was more temperate. Under the stress of the Napoleonic wars, the Bank of England suspended cash payments in 1797. This nullified the force which automatically limited overissue. The bank resumed cash payments in 1821. During much of the intervening period of paper money, prices in paper were very high. The following table of Jevons shows the relative prices in notes and specie from 1801 to 1820:

Year	Gold Standard	Paper Standard
1801	140	153
1802	110	119
1803	125	128
1804	119	122
1805	132	136
1806	130	133
1807	129	132
1808	145	149
1809	157	161
1810	142	164
1811	136	147
1812	121	148
1813	115	149
1814	114	153
1815	109	132
1816	91	109
1817	1171	120
1818	132	135
1819	112	117
1820	103	106

The causes of the rise of prices, were discussed in the famous Bullion Report. The general conclusion reached was that a "rise of the market price of gold above its mint price will take place," if the local currency of any particular country, "being no longer convertible into gold, should at any time be issued to excess. That excess cannot be exported to other countries, and, not being convertible into specie, it is not necessarily returned upon those who issued it; it remains in the channel of circulation, and is gradually absorbed by increasing the prices of all commodities. An increase in the quantity of the local currency of a particular country will raise prices in that country exactly in the same manner as an increase in the general supply of precious metals raises prices all over the world. By means of the increase of quantity, the value of a given portion of that circulating medium, in exchange for other commodities, is lowered.

In other words, the money prices of all other commodities are raised - that of bullion with the rest." This is an excellent statement of the philosophy of irredeemable paper money when that money is sufficiently within bounds to remain in general use. No mention is made of partial or complete abandonment of use because of worthlessness. The reason is doubtless that in England the paper money never reached this pass, as it undoubtedly did in many instances in France, Austria, America, and elsewhere.

Paper Money in Austria

Austrian experience with paper money is instructive. Like so many of the European banks, that of Austria was used by the government as an instrumentality for obtaining loans. This was done by allowing the bank to issue large sums 'in notes. The wars with Napoleon demanded supplies, and during these wars the issue was largely increased. In 1796 the note issue was 47,000,000 gulden; in 1800 it was 200,000,000; in 1806, it was 449,000,000. The notes were much below par. In 1810 the bank notes fell successively to 1/5, 1/8 and about 1/11 of par.

In 1811 a proclamation openly valued them at one fifth of their nominal value and decreed their exchange at this rate for redemption notes, called the Viennese legal tender, which became the Austrian legal-tender currency. But even these new issues soon fell to 1/216 of their face value (May, 1812) and 1/338 of their face value (June, 1812), while the bank notes were at 1690 to 100 in silver. New issues were added under a different name until, in 1816, the amount of paper money was over 638,000,000, with prices, of course, tremendously inflated. In 1816 was founded the Austrian national bank, which was intended to draw in the paper money. From time to time thereafter the amount of paper circulation was reduced, but not without occasional relapses. At the present time Austria has no paper money which is not at par.

Early American Paper Money

Many of the American colonies had experience with paper money. In fact, one of the grievances against England was the parliamentary prohibition of paper money issues! In practically all cases there was overissue and depreciation. This was true, for example, in Massachusetts, where paper money was issued to pay the expenses of the expeditions against Canada, and in Rhode Island, which suffered more, perhaps, from paper money than any of the others. Following are figures for Rhode Island taken from the account book of Thomas Hazard (the entries and memoranda extending from 1750 to 1785), which show the height and variability of prices.

1755. Hat £20 Per Load

Corn Per Bushel		Butter Per Pound	
1751	25s.	1751	7s,
1758	50s.	1760	16s.
1762	100s.		

Wool Per Pound		Potatoes Per Bushel	
1752	8s.	1750	10s.
1756	12s.	1753	20s.
1759	28s.	1774	35s.
1768	32s.		

We had also during the Revolution a national experience with Continental paper money which gave rise to the derogatory phrase, still current, "not worth a continental." Depreciation began almost from the moment of issue (1775), and finally the money was recognised by Congress itself to have reached 1/40 of the nominal value. All prices, of course, were tremendously high.

Even the new tenor paper given for the old emissions at the rate of a dollar for forty declined rapidly in value. A bushel of wheat was worth, at one time, seventy-five dollars, coffee four dollars a pound, and sugar three dollars a pound. It is interesting to observe that, in this case, the depreciation seems to have been accentuated far beyond what mere overissue tended to produce, by a distrust of the money and a refusal to receive it in trade.

Several classes were disinclined to receive it to begin with, and as confidence waned, the number who were unwilling to receive it increased. Barter frequently took the place of trade with money. The depreciation was doubtless much greater because the paper money of various colonies helped to overflow the circulation, competing with the congressional money and limiting its sphere of circulation.

The Greenbacks

The effects were so disastrous that, in the Constitution of the United States, a provision was incorporated prohibiting any state from issuing 'bills of credit'. But, during the Civil War, the temptation again came to resort to this easy way of securing means of payment; and the federal government itself issued United States notes or 'greenbacks.' The banks had already suspended specie payments so that gold was at a slight premium in bank paper.

These greenbacks were issued from time to time during the war with resulting depreciation as their quantity increased, — a depreciation greater or less also according as failure or success of the Union armies affected confidence in the paper money. The amounts issued were: $150,000,000 by the act of February 25,

1862; $150,000,000 by act of July 11, 1862; $150,000,000 authorised by acts of January 17 and March 3, 1863. Besides the greenbacks (issued in denominations in no case under a dollar), there was some issue of fractional currency and of interest-bearing notes running for a brief period, both of which were also made legal tender. The rise in prices is shown by the following table:

Index Numbers of Prices During Geenback Depreciation
INDEX NOS. OF NORTHERN PRICES (1860 = 100)

Year	Price of Gold in Greenbacks	Falkner In Gold	Falkner In Paper	Dun in Paper	Mitchell Median in Paper
1861	100	94	94	89	96
1863	144	91	132	150	134
1865	163	107	232	169	158
1867	138	123	166	164	150
1869	136	112	152	143	158
1871	112	123	136	132	130
1873	114	115	129	124	130
1875	115	115	129	117	121
1877	105	107	114	95	100
1879	100	95	95	85	85

It has been asserted that the rise of prices during the greenback depreciation was not due to the quantity of the greenbacks, but to the public distrust of greenbacks. The truth is probably that it was due to both. Distrust was evident and restricted the sphere of greenbacks very materially. California and, in fact, all the region west of the Rocky Mountains, made strenuous efforts to prevent the circulation of greenbacks, - efforts which were largely successful. And naturally the greenbacks could not circulate in the South. These restrictions alone would confine their circulation to a population of about 20 millions out of a total population in 1860 of 31 millions, that is, to less than two thirds of the entire population. Therefore the volume of trade for which the greenbacks were used must have been greatly reduced.

The total circulating currency during the war is not known with certainty; but the best estimates of the various forms of circulating

Historical Backdrop

media are those compiled by Mitchell. Though he modestly warns the reader against any attempt to cast up sums, his results may be considered as at least of some value. The totals, omitting money in the Treasury and interest-bearing forms, which were known to have only a very sluggish circulation, we find to be as follows:

Year	Roughly Estimated Circulation in Loyal States Importance, Comprising	Prices of All Articles Averaged According to 68.60 % of Total Expenditure
1860	433	100
1861	490	94
1862	360	104
1863	677	132
1864	708	172
1865	774	232
1866	759	188

Considering the unreliability of the figures for currency and the lack of data as to the other magnitudes in the equation of exchange, there is here a rough correspondence between the volume of the currency and the level of prices.

Confidence in the Greenbacks

It is necessary to remember that the confidence with which we have to deal is not primarily confidence in redemption, but confidence in the paper money,-its purchasing power. This confidence may rest on expectation of redemption or on other conditions, particularly the expectation of further inflation or contraction. The explanation of the value of the greenbacks appears to me to be in brief as follows:

The Redemption Act of 1875 announced the intention of our government to redeem the greenbacks on and after January 1, 1879. Each greenback being thus kept equal to the discounted value of a full dollar due January 1, 1879, they rose steadily towards par as that date approached. Some of them were withdrawn from circulation to be held for the rise. The value of a greenback dollar could not be much less than this discounted value of the gold dollar promised in 1879; otherwise speculators might withdraw the greenbacks wholly. This would pay them well provided they were certain that the government's promise would be fulfilled.

On the other hand, the value of greenbacks could not, with paper money redundant for trade, be greater than said discounted value, because in that case speculators would return it all to the circulation, the prospective rise being "too small to repay the interest" lost in carrying it. Thus speculation acted as a regulator of the quantity of money. Thus the rise in value of the greenbacks, like other coming events, cast its shadow before. It was "discounted in advance." It is quite true that confidence in redemption was here the ultimate cause of the appreciation of the paper money; but the readjustments caused by this confidence include a reduction in the quantity of the money in circulation.

Without such readjustment the appreciation would be impossible, as the equation of exchange plainly shows. One should note, however, that if the price of the currency were already sufficiently high, the prospect of future redemption would not further raise it. It might happen that the value of the currency was already above the discounted par value promised at the time set for redemption.

In such a case there need not be any speculation or any immediate rise in value until the date of redemption drew near enough to make itself felt. On the other hand, when, during the war, the government announced a further issue of a paper currency already depreciated, the public anticipated its further depreciation by releasing such hoards and stocks as were available; in other words, by accelerating the circulation of money.

Each man hastened to spend his money before an expected rise of price, and his very action hastened that rise. Announcements of federal defeats in the war acted in the same way, being signals that further issues of greenbacks might be required; while announcement of victories acted in the opposite way, being like

Historical Backdrop 111

signals of probable redemption. When appreciation is anticipated, there is a tendency among owners of money to hoard or hold it back, and, among owners of goods, to sell them speedily; the result being to decrease prices by reducing the velocity of circulation and increasing the volume of trade. When on the contrary, depreciation is anticipated, there is a tendency among owners of money to spend it speedily and among owners of goods to hold them for a rise, the result being to raise prices by increasing the velocity of circulation and decreasing the volume of trade. In other words, the expectation of a future rise or fall of prices causes an immediate rise or fall of prices.

These anticipations respond so promptly to every sign or rumour that superficial observers have regarded the rise and fall of the greenbacks as related directly and solely to expected redemption and as having no relation to quantity. These observers overlook the real mechanism at work; they fail to see that these effects, though quick, are slight and limited. They are the simple adjustments of transition periods described. It would be a grave mistake to reason, because the losses at Chickamauga caused greenbacks to fall 4 per cent in a single day, that their value had no relation to their volume.

This fall indicated a slight acceleration in the velocity of circulation, and a slight retardation in the volume of trade; but, under ordinary circumstances, it is only slightly that the velocity of circulation can thus be accelerated; while to make trade stagnate long or completely would require a cataclysm.

Confederate Paper Money

In the South it is "impossible to state even approximately how many Confederate treasury notes were outstanding at any time." Professor Schwab has, however, given the value of gold in Confederate currency and index numbers of prices in the South. He concludes:

"This movement of the gold premium corresponds roughly with the amount of government notes outstanding in each period. The relatively rapid increase in the issue of notes after August,

1862, during the last months of 1863, and again during the last months of the war, is reflected in the rapid increase of the gold premium at those three times.

When the amount of outstanding notes remained stationary at the beginning of 1863, there was a somewhat slower advance of the gold premium during those months; while the shrinking of the outstanding notes during the first half of 1864 is distinctly reflected in a temporary decline of the premium.

"In the North during the Civil War the course of gold premium only remotely suggested the amount of notes outstanding at any time. The premium rose most rapidly, or, in other words, the notes sank in value most rapidly, at the beginning of 1863, recovering again during the second quarter of that year, declining after August, 1863, to their lowest point in the summer of 1864, and rising again during the last months of the war. The value of the 'greenback' was much more a barometer of popular feeling as to the eventual outcome of the war than a gauge of their amount in circulation, for the latter did not materially increase after July, 1863, and certainly not after July, 1864. In fact, the gold value of the federal 'greenback' ran closely parallel with the gold value of the federal bonds during the war. This is also true of the confederate bonds and treasury notes. These two sets of parallel fluctuations were evidently caused by the changing credit of the two governments concerned.

"A general index number for either section, based both on a simple and a weighted average, can be constructed. The lines plotted to indicate these two sets of figures do not run parallel, but converge and diverge during different periods of the war, converging at those times when events in the military, the political, or the financial field discouraged the South, and correspondingly encouraged the North in the general belief that the war was approaching an end; diverging at those times when federal reverses, or similar events in other than the military field, raised the hopes of the South, and led to belief on both sides that the war would be protracted."

Thus, redundancy of issue produces a rise of prices, not only because of increased quantity, but because of decreased confidence, which affects the sphere of use of the money and therefore the volume of trade performed by the money, and accelerates its velocity.

Deposit Currency and Crises

We have given historical instances of the effects on prices of changes in the precious metals and in paper money. There remain to be considered historical instances of the effects on prices of changes in deposit currency. The price movements due to changes in deposit currency usually include those culminations called crises and depressions.

The economic history of the last century has been characterised by a succession of crises. Juglar in his description of the conditions preceding crises mentions the signs of great prosperity, the enterprise and the speculation of all kinds, the rising prices, the demand for labour, the rising wages, the ambition to become at once rich, the increasing luxury, and the excessive expenditure. A crisis is, as Juglar in fact defines it, an arrest of the rise of prices. At higher prices than those already reached purchasers cannot be found. Those who had purchased, hoping to sell again for profit, cannot dispose of their goods.

The analysis has shown us that, before a crisis, while prices are ascending, there is a great increase in bank deposits; and that these, being a circulating medium, accelerate the rise.

It has been pointed out that, with trade international, the rise of prices, resulting from expansion of deposits, is also international. Even if, in some of the countries, deposits should not expand, a rise of the price level would nevertheless occur. The expansion of deposits even in one country of considerable size would, by tending to raise prices there, cause the export of gold. Thus, in other countries the supply of money would increase and prices rise also.

This would tend to stimulate expansion of deposits in these other countries and bring about a further rise. Even, therefore, if credit expansion did not begin at the same time in all the principal commercial countries, the beginning of it in one country would be quickly communicated to others.

For the same reason the arrest of rising prices and the beginning of falling prices would occur at about the same time in most of the principal countries. As a matter of fact this is what we find to be the case. Juglar has made out a table showing the crises in England, France, and the United States from 1800 to 1882.1 With the addition of the dates of later crises the table is as follows:

France	England	United States
1804	1803	
1810	1810	
1813-1814	1815	1814
1818	1818	1818
1825	1825	1826
1830	1830	
1836-1839	1836-1839	1837-1839
1847	1847	1848
1857	1857	1857
1864	1864-1866	1864
1873	1873	1873
1882	1882	1884
1889-1890	1890-1891	1890-1891
	1893	
1907	1907	1907

Particular Crisis

In general, bank note circulation and bank deposit circulation increase before a crisis and reach a maximum at the time of the crisis. Index numbers of prices show the same general trend. Thus, for the United States, the crisis of 1837-1839 shows that circulation of state banks increased each year from 61 millions in 1830 to 149 in 1837 and fell to 116 in the next year; that individual

Historical Backdrop

deposits rose each year from 55 millions in 1830 to 127 in 1837 and fell to 84 the next year; that from 1844 to 1848, the date of the next crisis, circulation rose from 75 millions to 128, falling back to 114 the next year, and that the deposits rose from 84 millions to 103, falling back to 91; that from 1851 to 1857, the date of the next crisis, circulation rose from 155 millions to 214, falling the next year to 155, and that the deposits rose from 128 millions to 230, falling the next year to 185.

These facts-that prices and deposits rose, culminated, and fell together in reference to the crises of 1837, 1846, and 1857 — are confirmed by figures for per capita circulation and deposits given by Summer. These show the characteristic sharp check to expansion in the crisis years, mild in the mild crisis of 1846 and pronounced in the more pronounced crises of 1837 and 1857.

Corresponding phenomena occurred at the next crisis, 1863-1864. After this time, the chief statistics are for national banks, and these show similar results. Thus, from 1868 to 1873, national bank circulation rose from 295 millions to 341 and then fell, while in the same period deposits rose from 532 millions to 656 and then fell. Similar, though less marked, movements occurred in the milder crises of 1884 and 1890, which is the last included in Thom's tables. The crisis of 1893 was exceptional and largely confined to the United States, being chiefly due to the fear as to the stability of the gold standard without much reference to currency and deposit expansion. Whereas in the typical speculative cycle the ratio of deposits to reserves gradually increases until it reaches a maximum just before the crisis, as it did in 1873, 1884, and 1907, this did not happen in 1893.

It is true that the deposits of national banks were larger in 1892 than in 1890 or 1891, but they were no larger relatively to reserves, though possibly this fact is to be accounted for by an increase of reserves following the slight crisis of 1890-1891. It is true, also, that the ratio of the deposits of national banks to reserves was high in 1893, but this was due, not to an expansion of deposits, for deposits decreased during that year, but to the runs on the banks and consequent depletion of their reserves. The crisis of 1907, on the other hand, was, like that of 1857, typically a crisis of currency expansion. The facts in reference to this crisis will be discussed. In France the same tendency of circulation and deposits to reach a maximum at or about a crisis and recede immediately afterwards is illustrated fairly well, especially for deposits. For the Bank of England one finds the same general correspondence between crises, circulation, and private deposits.

Velocity of Deposits and Crises

Not only do money and deposit currency (M and M') rise regularly to a maximum at the time of a crisis, but their velocity of circulation, so far as statistics indicate, goes through the same cycle. Pierre des Essars has demonstrated this beyond peradventure, so far as velocity of circulation of deposits is concerned. For the United States there are scarcely any statistics of velocity of circulation of deposits, but those for two New Haven banks and for an Indianapolis bank, which I have secured for the last few years, show a maximum in the crisis year 1907.

After a crisis, a decrease occurs in M, M',V, and V'. Bank reserves are increased, and this causes a decrease in M. Since, then, currency and velocity both increase before a crisis, reach a maximum at the crisis, and fall after the crisis, it is small wonder that prices follow the same course. That they do is the real meaning of a crisis. In fact, as we have seen, Juglar defines a crisis as an arrest of a rise of prices.

The index numbers of prices show the rise, maximum, and slump for almost every crisis year for which price statistics exist. The following figures are designed to present a picture of the crisis of 1907 in the United States as illustrating the culmination of a typical credit cycle:

1904	3.31	658	5.0	113	228	113.2	.7	4.2	3.5
1905	3.78	649	5.8	144	279	114.0	5.3	4.3	−1.0
1906	4.06	651	6.2	160	315	120.0	6.6	5.7	−0.9
1907	4.32	692	6.2	145	323	127.9	−1.7	6.4	8.1
1908	4.38	849	5.1	132	294	125.7	—	4.4	—

Historical Backdrop

In the first column, a steady and rapid increase in the deposits of national banks up to, and including, the crisis year. Though deposits for 1908 do not decrease, yet they remain almost stationary as compared with those of the previous year. The second column, that for reserves, shows, as we should expect, a large increase in the year after the crisis, the banks having fortified themselves against the decrease of business confidence. We find, then (third column), an increase in the ratio of deposits to reserves, the highest ratio being reached in 1906 and 1907, not because reserves were depleted, — on the contrary, they were expanding, but because deposits were expanding still more rapidly.

It is precisely this high ratio of deposits to reserves, brought about by failure of interest to rise with rise of prices, which forced the banks to raise their rates of discount and so check further expansion of credit. Then came the crisis and the short succeeding depression. The next column, headed 'clearings', is indicative of the volume of check transactions, the circulation of deposit currency. As a fairly constant proportion of checks is settled through the various clearing houses of the country, clearings may fairly be regarded as somewhat of a criterion of $M'V'$.

The fifth column is derived from the fourth and from other data, and is intended as an estimate of $M'V''$. These two columns increase through 1906, but (since they relate to the whole year and not to a point in the middle of the year) begin to show the effects of the credit slump in the fall of 1907, so that their growth is arrested somewhat in that year, and still more in the year after. We should expect to find, then, a rise of prices reaching a maximum with 1907 and falling in 1908, and this we do find in column six. Column seven shows the per cent rise during each year.

Thus, for January, 1904, the index number or P is 113.2, and for January, 1905, it is 114.0. The rise, therefore, is a little less than 1 per cent. The minus sign signifies a fall The eighth column is for rates of interest and indicates, as we should expect, a rise, culminating in 1907. Virtual interest - that is, the interest in terms of commodities - was exceedingly low during the years immediately preceding 1907, because prices were rising so fast. This is shown in column nine, where the nominal interest (measured in money) is corrected by the rise or fall of prices to give interest as measured in actual purchasing power. With the culmination of the cycle in 1907 and the resultant fall of prices, we find virtual interest suddenly becomes very high. No wonder that borrowing enterprisers often found it hard to make both ends meet.

The facts as to credit cycles, then, completely confirm the analysis and indicate that prices rise and fall with cycles of currency and velocity. For the benefit of those who doubt whether the expansion of deposit currency raises prices, or whether the rise of prices creates deposit currency, it may be added that facts, as well as theory, show that the former relationship is the true one (although temporarily, as during 1904-1907, there exists a reaction of prices on deposits). Miss England has shown, for instance, that loans and deposits expand before prices rise, and that, though prices often fall before loans and deposits shrink, this anomalous order of events is explainable by the revival of trade following a crisis. No attempt has been made in all the phenomena or even all the typical phenomena of crises. We are not here concerned with crises except in relation to currency. Our concern is with the magnitudes entering the equation of exchange, especially M, M', and V', for these are the immediate elements the variations in which affect the price level and cause it to rise and fall.

Summary

This was a historical study of changes in the quantity of currency and of the effects of these changes on prices, on the whole, increases in the amount of money have tended to raise prices from century to century during the last thousand years, and especially since the discovery of America. The changes in the last century, or more exactly, from 1789 to 1909, have been considered in somewhat more detail, covering five periods of alternately rising and falling prices. We have seen evidence to connect these price movements with changes in the quantity of money and in the volume of business. The periods 1789-1809, 1849-1873, and 1896-1909 were periods of rising prices and large increases of the

Historical Backdrop

money supply. In the period 1809-1849 prices fell presumably because of a falling off in gold and silver production and a continuing increase of business; while between 1873 and 1896, although the world's stock of precious metals was increasing slowly, prices in gold countries fell, because in addition to the increasing volume of business there was a stampede of nations to adopt the gold standard and demonetise or limit the coinage of silver.

It is observed the recent continual increase of gold production and found reasons for the tentative prediction that the gold production of the future would continue excessive and probably cause the present rise of prices to continue for some time in the future. There are some of the chief examples of paper money inflation and shown that the records for circulation and price changes bear out in a general way the principles set forth. The paper money experiences of France during the French Revolution, of England during the Napoleonic wars, of Austria, the American colonies, the United States, and the Confederacy have been briefly reviewed. We have noted that in these cases, as in others, prices depended on the quantity of money, its velocity, and the volume of business. We have seen that the apparent exceptions due to lack of confidence in paper money are not really exceptions, because lack of confidence works itself out through the magnitudes in the equation of exchange.

Distrust increases the velocity of circulation, and decreases the trade performed by the money. We have shown that the general effect of irredeemable paper money issues, which are almost always in large quantities, despite pledges to the contrary, has been to raise prices. Finally, our study of deposit circulation and crises has afforded further illustration. Preceding a typical crisis, there is, in general, a tendency for deposits to increase and also for their velocity of circulation to increase, while prices tend to rise. Following the crisis comes a decrease in bank deposits and their velocity of circulation, an increase in bank reserves, with a corresponding tendency to diminish money in circulation, and a fall of prices. In the years of the principal crises these took place simultaneously in different countries.

Purchasing Power of Money

Circulating Media

An old account tells us:

The money is what is generally acceptable in exchange for goods. The facility with which it may thus be exchanged, or its general acceptability, is its distinguishing characteristic. The general acceptability may be re-enforced by law, the money thus becoming what is known as 'legal tender'; but such re-enforcement is not essential. All that is necessary in order that any good may be money is that general acceptability attach to it. On the frontier, without any legal sanction, money is sometimes gold dust or gold nuggets. In the Colony of Virginia it was tobacco. Among the Indians in New England it was wampum. "In German New Guinea the bent tusks of a boar are used as money. In California red birds' heads have been used in the same way. "Stone money and shell money are so used in Melanesia." In Burmah Chinese gambling counters are used as money. Guttapercha tokens issued by street car companies in South America are said to be used in the same way." Not many years ago in a town in New York state, similar tokens got into local circulation until their issue was forbidden by the United States government. In Mexico large cacao beans of relatively poor quality were used as money, and on the west coast of Africa little mats were used. The list could be extended indefinitely. But whatever the substance of such a commodity, it is general exchangeability which makes it money.

On the other hand, even what is made legal tender may, by general usage, be deprived of its practical character as money. During the Civil War the government attempted to circulate fifty-dollar notes, bearing interest at 7.3 per cent, so that the interest amounted to the very easily computed amount of a cent a day. The notes, however, failed to circulate. In spite of the attempt to make their exchange easy, people preferred to keep them for the sake of the interest. Money never bears interest except in the sense of creating convenience in the process of exchange. This convenience is the special service of money and offsets the apparent loss of interest involved in keeping it in one's pocket instead of investing.

There are various degrees of exchangeability which must be transcended before we arrive at real money. Of all kinds of goods, perhaps the least exchangeable is real estate. Only in case some person happens to be found who wants it can a piece of real estate be traded. A mortgage on real estate is one degree more exchangeable. Yet even a mortgage is less exchangeable than a well-known and safe corporation security; and a corporation security is less exchangeable than a government bond.

In fact persons not infrequently buy government bonds as merely temporary investments, intending to sell them again as soon as permanent investments yielding better interest are obtainable. One degree more exchangeable than a government bond is a bill of exchange; one degree more exchangeable than a bill of exchange is a sight draft; while a check is almost as exchangeable as money itself. Yet no one of these is really money for none of them is 'generally acceptable'.

If we confine our attention to present and normal conditions, and to those means of exchange which either are money or most nearly approximate it, we shall find that money itself belongs to a general class of property rights which we may call 'currency' or 'circulating media.' Currency includes any type of property right which, whether generally acceptable or not, does actually, for its chief purpose and use, serve as a means of exchange.

Circulating media are of two chief classes: (1) money; (2) bank deposits, which will be treated fully. By means of checks, bank deposits serve as a means of payment in exchange for other goods. A check is the 'certificate' or evidence of the transfer of bank deposits. It is acceptable to the payee only by his consent. It would not be generally accepted by strangers. Yet by checks, bank deposits even more than money do actually serve as a medium of exchange. Practically speaking, money and bank deposits subject to check are the only circulating media. If post-office orders and telegraphic transfer are to be included, they may, be regarded as certificates of transfer of special deposits, the post-office or telegraph company serving the purpose, for these special transactions, of a bank of deposit.

But while a bank deposit transferable by check is included as circulating media, it is not money. A bank note, on the other hand, is both circulating medium and money. Between these two lies the final line of distinction between what is money and what is not. True, the line is delicately drawn, especially when we come to such checks as cashier's checks or certified checks, for the latter are almost identical with bank notes.

Each is a demand liability on a bank, and each confers on the holder the right to draw money. Yet while a note is generally acceptable in exchange, a check is specially acceptable only, i.e. only by the consent of the payee. Real money rights are what a payee accepts without question, because he is induced to do so either by 'legal tender' laws or by a well-established custom.

Of real money there are two kinds: primary and fiduciary. Money is called 'primary' if it is a commodity which has just as much value in some use other than money as it has in monetary use. Primary money has its full value independently of any other wealth. Fiduciary money, on the other hand, is money the value of which depends partly or wholly on the confidence that the owner can exchange it for other goods, e.g. for primary money at a bank or government office, or at any rate for discharge of debts or purchase of goods of merchants.

The chief example of primary money is gold coin; the chief example of fiduciary money is bank notes. The qualities of primary money which make for exchangeability are numerous. The most important are portability, durability, and divisibility. The chief quality of fiduciary money which makes it exchangeable is its redeemability in primary money, or else its imposed character of legal tender.

Bank notes and all other fiduciary money, as well as bank deposits, circulate by certificates often called 'tokens.' 'Token coins' are included in this description. The value of these tokens, apart from the rights they convey, is small. Thus the value of a silver dollar, as wealth, is only about forty cents; that is all that the actual silver in it is worth. Its value as property, however, is one hundred cents; for its holder has a legal right to use it in paying a debt to that amount, and a customary right to so use it in payment for goods.

Likewise, the property value of a fifty-cent piece, a quarter, a ten-cent piece, a five-cent piece, or a one-cent piece is considerably greater than its value as wealth. The value of a paper dollar as wealth—for instance, a silver certificate - is almost nothing. It is worth just its value as paper, and no more. But its value as property is a hundred cents, that is, the equivalent of one gold dollar. It represents to that extent a claim of the holder on the wealth of the community.

The classification of all circulating media in the United States. The total amount of circulating media is about $8\frac{1}{2}$ billions, of which about 7 billions are bank deposits subject to check and $1\frac{1}{2}$ billions, money; and that of this $1\frac{1}{2}$ billions of money, 1 billion is fiduciary money and only about $\frac{1}{2}$ a billion, primary money.

The consideration of bank deposits or check circulation and confine our "attention to the circulation of money, primary and fiduciary. In the United States, the only primary money is gold coin. The fiduciary money includes (1) 'token coins, viz. silver dollars, fractional silver, and minor coins (nickels and cents); (2) paper money, viz. (a) certificates for gold and silver, and (6) promissory notes, whether of the United States government (greenbacks), or of the National banks.

Checks aside, we may classify exchanges into three groups: the exchange of goods against goods, or barter; the exchange of money against money, or changing money; and the exchange of money against goods, or purchase and sale. Only the last-named species of exchange makes up what we call the 'circulation' of money. The circulation of money signifies, therefore, the aggregate amount of its transfers against goods. All money held for circulation, i.e. all money, except what is in the banks and United States government's vaults, is called 'money in circulation.'

The chief object of this discussion is to explain the causes determining the purchasing power of money. The purchasing power of money is indicated by the quantities of other goods which a given quantity of money will buy. The lower we find the prices of goods, the larger the quantities that can be bought by a given amount of money, and therefore the higher the purchasing power of money.

The higher we find the prices of goods, the smaller the quantities that can be bought by a given amount of money, and therefore the Tower the purchasing power of money. In short, the purchasing power of money is the reciprocal of the level of prices; so that the study of the purchasing power of money is identical with the study of price levels.

3

Money and Practical Life

Something like "money doesn't grow on trees", or "money is the root of all evil", or maybe "all rich people are greedy"? Well, how do you expect to become a success financially if you believe these things? You attract into your life what are thinking about and what you believe. If you think there is not enough money in this world for everyone you will never have enough money. That is called the Law of Attraction.

First of all, believing that "money doesn't grow on trees" is an example of what's called lack or scarcity programming. Our parents taught us that there was never enough money to go around, and that it was not readily available or abundant. But in truth, the universe is very abundant, and there is lots of money to go around for everyone. Just think what you could do if you have so much money how much your heart desires. What wonderful things you could do with it: travel to the countries you have always dreamt of, buy a house you even scared to think about it, attend meditation classes so you could spiritually grow, donate money to your favourite charity, spend more quality time with your family and the list goes on.

The key is to start thinking that you deserve the money and that there is lots of it available for you, and then you can start attracting it into your life. That's abundance thinking, which is the opposite of lack or scarcity thinking. When you start thinking about the abundance the Law of Attraction will do the rest.

You do not need to know how it is going to happen just make the first step, first thought. Starting is already winning. And what about thinking that "money is the root of all evil"? Can you really expect to become a success if you believe that money is the root of all evil? Unless you have a desire to be an evil person, your subconscious will not let you have money if you believe deep down that it is the root of all evil.

By the way, that quote is taken out of context in the first place. It was originally stated as "the love of money is the root of all evil". So it has nothing to do with the money itself. The money is in fact good. You can help people with money. You can stimulate the economy with money.

Even the most kind-hearted spiritual person, who says they don't need money, can do more to make the world a better place with money than without it. And what about thinking that "all rich people are greedy"? Well, that creates us versus them, whereby you have labelled all of "them" greedy in your mind. You, on the other hand, are very giving in your mind. That's why you don't have money, because you're not greedy.

Sure, there must be some rich people in the world who are greedy. But there are also poor people who are greedy. There are both rich and poor people who are very giving as well. The amount of money you have has nothing to do with these character traits. In fact, a lot of rich people got there by not being greedy. Having a giving attitude opens up a flow of money that often brings them more. You will find the same thing... give away money joyfully to a friend, and notice that it comes back to you in some other form.

The world needs to be a balance of give and take, and being joyful both as you give and receive will ensure that you always go with the flow. And changing your mindset from what you were taught as a child to a healthier view of money will allow you to become the financial success you deserve to be, to become real you.

Social Development and Money

With the rise of large commercial urban centres, the principle instrument for development shifted from physical matter to social institution — from arable land to money. Money has been the single greatest organisational invention of the past five thousand years. The emergence of money as a pre-eminent social institution vividly illustrates the central role of organisation in the process of social development.

The creation of money was made possible and spurred by the generation of food surpluses. One of the earliest forms of money was the receipt issued for grain deposits at government warehouses in ancient Babylon, which gradually became transferable to third parties. The capacity of early farmers to produce more food than was required for consumption by the family naturally prompted them to trade their surplus for other goods or services. As long as these exchanges were conducted by means of barter, they were severely limited both in volume and speed. Barter exchange required the double coincidence of a buyer and seller both wanting what the other possessed in surplus. It also involved a very complicated form of valuation, since every type of commodity would have a different price depending on the goods or service for which it was to be exchanged.

Direct barter involving 1000 different commodities would require 500,000 rates of exchange. Barter transactions worked best within a narrow geographical area due to the physical difficulties of transporting products over long distances. The perishable nature of many products also limited barter exchanges. Producers had no incentive to produce more than they were confident of either consuming or exchanging with other consumers during the period before a product deteriorated.

The use of money spread gradually from one country to another by a process of imitation similar to the manner in which ideas, technologies and other social institutions are transmitted from one place to another and bear fruit wherever the soil is sufficiently prepared.

The adoption of money in place of barter had a tremendously liberating and expansive impact on early society. As urbanisation increased the number, size and speed of transactions by bringing many more people into proximity, money increased the number, size, speed, and efficiency of transactions even over long distances. The capacity to convert the fruits of one's labour into money meant that those fruits could be stored indefinitely, overcoming the limitations of time and providing an incentive for people to exert themselves much harder and longer than if what they produced must be consumed immediately.

The capacity to convert physical goods into portable money overcame the limitations imposed by space. Whereas products could be transported long distances only at considerable cost and difficulty, money could be moved quickly and inexpensively, making possible trade over much larger geographic areas.

Money also provided a common standard for valuation of all products and services, thereby vastly reducing the complexity of exchange rates. By eliminating the necessity of the double coincidence required for barter trade, money made it possible for a much larger number of transactions to be completed. At the same time, its ease of movement and accounting enormously increased the speed of commercial transactions. The increasing volume and speed of transactions made possible by money combined with the increasing size and density of urban population had an exponential impact on the development of society.

Money had a transforming effect on society equivalent in magnitude to that brought about by the emergence of urban communities. It helped liberate society from the strict confines of the land and the retarding influences of tradition, spurring the evolution from the physical to the vital stage of social development.

Money and Practical Life

Before money, land was the principle productive resource and source of wealth. Those who controlled the land controlled the wealth of society. The hereditary transmission of property rights during the feudal period left little incentive for individual initiative and little room for individual advancement.

During the Middle Ages, European society actually reverted for a time to barter before money returned and gained ascendance. The return of money and the rise of commerce in European society coincided with the demise of the agrarian based feudal system. Money gradually replaced heredity not only as a source of wealth, but as a source of social power and privilege as well.

The moneyed commercial classes became increasingly influential, creating the backdrop for the emergence of democratic values and forms of government a few centuries later. Money freed the individual from servitude to the soil. A person could earn money and use it to purchase whatever was required for personal sustenance and also utilise it as capital to earn a living. It impersonalised and democratised transactions, empowering the possessor with economic voting power that drastically reduced discrimination based on class and status. Money increased the individual's freedom of choice and gave greater scope for the development of individual talents and potentials.

Social organisations that spur development at one stage tend to ossify and die out later on, as hunting tribes, guilds, East India companies and colonial empires, feudal and monarchical institutions have in the past. Some institutions exhibit the capacity to evolve along with society, adapting and changing to match the character of the times. Money has exhibited this capacity to evolve with the times. Sharing the characteristics of this physical stage of development, early money was itself a physical commodity, grain, gold or silver.

Only gradually did representative forms of money appear, but these too were full-bodied commodity money, convertible at any time into the commodity that they represented. During the vital stage, more symbolic forms of money such as certificates of deposit, bank notes, checks, letters of credit, bonds and other forms of negotiable securities came into prominence. The complete separation of money from its physical roots came at a much later stage of social development with the appearance of fiat money that does not have a commodity value and cannot be redeemed for a commodity.

Role of Money in Society

A first definition of money is to define money as the mean of exchange between individuals. In a capitalist economy, this is a too simple definition. The fundamental purpose of money is a way to distribute the ownership in the society. And, by a consequence, money is also used as a mean of exchange. But, if you analyse the way that money works you will understand that as a tool to help exchange that money is a very imperfect tool. Furthermore, it should be analysed that money is also a social instrument which help to coordinate social relation between individuals.

Three Stages of Social Development

The historical perspective presented thus far may create the impression that the development process is essentially a linear progression from less organised to more organised conditions generating greater benefits for society. While this is true, it is an oversimplification of what actually occurs. This complex multidimensional process of organisational development directed and fuelled by social awareness and aspiration is further complicated by the gradual evolution of the society through three stages of development. By this evolution society is progressively infused by the release of greater vital energy and by the acquisition and practical application of more conscious and complete mental knowledge.

Society advances through three overlapping stages of development involving changes in the relative roles of three fundamental components of individual and collective human consciousness. We term these three components physical, vital and mental. All three components coexist and play a role in all stages of development. The intensity of each and their relative predominance create a series of overlapping stages, rather than clearly demarcated steps. Different societies move through these stages at different times, at different rates and with variations in the relative mix of the three components. Yet despite these differences, three distinct stages can be discerned in the development of every society and in the overall development of the human community.

In the first stage there is a prevalence of the physical component. The dominant characteristic of society at this stage is a preoccupation with physical survival, protection and preservation of the status quo. There is a strong tendency towards tradition and conservatism. This is the agrarian and feudal phase where land is the primary source of wealth and the most productive resource. The primary political and social systems are based on physical, hereditary principles. Children inherit the wealth, power, occupations and social position of their parents. There is little social mobility, especially upwards.

The organisation of society during this stage centres around the military and land, feudal lords controlling small fiefdoms. Commerce and money play a relatively minor role. Beliefs are grounded in the past. There is little emphasis on education, experimentation or thinking outside established guidelines defined by tradition and religious authority. Skills are passed down from generation to generation by a long, slow process of apprenticeship. Guilds restrict the dissemination of techniques.

The church or state controls the dissemination of knowledge. The contribution of the human resource is predominantly in the form of physical labour. Apart from a small, privileged ruling elite, the society accords little respect, rights or value to other human beings. The pace of change during this stage is quite slow, because those factors that promote rapid development are only minimally present.

The maturation of the physical stage occurs when the physical organisation of society develops to the point where the increasing productivity of physical resources generates surplus produce, energy and wealth. The reorganisation of agriculture in Europe following the end of Feudalism provided the basis for the rise of commerce and later industry. The vital and mental principles become more active. The generation of surplus energy and capacity in society begin to break the bonds of tradition and overflow into new fields of activity.

During the next stage, the vital factor plays an increasingly active role. The dominant characteristics of this phase are dynamism and change. The energy level in society rises. It becomes increasingly inventive, outward looking and adventurous. This was the phase in which Europe began to explore the seas, leading to the discovery of new trade routes and new lands and ushering in the age of mercantilism.

The greatest invention and discovery of this phase is the power of money. Commerce replaces agriculture as the predominant source of wealth. Money replaces land as the most precious and productive resource. The centre of society shifts from the countryside to the cities and towns, where opportunities for trade and enterprise attract more and more people.

The great urban centres grow rapidly. The rise of a merchant class wrests power from the hereditary aristocracy, at first gaining the support of ruling monarchs in exchange for economic rights and later leveraging its increasing wealth to make monarchs subordinate to Parliaments. The organisation of society expands rapidly during this period. New types of organisations proliferate. In order to provide an attractive environment for commerce, the rule of law and stable economic policies of the state gradually replace arbitrary decrees. Banks, shipping companies and trading houses proliferate. Religious institutions lose much of their political influence.

New ways of life are accepted rather than frowned upon because they generate practical benefits. The practical comes to take precedent over the traditional. The mental influence increases markedly with the growth of experimentation, scientific discovery and new technologies. Increased travel, interaction between societies and greater flows of information engender greater tolerance and openness to new ideas and different ways of life. Expansion of commerce and rule of law increase the demand for and spread of education among the more prosperous classes.

Maturation of the vital stage through commercial and industrial expansion generates higher levels of surplus in society. Capital accumulation occurs on a large scale. An abundance of goods is produced and is available.

The middle and upper classes grow in absolute and relative proportion, meaning that more people have surplus time, energy and money for consumption, education, travel and recreational pursuits. The aspiration for luxury and leisure penetrates to lower levels of society, inspiring the common man to yearn for more.

The third stage of development is one in which the mental component becomes more and more predominant. This stage has three essential characteristics that demarcate it from those that came before – a great increase in the practical application of mind to generate new inventions, in the social application of mind to generate new and higher levels of organisation, and in the political application of mind to elevate the status and rights of individual human beings.

The first distant origins of this phase in Europe can be traced back to the Renaissance and the Enlightenment, when ideas began to gain freedom from domination by church doctrine and traditional superstitious beliefs.

The mental component gained influence after the Reformation, which empowered the individual to seek direct relations with God. It led eventually to the proclamation of the political ideals embodied in the American and French Revolutions and the establishment of human rights, at first in principle and much later in practice. The onset of this phase gave rise to the birth of modern science and practical experimentation.

This led ultimately to the explosion of technical innovations that ushered in the Industrial Revolution, which has continued with increasing momentum for the last 150 years. Industry gradually replaced commerce as the greatest source of wealth. Technology began to challenge the position of money as the most powerful and productive resource.

Organisation is a product of the mind. Therefore it is not surprising to find that the mental phase has given birth to an incredible number and variety of new forms of social innovation, equalling or perhaps even exceeding the number and variety of new technical inventions generated during this period. Huge commercial organisations have emerged, larger and more wealthy and powerful in some cases than entire countries.

The world, which was criss-crossed by sailing ships in previous centuries, is now linked together and wired by a profusion of systems and structures that connect people and activities around the globe.

The physical application of mind for scientific discovery and technological invention and the social application of mind for organisational innovation have been powerful forces for social development over the past few centuries. However, the highest power of mind expresses in the field of pure ideas.

It is here that mind has introduced the most far-reaching changes that are destined to transform life in the coming centuries. Ideals and ethical ideas are as old as civilization, but the practical extension of high ideas to social life has never before been accepted and attempted on such a massive scale as it is today.

The mental stage has established the principle of human rights and proclaimed the value of the individual. The 20th Century has been heralded as the century of the common man. Never before has society as a whole accorded such value and consideration for the poorest and lowliest of its citizens.

The granting of universal suffrage and acceptance of the goal of universal education are unprecedented steps. Actual practices fall far short of the ideal in every society, but the direction of the social movement is clear. With every passing year new measures are introduced to extend greater physical and economic security to larger sections of the population in more countries around the world. Once this goal has been accepted by the mind of humanity, it exerts an inexorable pressure for further progress.

It is evident that the content of these three stages and the timing and circumstances of the transition from one stage to the next may vary widely between countries.

However, the stamp of the physical, vital and mental components of human consciousness is remarkably similar and can be discerned even in societies that otherwise appear to have little in common. It is also evident that each country's experience is influenced by the experience of other countries that have passed before it and by those with which it is in contact or proximity at any given time.

Thus, the circumstances in which universal primary education was introduced in the Netherlands after 1618 were naturally different than the circumstances faced by Japan after 1872 or in other Asian countries after 1950 when education gained momentum in these countries.

The Dutch were pioneering a new concept, whereas the Japanese were spurred to imitate the example of technologically advanced US and Western Europe, and other Asian countries to imitate Japan. This is one reason why the pace of development continues to accelerate as the world accumulates greater experience and more successful models for emulation.

The figure depicts the increasing contribution of the vital and the mental components to development in recent centuries. As the vital and later the mental components gain in their contribution to productivity, the rate of development accelerates.

It is worth noting that the emergence of the higher component reduces the relative, but not the absolute, contribution of the previously dominant one. In fact, each successive advance to a higher level has an invigorating effect on that which it supercedes. This is illustrated by the fact that spread of education, a contribution of the mental component, increases physical productivity.

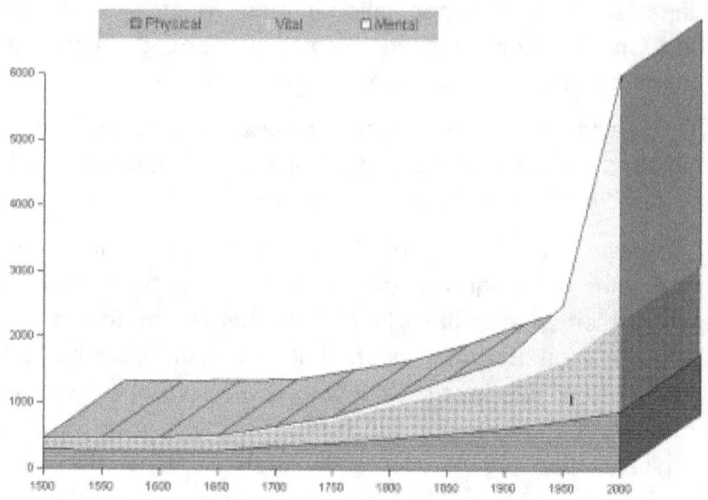

Figure: Contribution of Three Components to Development

It should also be apparent that although we seem to suggest that each society passes from one stage to the next in mass, this is rarely, if ever, the case. The movement to the next phase invariably begins among the most advanced parts of the society, which means the urban centres, and among the most educated, wealthy and worldly classes.

Thus New York, Paris, London, Moscow, Tokyo and Bombay have advanced much faster and further than isolated rural areas such as Appalachia, the Scottish Highlands, Siberia, Hokkaido and Bihar. Even today we can find the anachronism of near feudal communities existing almost side by side with the most modern industrial societies within the same nation state.

Money as an Organisation

Money plays a crucial role in development. Money is the product of organisation. In earlier societies, land was the principal form of wealth. The productivity of the land was the primary resource for development and that productivity depended on the organisation of society for agricultural production. The growth of commerce depended on creation of more liquid forms of wealth that could be moved and traded for precious goods. Money replaced land as the principal form of wealth. But money by itself has no inherent value and cannot produce or develop anything. Money depends for its productive power on organisation.

The creation and operation of a money economy depended from the beginning upon the establishment of governmental organisations that could issue new forms of money, financial organisations that would honour, store and transfer it, and commercial organisations that would accept it in exchange for goods and services.

Money not only depends on organisation; it is itself an organisation. Money is a commodity such as gold or an officially issued coin or paper note that is legally established as an exchangeable equivalent of other commodities and is used as a measure of their comparative values on the market. It is an abstract unit of account in terms of which the value of goods, services and obligations can be measured. The systems of exchange, valuation, issuance and conversion of one form of money into another constitute elements of that organisation. The value of money depends directly on the level of this organisation. The more developed it becomes, the greater the productive power of money.

Money is often regarded as a unique social institution, but actually it derives its productive power from characteristics which it shares in common with other forms of social organisation. Like other organisations, the development of money has occurred on the foundation of four types of organised infrastructures. In early times, a physical infrastructure of towns, ports, and roads provided the necessary conditions to stimulate the growth of commercial transactions based on money. A social infrastructure was also necessary to support the evolution of money from a commodity into a symbol.

An essential requirement was for a stable government to issue and redeem the symbol for the underlying commodity. The development of money coincided with the emergence of nation states that possessed the stability and continuity necessary to stand surety for symbolic forms of money. In addition, the development of banking, stock exchanges, legislative, judicial and administrative infrastructures became essential supports for the growing use of money. In modern times, the role of money has been expanded enormously by the development of complex mental infrastructures consisting of an intricate web of technology, organisation and information. Systems for international banking, telecommunications, and computerised financial transactions serve as essential infrastructure for the rapid movement of money around the world.

The emergence of money also required the development of a sophisticated psychological infrastructure in society. The progression from physical to symbolic forms of money involved a huge leap of faith for early physical man still struggling, against the direct evidence of his senses, with the concept that a round earth revolved around the sun. It must have required an irresistible urge for accomplishment and great spirit of adventure to forego the security of pure commodity money for pieces of paper and promises of redemption.

The magnitude of that psychological leap is evidenced by the persistent preference of some Asian population today for the certitude of gold in an age where much higher returns and greater security are offered by symbolic forms of money. The development of money required that people accept record keeping and systematic functioning as a way of life and have sufficient trust to deposit their funds with others. Money has long since passed from the stage of organisation to that of an ubiquitous global, social institution that derives support from many organisations but does not depend on any for its existence.

As an organisation, the power of money is based on authority. The value and productive power of money depends directly on the perceived strength of the issuing government and the authority conceded to it by the population. This authority has an economic aspect, its capacity to maintain fiscal discipline, to collect taxes, to prevent counterfeiting. It also has a wider political and social aspect. The value of money issued depends on the perceived

Money and Practical Life

strength and stability of the government, the military strength and stability of the country and its relationship with other nations, and its capacity to enforce rule of law among its citizens.

Authority and trust are complementary forces. Ultimately the strength of a currency depends on the extent to which it gains the trust and confidence of society, which today means the global financial community. Remove this trust and confidence, as occurred during the US banking crisis of the Great Depression or during the recent financial crisis in Asia, and the entire monetary system is threatened with collapse. The ultimate foundation that gives force and effectiveness to this greatest of social institutions is not hard core physical assets but an intangible human value.

As an organisation, money also derives power from the systems of which it is constituted and through which it acts. The value and productivity of money is directly proportionate to the quality of systems for minting, storage, accounting, transfer, exchange, savings, borrowing, investment, credit and information flows. It is indirectly proportionate to systems for administrative decision-making and enforcement, trade, manufacturing, R&D, transport, telecommunications, education and training. The productivity of money depends upon the velocity with which it circulates through these systems. Each system contributes directly or indirectly to determine the overall speed of circulation, which increases with each advance in social development. The establishment of a sophisticated global communications system now enables hundreds of billions of dollars to flow back and forth around the world on a daily basis in search of higher rates of return.

Organisations derive their power from the complexity of the activities to which they relate and the breadth of activities with which they are integrated. As the complexity of the interconnections between the synaptic junctions in the human brain determines the degree of intellectual capacity, the intricate interrelations forged between activities determine the degree of social development. Money has a powerful catalytic effect on development arising from its capacity to relate to, integrate with and energise virtually every other activity in society.

Not only every variety of product and service, but also every variety of social activity has come to be valued in monetary terms. Late during the monarchical period, aristocratic titles became available to wealthy merchants for a price.

Education, the traditional mark of the nobility, opened up to all with the money to acquire it. Marriage, civil claims and personal injury suits, civil and criminal judgements, tithes for religious salvation, political election and appointment, copyrights, patents, knowledge, information and even artistic inspiration have been translated into monetary terms and stimulated in their own development by the development of money.

Although this characteristic of complexity and integration is most apparent with regard to money, every social institution has a similar type of impact on existing social activities. Thus, the creation of a national organisation of highways or a national system of education promotes national defence, agriculture, industry, trade, tourism, recreation, education, immigration, publishing, and so forth.

The ultimate determinants of the power of social organisation are the values of society. The institution of money has been so deeply accepted and internalised by every society in modern times that it would appear to have assumed the status of an ultimate value in itself.

The constitutional and legal framework of the nation state provides protection for all types of property rights. Monetary incentives are utilised everywhere to encourage higher levels of individual productivity and group performance. Brushing aside hereditary claims for social status, society accords the greatest respect to those individuals, organisations and nations that have amassed the most wealth. But this apparent pre-eminence of the money value is misleading. The remarkable creativity and productivity of money is itself based on a bedrock of other social values without which it could not produce anything of worth.

The value of money depends directly on all the values that support its functioning as an organisation. These include physical values such as accuracy, orderliness, punctuality, regularity and efficiency; organisational values such as discipline, standardisation, systematic functioning, communication, coordination and integration; and psychological values such as trust, integrity, harmony and creativity. Take away these intangible but priceless social accomplishments and the value of money quickly vanishes into obscure symbolism. Money is a tremendously productive social organisation, but like every social organisation it depends on an incorporeal human foundation for its existence.

The ultimate foundation for the value of money is not material wealth but the value of human beings. Money has grown in its power and productivity not because society has accorded it ultimate value, but because it has become an instrument and medium for fulfilling human aspirations and elevating people. The more society has come to recognise the inherent value and potential of the human being, the more productive the individual, society and money have become. Money has served as a symbol of the infinite potential for human accomplishment. As such it has released enormous energy, creativity and initiative in society. But the ultimate source of that unlimited creative energy is the individual and the society, not money."

A World without Money

France is a country where money has a monopoly in term of exchange so people can't imagine what would happen in a world without money. It is interesting to have a look in society where money exists but exchange are just partly base of money. Other system are the solidarity system. People give with the expectation that the receiver will give them something back. This system has the advantage to be simple and so no accounting is needed.

It is working with a society of people of common value and understanding. You should note that this system is based on trust and does not work in place where the population is moving (big city). The solidarity relation is also disappearing when money (called prosperity) is commonly used by the middle class as when people are capable to sell their service against money they prefer the guarantee of money than the guarantee of trust.

Money: Greediness or Generosity?

In the current culture of media in France, it is current thinking that people who are money mind are greedy. Money is considered to be the tool of greedy people. Good people are supposed to work (or sell) freely. If follow, this contest should lead to the suppression of money.

So, the question is, "Why money has been created?" If you consider the money in the antic world, money was a way to take in account action of individual in order to guarantee an equivalent action. It is then more generosity to give out of money than against money.

Attraction for Giving

All psychologist will agree that people are bound to give to other people. So, why not simply give. Why money should be used to take account giving?

The reason is that people wants to choose what they are giving to others. And, others people wants to choose what they are receiving from you. And in most case, they are a strong discordance between what the receiver wants to receive and what you want to give. If you try to live in society where the practice of solidarity is the main way of exchange. You will notice that giver are very happy but receiver are not so happy. In most case, receiver has to pretend to be happy by the generosity of the giver. But, in his inner being, he is thinking "I don't need this".

In a money leaded society, receiver (called "consumer") are very happy while getting (called "buying"). But, the giver (called "worker") is very often thinking that he is forced by money to do think that he doesn't want to do. So, he will complain about money as money is the institution which create the gap between what he is giving (called "selling") and what he wants to give. They will be happy if they are chosen what they are giving to

Money and Practical Life

others. If it is the receiver who choice what the person gives. In summary, money is a regulator between what people want to do and what other people want to receive.

Interest Rate

In Europe at the end of the XIXth century, a practice in the past forbidden by the religious instance has been institutionalised "interest rate". Interest rate has completely revolutionised the institution of money. Before money if based on gold was in an insufficient quantity or lead to inflation. Interest rate has bring price stability as money got value on itself. Before money has no value in itself so it was preferable to keep goods than money. But with interest rate, money creates money. So, it start to be interesting to keep it.

The fact that people are ready to keep money a long time as make possibly long time perspective investment and industrialisation. Interest rate has made industrialisation possible. And, the main reason of not success in industrialisation itself is due to the absence of practice of interest rate.

An industrialisation should be planned on a term of more than 5 or 10 years. If you can't wait so long to receive to receive back your "right to buy", you are not going to accept that you can not use your money for you. The difference between investing and buying is in investing that: with buying you are choosing what you are spending for, with investing another person is choosing for you what he is spending for.

Before, interest rate, investing was not possible so as industrialisation. With interest rate, the person who is spending promise you to give it back your "right to buy" (and to buy in a bigger amount). If the person only give you back the same right of buying back while giving up the right of buying back. So, interest rate appears with interest rate you can't buy now but you will buy more in the future. So, you can accept the another person is taking your right to buy because he will give you back this right with increase.

Industrialisation means making machine to do thing instead of directly doing thing. If you are directly making a shoes by hand, you will get your shoe fast. If you are making a machine to speed up the process of making shoes, it will take the time to make the machine and the time to make the shoe with the machine. So, it will take more time. If you are making shoes with machine, you will make much more shoes per hour of work. You are giving more to the society so you can receive more from it (called " making more profit").

The person who had given to the investor the right to buy (called " lending money") has created the possibility for you to make the machine as however it might not have been possible for the investor to live or buy what is needing to create the machine. So, the person receives a part of this more profit made possible on the form of " interest rate". It is while the society does not succeed to be industrialise before interest rate has been institutionalised.

Freedom of not Receiving

In a market economy, every body is free of not buying what he doesn't want. This freedom has created unemployment and social misery. A question commonly asks in France: Is it " the choice of buying" socially acceptable? Suppose that you live in a society where half of the population are professional actors. There will have drama, movie and no public to look at them. But, in society where the freedom of not buying is guarantee, professional are working for money so no public means no money and a great number of actor will have to look for another job.

Money is the basis of a social organisation in the capitalist society as there is a strong discordance between what individual wants to do to the society and what society needs from individual. For example, most people wants to be artist, politician, business men and these people want to eat, buy houses, car, dress. People are trying to spend their time in what is the most interesting for them. And, unfortunately, goods that people want to buy don't lead to the job that people wants to do.

Money and Practical Life

Money: a Tool to Select the Decision-maker?

A common tendency in an organise society is to select a single or a small number of individuals in order to decide for many others. As in a professional environment, a professional individual has a very high probability to decide the same way than any other professionals. The hierarchisation of the social organisation appears to have one individual deciding with eventuality a veto of others individuals appear to be more functional than many individuals with an equal status in a perpetual negotiation to find a compromise. A negotiation generally consists to put everybody at a equal status in term of understanding of the situation and information and in a complex environment could be a very time consuming operation. Furthermore, when people are talking, they are not producing so reducing the talking time increase the productivity.

The industrial phases has increased this tendency as the environment became so complex than it necessitates years of experience before becoming enough competent in taking a decision. So, instead of putting everybody to an equal understanding, selecting a person (or a small group) with the best understanding and knowledge appear to be the most practical. (The ultra democrat could pretend the opposite).

Money is the tool who define the position of the individual in the society. Money has been the tool which create the social disparity between individuals. So, many people consider that the use of money creates inequality between the distribution of wealth between individuals. In fact, it is the industrialisation which necessitate the inequity between the distribution of wealth between individuals. In an industrialised society, all worker fell inequity face to manager whatever money is used or not.

How does Money Create a Hierarchical Society?

People who have no money, should work for other people. And between people who has no money some will have money to create small business as restaurant as other people will be in position to create a big factory. In society socially regulated by money, it is socially needed that some people have an huge amount of money otherwise there will never have industrial investment.

Role of Money in the Communist System

The Marxism is based on the refusal to use money as an instrument to socially organise the society. In the communist USSR, money was as reduce a way to take in account what individual are doing for the society. So, as communism society has to be industrialised, a system of individual hierarchisation has to be created.

In the communist, social position has to be fixed according to exam success or the promotion through the party. Ambitious people was then involve in a political game which is opaque and more base on appearance than capability. Then, market economy has the advantage to be more pragmatic and more based on individual capability than individual appearance. In the market economy, a business manager acquiring power is acquiring money. A business manager who is acquiring money is selling with profit. Succeeding a sell is like a grant of satisfaction from the customer to the business manager. So, power concentrates to the business manager who creates the highest satisfaction to other individuals (called customer). Then, capitalist could be considered as a meritocratic system based on the capacity to satisfy the material claim of others.

Another advantage of a hierarchisation based on money (capitalist system) to a hierarchisation based on relation (communism system). A business manager who analyses a market and looks how to satisfy customer is involved in a more rational activity than a politician who will to have the power from others (his superior in totalitarian system or the majority in democracy). The bank account makes an history about how successful business people handles their business to succeed.

If money movement were on Internet so as every body in the world can understand how rich people succeed to get rich. The problem about how, why, who get rich could be analysed and help individual to get the capability of succeeding with money simply in understanding how rich people manage to be rich. But, that is something which is today technically possible but whom the obstacle are used. The Institute of Research about Entrepreneurship is strongly interested about the possible change and the transparency of world exchange.

Is it the Best Social Measurement System?

Money is the most sophisticated social measurement system uses in our days. It has played a major role in the industrialisation of our society and in the development of our economy. Its major success is that undeveloped countries which adopts a western style banking system has managed a strong development while others stay underdeveloped. However, despite this success, money is still strongly contest everywhere in the world. Many of this contest came to see mainly money as a tool of exchange which is a half false view, money is before all tool of social development and hierarchisation which has made industrialisation possible.

Another view is to consider that at the age of computerisation. Money is may be too simple system to be optimum? And, the best way to develop this analysis to model another system much more optimised which can be called a collaborative system. Another alternative less innovative is to analyse the advantages and inconvenient of a multi-monetary economical system with money of various hardness.

Quality of Money in Terms of Social Measurement System

The current hard-currency monetary system offers to the society the following advantages:

Right of buying everything on sell: Money offers the possibility to acquire everything that people are ready to abandon there ownership right. This is the best quality of money and the counterpart is that there is no guarantee that everything on sell can be sold (unemployment !).

Right of Saving: Selling with profit increases the personal freedom towards the society. This is the consequence of the interest rate system. Each profit can be put on saving with interest rate. From saving, the individual has the guarantee of a regular revenue and escapes from the constraint of work. The reality between this is that most of the work is made by the working equipment (probably more than 90 per cent if you compare the productivity between an artisanal tribal society to a modern industrialised society). Saving means buying "work equipment". So, the interest rate is in reality the revenue of the "work equipment". The current monetary system guarantees that the person which makes the investment and so is the cause the production of the "work equipment" receives the revenue of this work equipment.

Pragmatic Hierarchisation of the Society: This last point is the less considered but it is one of the major role of money as it permits the person to acquire a position in the society according to their realisation and not the talk. One the biggest cause of failure in social system is the concentration of responsibility and talent to the political world instead of entrepreneurs world. This last point should be kept in consideration as it is easy to conceive better social measurement system than money.

Weakness of Money in Terms of Social Measurement System

The analyse of the weakness in term of social measurement system should be made on the concept of lost of information (in the sense of the physician concept of entropy). So, money is a good system in the sense of keeping the debt between individuals. But, many information concerning the society are not kept and could be kept in the present capability of the computerised society.

A Different View

A warning is in order, that we are entering sacrilegious territory. For in today's times, when money is the new God, deified as the sole yardstick and *raison d'être* of our existence, it is nothing but blasphemy to even think of a different point of view. There is too much all around us, on why money is so very important and what one needs to do to become rich, the top 10 ways to make money, etc., etc., that one thought a slightly different flavour may do the palate some good. A refreshing change - a diversion - nothing

Money and Practical Life

more. This discussion about money in a very loose way to include money and all the investment avenues and assets that constitute the changing forms of money. Let's say wealth is what is being alluded to when talking about money. So, first the incontrovertible facts. Money is strange. Everybody needs it. Nobody has enough of it. It is believed to have a very central and pivotal role in our existence today and yet very few understand it completely. Yet there are enough and more who are willing to guide you on how to handle it (mostly for a fee) although, in most cases the risk is yours, if things go wrong later.

If you consider the erosion in value of money as inflation takes its toll, and the way exchange rate movements affect the international value of your money it all adds up to something fascinating to keep you engaged for a lifetime. Money evokes varied reactions:

"Money is better than poverty, if only for financial reasons"
– *Woody Allen*

"Money can't buy me love"

– *Paul Mcartney from the Beatles song Can't Buy Me Love*

"He is truly a man to whom money is only a servant; but, on the other hand, those who do not know how to make a proper use of it, hardly deserve to be called men." – Ramakrishna Paramahamsa, (famous Indian mystic saint).

Now we come to the pointers to support my argument for a different way of looking at money. If one looks around there is enough to suggest that the present structure suffers from numerous flaws. Some of these flaws are evident to anybody studying the global imbalances and the ongoing economic problems affecting several countries. Similarly global warming is also an indicator of serious flaws that need corrective steps. Now what does all this have to do with money? On the face of it nothing. In fact money may be seen to be the solution for all these problems. It is therefore necessary to point out some of the pernicious effects of money so that the linkage with today's burning problems becomes clear. Fortunately for us money has occupied the centre stage over the last fifty years and therefore if we look at the difference between then and now, the conclusions are clear.

- *Degradation of Values:* When I was a young boy, it was not only the wealthy who were emulated or served as role models for inspiration. There were achievers from all walks of life, some of them moderately rich and some even poor who commanded respect, either for the sheer brilliance of their intellect or for their artistry, or for their sportsmanship, valour, or strength of character, Also a person who had money from ill-gotten means did not command attention and was instead seen as a freak case – an exception to the rule that honest hard work alone pays. "God knows how he made his money and got away with it," would be the refrain when somebody like that was discussed. In those innocent (or backward) times, it was believed that wrongdoing would get you nowhere and that when you are caught it's not possible to talk your way out of the situation. How different the present times are ! It's not necessary for me to elaborate.

- *Erosion of Institutions:* With the centrality that money and commerce have assumed, all other human activities have had to wither and vanish or get reduced to being a small part of a giant enterprise in a global bazaar, where everything is bought and sold. What can be monetised or traded finds value and is allowed to flourish while the rest of it finds its way to the trashcan. Wombs can be rented and awards purchased. In the old days, schools and hospitals had dedicated doctors and teachers providing selfless service. Today, we have money-churning enterprises that leave you cold. Human life is reduced to a lifetime of buying and selling and institutions merely sub serve the cause.

- *Perversion of Perspectives:* Money being the yardstick, anything that makes sense from a money point of view becomes a truth that cannot be challenged. I remember an article about a group of economists in the seventies, who argued that money is highly inappropriate as a measuring rod to evaluate outcomes. They suggested that better alternatives need to be thought of and suggested that energy can be considered. Now the interesting point is that if energy is used as a measuring rod then one would get completely different results. For example, the increased output from adoption of modern agronomical practices would vanish because of the high energy cost of manufacturing fertilizers. Traditional farming would seem to be a highly energy efficient process.

These are some of the pointers that would make it appear that it's not less money but the central role given to money that is at the root of all evils and pains that we are suffering. Ancient Indian thought prescribed a fine balance between the four Purusharthas or aims of human life – Dharma (righteousness/duty and moral order), artha (wealth and prosperity), kama (worldly desires) and moksha (liberation). It is obvious that in today's world, we have extolled the value of artha (wealth) and subjugated and relegated the other three purusharthas. The world would be much better if we restored the balance. Not that money is irrelevant or of no use – just that the balance needs to be restored.

4

Money and Economic Development

In the first half of the twentieth century, the miners in the western world, used to keep canaries in coal mines as an early warning device. If the air was so bad that it killed the canary, the miners would soon be next. Japan may be the canary for the out-of-control deficit spending policies now being pursued in the United States and the United Kingdom. In an article in the Daily Telegraph called "It Is Japan We Should Be Worrying About, Not America," international business editor Ambrose Evans-Pritchard wrote:

> "Japan is drifting helplessly towards a dramatic fiscal crisis. For 20 years the world's second-largest economy has been . . . feeding its addiction to Keynesian deficit spending – and allowing it to push public debt beyond the point of no return. The rocketing cost of insuring against the bankruptcy of the Japanese state is telling us that the model has smashed into the buffers.

"... Tokyo's price index fell by 2.4 per cent in October, the deepest deflation in modern Japanese history.... The government could stop this .... It could print money a l'outrance to stave off deflation. Yet it sits frozen, like a rabbit in the headlamps.

"Japan's terrible errors are by now well known.... QE was too little, too late, and this is the lesson for the West. We must cut borrowing drastically over the next decade, and offset this with ultra-easy monetary policy. Does Downing Street understand this? Does the White House? ... Clearly not."

In case you too have forgotten your high school French, "a l'outrance" means "to the uttermost." "QE" is "quantitative easing" – printing money. Evans-Pritchard's proposed solution to the mounting fiscal crisis is that the government needs to quit borrowing money and start printing it.

Economy and Role of Money

The answer to the question of the role of money is not merely a philosophical one. Rather the very answer to this question is the key to understanding the realm of the world's economic problem today and is indeed the starting point to finding a solution.

As human societies evolved so did both human needs and the goods and services human produces. As needs grew and became more diverse, humans became less self sufficient and more co-dependent on one another. Instead of surviving on few items of food, shelter, and clothing, humans used a basket of numerous goods and services.

Combination that makes such baskets varied from one person to another and items that make up such a combination started to come from different sources producing same or similar items. Exchange that allows producer of a commodity to trade it in for one that is produced by another needed a medium to make such an exchange easy or even possible. It is that need to facilitate exchange of goods and services between various producers and

Money and Economic Development

consumers is what gave rise to the need for money. Thus money was invented as a means to facilitate exchange.

The function of money as medium for exchange required that money acts as a measure of value, otherwise how else would we know how much one item is measured in terms of other items? So human need to facilitate exchange is what gave rise to the role of money as both measure of value and medium of exchange. So far there would be little or no argument as to what money or its role are. As measure, money in and by itself has no value except in terms of the goods and services you can get in exchange for giving up an amount of that money.

As a measure, money also is a neutral medium where it only shows how much each commodity is worth in relation to another commodity. A tape measure is the same tape measure whether you are measuring carpet, a pipeline, or how tall or short you are. The value is not in the tape except for the function of standard measuring it provides. It is in what the tape is measuring, and such a value is weighed in relative terms. The distance a taxi travels is measured in terms of money which the driver gets in return for the service of travelling such a distance, which is the same amount of money the passenger pays the driver in return for the service.

Neutrality of money is a guarantee that money does not distort the terms of exchange as the relative value of things would be measured of how much one is willing to sacrifice in terms of one commodity in return for another. Once neutrality of money is violated then its very role in facilitating exchange and promoting economic growth of producing more and consuming more in and by itself is compromised.

Placing value on money itself then becomes a distorting factor where things are no longer only weighed in terms of relative values to buyers and sellers. A new player comes into play where terms of exchange are now affected by how much value a "money supplier" places on that money where money abandons the role it was created for to become a commodity in itself.

The fact that someone placed value on what is essentially neutral means of measurement and medium of exchange is at the heart of our economic melt-down today. When you buy a house today, you take a loan called mortgage to pay for that house. The amount of money you take out as a loan and agree to pay back has much more to do with the value the lender places on that money NOT on the house itself. A house could be worth a thousand dollars today, but when its purchase is financed by a loan which you agree to pay back over thirty years instalments, its price immediately jumps to about three times as much. In some cases you will have to pay that amount even if you decide to pay off your loan sooner than those thirty years. The mechanism by which your loan tripled is called interest, measured by interest rate, and is argued to be the value of money or the cost of borrowing.

That is precisely where the problem is. When you take out a loan, such a loan is no longer valued by the lender in terms of the money you took out rather by the amount you owe. To have money to lend to other people, the bank sells the amount you owe to another bank much earlier than the end of those thirty years for a discount, and new markets emerge where money is valued and exchanged in terms of contracts. But contracts are not money, and money is no longer a neutral means of measurement and exchange, thus just like everything else we lost our standard of value.

We started to hear terms such as "toxic assets." I can understand using the word toxic to describe food or waste that harms or kills you, but how can neutral meaning harmless means such as money be toxic? When money is assigned value in terms of interest it becomes less and less payable as you end up having to pay back more than the money you took. As you become less able or certain to pay back your loan, chances of defaulting on your loan increase. When banks bundle uncollected or uncollectable loans along with other loans in new financial products to conceal such a risk, then we end up having a form of money circulated called "toxic asset" because it kills the economy of goods and services we exchange thus providing the exact opposite role for which money was created to start with.

When neutrality of money is compromised so are its role and function of facilitating production and trade. Instead of acting as stimulus for growth and prosperity, money becomes a barrier to trade and production and a catalyst for poverty and misery. When banks knowingly and intentionally defraud investors by selling them those toxic assets we are all taken for a ride, and this time not in a taxi.

Interest is the mother of all economic ills. It assigns a role to money other than what money was created for, and that role is a store of value. When money is a store of value people no longer put money to good use by investing in producing more goods and services, and whole fanatical markets such as money and financial markets emerge where greed instead of utility is traded.

Next time you take a taxi, remember that you are not buying the distance you are travelling. You are merely paying for the service of travelling that distance. This way someone else can travel that same distance. You get your mission accomplished, the cab driver is happy to collect the fare, and someone else is happy to travel that same distance or even further.

Role of Money

The classical economists were of the view that money was discovered to remove the defects of barter. The important functions of money for them were to serve as a medium of exchange and standard of material. They examined in detail the characteristics of a good money material and the forces which operate in determining the value of money. The classical economists were of the view that the volume of output, the quantity and quality of the goods to be consumed, the volume of exchange, distribution of wealth, rate of saving and investment, etc., are not to be influenced by the use of money. They, therefore, regarded money as neutral. To quote Adam Smith "The gold and silver money which circulates in any one country may very properly be compared to a highway which while it circulates and carries to market all the grass and corn of the country, produces not a single pile of either." In the words of Jevon, "Accustomed from our earliest years to the use of money, we are unconscious of the inestimable benefit which it confers upon us and only when we recur to oblige their different states of society we can realise the difficulties which arise in its absence. Robertson in his book Principles of Money' states "Money enables man as consumer to generalise his purchasing power and make his claims on society in the form which suits him most."

The modem economists fully recognise the economic role of money as a medium of exchange and standard of value. They regard it as an economic catalyst. They emphasise that in a capitalistic economy, money exercises a decisive influence on the volume of production, distribution of wealth and income, direction and volume of exchange and on the rate of saving and investment in the country. We, here, discuss in brief the significance of money in a capitalistic and centrally controlled economy.

Role of Money in a Capitalistic Economy: Money is the sovereign Queen of all delights. For her the teacher teaches, the lawyer pleads, the dancer dances, the soldier fights. In a capitalistic economy, money is the pivot around which all economic activities cluster. Money is an indicator as well as a surveyor of wealth. The importance of money can be judged from the powerful influence which it exercises on the (1) Volume of production; (2) Direction of production; (3) Pattern of consumption; (4) Method of distribution; (5) Direction and volume of exchange; and (6) Rate of saving and mi investment in the country.

Production Decisions: Production has been greatly facilitated by the introduction of money. Money makes possible the accumulation of wealth in those hands which are. Able to organise the production. The captain of the industry hires the various factors ' of production in order to meet the future demand for goods and services and pays them in terms of money If the reward was to be paid in commodity, then the exchange of goods would have been very limited and so the production on a small scale Production without the use of money cannot be organised

Money and Economic Development

on a large scale and run efficiently and economically. The decision of what, where, when and how much to produce are all guided by the amount of money offered in exchange of goods and service. The cost of production is also estimated in terms of money. The profit or loss which is the difference between the sales proceeds and the total money cost is also expressed in terms of money. With the introduction of money. The consumption can be easily postponed and the assets can be stored for use to a future date.

Exchange Transactions: In a moneyless economy, exchange of goods was a very inconvenient process. People used to face the difficulties of double coincidence of wants. There was also no common measure of value. The use of money has successfully removed the awkwardness of barter. Money, by acting as a medium of exchange, has greatly stimulated the exchange of goods. It splits up exchange process into two parts, sale and purchase and thus facilitates flow of goods and services from producers to consumers.

Distribution of National Dividend: The four factors of production, combining together, produce a net aggregate of commodities every year. The share of each factor of production, i.e., rent of land, wages of labour, interest on capital and profit to entrepreneur is paid in terms of money, if the share of each factor of production was to be paid by dividing joint products, it would have caused much inconvenience to each distributor. Imagine, a cloth producer paying the share of each factor of production in term of Cloth. As money is generally acceptable as a medium of "exchange and at the same time acts as a measure and a store of value, therefore, the distribution of national dividend through the medium of money greatly facilitates the processes of distribution. In the words of Jevon "Money subdivides and distributes properly and lubricates the activities of exchange".

Money in the Field of Public Finance: Money renders a very valuable service in the field of public finance. Public Finance in recent times aims at increasing the rate of economic activities and reducing inequalities of income. It also acts as an instrument of economic and social justice in a country. Money helps the state in the achievement of these objectives. The government can easily raise revenue through the medium of money and can spend it for the betterment of the people.

Money in the Sphere of Banking: We know it very well that money serves as standard of deferred payments. The general confidence in the purchasing power of money makes it the chief farm of credit. The debtor can safely borrow money for consumption or for production purposes. This has led to the building up of a gigantic superstructure of banking and credit system.

Attainment of High Level of Production and Employment: The introduction of money in the economy has facilitated exchange. It has led to high degree of specialisation and interdependence of economic units; If the money is properly managed, it ensures rising level of productions employment and real income in the Country. In case, the delicate instruments is not properly handled, it leads to decline in the prices, output and job opportunities. We, thus, find that the behaviour of employment, rate of output, level of price and distribution of national income are all directly related to the monetary forces.

More Funny Money?

Your response is liable to be that we are doing that already, in spades; and it does not seem to be working. The Federal Reserve is madly printing money (or writing it into electronic accounts), increasing the money supply to the point that pundits are screaming about hyperinflation. Yet the nation is just plunging further into debt, while the credit crunch continues to get worse.

And that is true, but it is only half the picture. M1 is shooting up, but M3 and bank lending are both shrinking. (M1 is readily spendable money – coins and dollar bills, or M0, plus chequebook money. M3 is the broadest measure of the money supply, including savings deposits, money market funds, and other forms of liquid assets that are traded as money.) The Fed is creating money as fast as it can find federal and bank borrowers to take the money off its hands, yet it can't keep up with the rampant deflation in the real economy. Bank lending has dropped by 17 per cent since October 2008, when the credit crisis was already in full swing. "There has been nothing like this in the USA since the 1930s," says Professor Tim Congdon of International Monetary Research. "The rapid destruction of money balances is madness."

The reason the level of bank lending is so important is that virtually all our money today originates as loans created by private banks. Most people think money is issued by the government, but the only money the government creates are coins, which compose less than one ten-thousandth of the money supply – about $1 billion out of $13.8 trillion (M3). Dollar bills are issued by the Federal Reserve, a privately-owned banking corporation, and lent to the government and to other banks. And coins and dollar bills together make up only about 7 per cent of the money supply. All of the rest is simply written into accounts on computer screens by bankers when they make loans.

Contrary to popular belief, banks do not lend their own money or their depositors' money. Every time a bank makes a loan, it is brand new money, simply written into the account of the borrower:

> "The different forms of money in government money supply statistics arise from the practice of fractional-reserve banking. Whenever a bank gives out a loan in a fractional-reserve banking system, a new sum of money is created. This new type of money is what makes up the non-M0 components in the M1-M3 statistics. In short, there are two types of money in a fractional-reserve banking system: (1) central bank money (physical currency, government money); and (2) commercial bank money (money created through loans) - sometimes referred to as private money, or checkbook money. In the money supply statistics, central bank money is M0 while the commercial bank money is divided up into the M1-M3 components."

If there were no banks, we would have no money except pennies, nickels, dimes and quarters. Money created as bank loans does not stick around, since loans eventually get paid back. When old loans get paid off and new ones aren't taken out to replace them, the money supply shrinks; and lately, new loans have fallen off dramatically.

Why? Banks insist that they are lending as much as they are prudently allowed to. The problem is that they have reached the lending limits imposed by the capital requirements set by the Bank for International Settlements. In the years of the credit boom, banks were able to leverage their capital into far more loans than are being created now.

This was because loans were taken off the banks' books by investors, allowing the same capital to be used many times over to generate new loans. These investors, called "shadow lenders," have now exited the market, and they are not expected to return any time soon. They left after it became clear that the credit default swaps allegedly protecting their investments were only as good as the solvency of the counterparties (typically AIG or hedge funds), which had a bad habit of going bankrupt rather than paying up.

An estimated $10 trillion disappeared from the money supply along with the shadow lenders, and the Fed has managed to get only a few trillion back into the market as replacement money.

Shadow Money

Along with the disappearance of the "shadow lenders," there has been a dramatic decline in something called "shadow money." The concept of shadow money was presented by two economists from Credit Suisse, James Sweeney and Carl Lantz, in a Bloomberg interview in May. As explained on Demand Side Blog, shadow money is money the market itself creates in order to finance a boom — "money" in the sense of a medium of exchange.

In a boom there is not enough cash to go around, so collateral is used as near money or shadow money. Shadow money can include government bonds, private bonds, asset-backed securities,

Money and Economic Development

credit card debt (which can be incurred and paid off without drawing on the M1 money stock), and even real estate (when it is highly liquid and easily tradeable).

In a fuller explanation on Zero Hedge, Tyler Durden (a pen name) quotes from Friedrich Hayek's Prices and Production (1935). Hayek said:

> "There can be no doubt that besides the regular types of the circulating medium, such as coin, notes and bank deposits, which are generally recognised to be money or currency, and the quantity of which is regulated by some central authority or can at least be imagined to be so regulated, there exist still other forms of media of exchange which occasionally or permanently do the service of money.
>
> "...It is clear that, other things equal, any increase or decrease of these money substitutes will have exactly the same effects as an increase or decrease of the quantity of money proper, and should therefore, for the purposes of theoretical analysis, be counted as money."

Lantz and Sweeney calculate that at the peak of the boom there were six trillion dollars in the traditionally-defined money stock (or money supply). The private shadow stock accounted for $9.5 trillion, and government-based shadow money accounted for another $11 trillion. Thus the shadow money stock dwarfed the traditionally-defined money stock. This can be seen in the chart below provided by Tyler Durden.

The blue strips at the bottom, called "outside money," are dollars printed by the Federal Reserve. The red sections, called "inside money," are money created as loans by the banks themselves. The green sections, called "public shadow money," are money created by the government and the Fed as debt (or loans). The purple sections, called "private shadow money," are the money created as private debt securities by the shadow lenders.

Lantz and Sweeney estimate the total drop in private shadow money (the purple blocks) during the current credit crisis at $3.6

trillion. This has been offset by an increase in public shadow money, both from the massive borrowing needed to finance the federal deficit and from the aggressive liquidity measures taken by the Fed in converting private securities into loans. Those measures helped prevent an even worse drop in the commercial money supply than actually occurred, but they were not sufficient to eliminate the credit squeeze from lowered commercial lending, which continues to act as a tourniquet on the productive economy.

Moreover, the lending situation is slated to get worse. At the G20 meeting in Pittsburgh in September, deadlines were set for increasing the amount of capital that financial institutions must set aside to cover their loans. That means that credit could get even tighter, further shrinking the global money supply and precipitating an even deeper depression.

Helicopter Money: not Such a Bad Idea after All?

Ironically, it was in Japan in 2002 that Ben Bernanke gave the speech for which he has been much derided, in which he maintained that deflation could be reversed simply by dropping money from helicopters. He said, "The US government has a technology, called a printing press (or, today, its electronic equivalent), that allows it to produce as many US dollars as it wishes at essentially no cost.... A money-financed tax cut is essentially equivalent to Milton Friedman's famous 'helicopter drop' of money."

But the Japanese froze in the headlights, as Evans-Pritchard writes. Instead of merely issuing the money it needed, the government borrowed from banks that issued it and lent it at compound interest.

Chairman Bernanke could not even implement his own plan in the US, because the Federal Reserve is not actually the government. The Fed Chairman is not authorised to print money and simply hand it over to the government or to spend it directly into the economy. The Fed has to lend it to the government and other financial institutions, which means finding willing and able borrowers; and today, creditworthy borrowers are in short supply.

Moreover, when they do borrow, they eventually pay the money back, shrinking the money supply once again. Only the government is in a position to simply roll its debt over from year to year. But when Chairman Bernanke announced last spring that the Fed would be funding $300 billion in long-term government debt, the Chinese expressed grave concern. He then backed off from this form of quantitative easing, evidently to keep the creditors happy.

How to Save $400 Billion Yearly in Interest: Monetise the Debt

Although the Federal Reserve cannot create money and simply spend it into the economy, Congress can. The Constitution authorises Congress "to coin money [and] regulate the value thereof." A former chairman of the House Coinage Subcommittee once observed that Congress could solve its financial problems just by minting some very large-denomination coins and paying off its debts. This solution is invariably rejected as dangerously inflationary; but when the "shadow money" is factored in, it actually wouldn't be.

Government bonds already serve as a medium of exchange, trading in massive quantities around the world just as if they were money. Paying off government bonds with newly-printed dollars and then ripping up the bonds (or voiding them out on a computer screen) would not significantly affect the size of the overall money supply, since "shadow money" would just be replaced with dollar bills (paper or electronic). In the chart above, green money (public shadow money) would become blue money (dollar bills and checkbook money), leaving the total money stock unchanged.

It might be argued that the money borrowed by the government has already been spent into the economy, and that if the bonds are now turned into dollars, the money will be out there twice. And that is true; but on the shadow-money model, the inflation has already occurred and cannot now be reversed.

It occurred when the government printed the bonds. The bonds are already out there serving as money. Whether the money stock takes the form of dollars or bonds, it will be used as a medium of exchange in the real economy.

Another argument often raised is that the money created as government securities and Federal Reserve loans has been "sterilised" by lodging it with central banks and commercial banks. When this money hits Main Street as dollars competing for goods and services, the floodgates will open and hyperinflation will be upon us. That is the alleged justification for keeping the stimulus money in the banks instead of in the marketplace. But then what was the point of the stimulus? If the money is only stimulating the banks, it is not doing anything for the real economy.

We want money out there in the marketplace generating demand for products, which generates jobs. Price inflation results only when "demand" (money) exceeds "supply" (goods and services). If the money is used to create goods and services, prices will remain stable. We have workers out of work and factories sitting idle. They need some "demand" (money) stimulating them to create supply, in order to make the economy productive again.

Other critics point to gold's recent rise as an indicator of inflation already being upon us. But the more likely explanation for gold's rise is that foreign central banks are looking for something besides US government bonds in which to park their money. They no longer want our bonds, so fine. We should tell them that no more are for sale. We will in the future sell our bonds to our own central bank, which will rebate the interest to the government after deducting its costs, making its credit the best deal in town. And we will use the money, not to feed a parasitic private banking empire by building up bank reserves, but for direct expenditures on infrastructure and other public projects that will put people back to work, add to the productive economy, and increase the collective well-being of the American people.

New Role of Money in Admissions

Affluent students in the UK are about to get a big leg up in the college admissions game. Under a new proposal, students will be able to buy a guaranteed spot at some of the top universities—like Oxford—that turn away thousands of candidates every year. It's a money making proposition for the schools since students admitted in this way will pay the same higher tuition rates that foreign students pay, $20,000 to $45,000 per year, depending on the student's course of study. The plan also sounds like a total death knell for the idea of a meritocracy.

Money is also playing a new role in college admissions stateside, albeit in a somewhat different way. The 10-campus University of California system is currently mulling over a plan that would charge students varying tuition depending on which campus they decide to attend. If a student chooses a more prestigious UC school, like Berkeley or UCLA, they'll pay more. Proponents say that in an era when budget cuts are gutting the system, such a plan could raise much needed money that the all campuses could share. Unfortunately, it could potentially also put the more elite UCs out of reach of middle-class and lower-income students.

There's no denying that many schools could certainly put extra money to good use. Over 86 per cent of American students borrow to pay for college, and our collective student loan debt is on track to hit $1 trillion this year. Universities that sell guaranteed spots or charge more for more prestige *could* use that money from rich families to beef up the scholarships and grants they offer to less well-off students.

But this is a really slippery slope to go down. What's to stop a college from allocating more and more spots for students from wealthy backgrounds every year? We need to make colleges more meritocratic and affordable, not less so. These new proposals, both here in the States and in the UK, just further undermine the ideal that a quality education should be a right—or at least an opportunity you can earn through hard work—not something you can simply buy.

Role of Organisation in Three Stages

The evolution of society through these three stages is accomplished by the progressive development of more productive, efficient and complex social organisations. At the same time, the nature of the predominant organisations also evolves from physical to vital to mental. Each transition from one stage to another results in a tremendous increase in social productivity by several orders of magnitude. An examination of the role of organisation in each of the three stages reveals the source of this phenomenal increase in the capabilities of society. In the following section, we examine the contribution of three different levels of social organisation to development – urbanisation during the physical stage, money during the vital stage, and Internet as an organisation of information during the mental stage.

Development can be likened to a chemical reaction. The speed and outcome of the reaction depends on the concentration of ingredients, the temperature and pressure, and the presence of catalytic agents. These elements determine the frequency, intensity and efficiency of contact between the substrates.

The greater the concentration, temperature and pressure, the faster the molecules move and the more frequently and forcefully they interact with each other. The presence of the appropriate catalyst speeds the reaction between compatible substances by serving as a medium for bringing the substrates into proximity over a larger area. Development also depends on the speed, frequency, intensity and breadth of contacts and interactions. Social institutions act as powerful stimuli for development by increasing the number, frequency and intensity of interactions between compatible elements.

Population Growth and Urbanisation

The most discernible trend during the physical stage of development is growth of population. In the physical stage, the primary goal of society was to ensure the survival of the community in the face of war, famine, and epidemic disease. The first result of progress in agriculture, defence and urban settlements was an increase in population. In the modern age of the population explosion, growth of population is often viewed as a barrier to development rather than a measure of it. But in prior centuries, population growth has always been limited by the capacity of society to sustain larger numbers of people. Until very recently, each improvement in agricultural productivity and food supply has resulted in a significant expansion of population.

Before the invention of cultivation about 10,000 years ago, the total population of the world probably did not exceed 10 million people. During the next 8000 years, the world's population increased about 30 times to reach 300 million in 1 AD. Since then it has grown another 20 fold. It reached 500 million in 1650, then doubled to cross one billion by 1800, doubled again to 2 billion by 1930, then tripled during the last six decades.

The 12-fold growth of population over the past 300 years as a result of tremendous increases in food production and public health is an indication of the order of magnitude of social progress during this period. Figure 1 utilises population growth as an index of the growth in social productivity over the last 500 years.

These enormous increases in population were made possible by tremendous advances in the organisation of society around urban centres. Historically, the first major organisational innovation was the transition of primitive society from hunting and gathering to cultivation and rearing of domesticated animals between the 7th and 3rd Millennium BC.

The capacity to generate reliable supplies of food from the land made possible the establishment of permanent sedentary human settlements. As agricultural productivity increased the supply of food, the surpluses freed more and more people from the necessity of producing and gathering food, so they could specialise in other activities. The size and location of these early settlements was limited by the productivity of the surrounding lands. Later, improved transportation made possible by the development of the wheel, roads, boats and canals enabled food to be carried over greater distances from fields to towns.

The concentration of population in early agricultural settlements led to development of fortified towns, providing physical security from external threats. The creation of towns represents the development of a higher type of physical organisation. With few exceptions, these cities were very small by modern standards, rarely exceeding 100,000 inhabitants, but more densely populated than the most crowded modern metropolises.

The formation of towns required the evolution of new organisations for governance, external defence, internal security, regulation of property rights, production, trade, distribution, education and religion. Within the town, the workforce divided and specialised into military, political, administrative, agricultural, industrial and commercial categories.

The concentration of larger population increased the frequency, speed and intensity of social interactions, providing far greater need and opportunity for economic exchange than occurred in sparsely populated rural areas. It created pressure on society to continuously increase food production. It created a growing market for goods and services that encouraged social inventiveness.

The growth of these population centres in turn depended upon and was facilitated by advances in the physical organisation of the settlement. Towns were organised into sectors. Roads were laid, bridges were built, markets were constructed and ports were developed.

In some instances aqueducts were built to transport drinking water and sewers were dug to carry away wastes and drain rainwater. This physical infrastructure enabled towns to grow into larger urban centres, further intensifying the number, size and variety of economic interactions.

Cities became centres for government, trade, manufacturing, education, recreation and cultural activities. These densely populated areas where people, capital and knowledge accumulated became powerful engines for development. Packed into close quarters, news and rumours spread swiftly.

The population became far more aware of what was taking place in other places. Pioneering inventions and innovations were quickly imitated by others. The growing frequency, efficiency, speed, complexity and intensity of human interactions through the organisation of urban communities was the basis for the significant developmental achievements of the physical stage.

The process of urbanisation that began with permanent agricultural settlements progressed very slowly up through the Middle Ages. The dual imperatives of defence and sustenance remained the principle rationale for cities and fortress towns under the feudal order. Urban communities in Europe grew more rapidly in size and number with the decline of feudalism and the rise of the mercantile era from the 12th Century onwards.

Commercial communities governed by merchant councils flourished throughout Europe and exerted continued pressure for increasing economic freedom and political autonomy from feudal and monarchical power, which led eventually to the emancipation of individuals as well.

The growth of merchant cities was made possible by the rapid development of a higher level of commercial organisation and the increasing role of money. The growth of the money economy ushered society into the vital stage and spurred the remarkable expansion of global economic activity that led up to the Industrial Revolution.

The growth of urban organisations did not occur until the sustained population explosion of the last three centuries. By the time world population crossed one billion in 1800, only three per cent of humanity lived in cities of 20,000 or more. Only 45 cities in the world had population greater than 100,000.

London was still too small to qualify for this elite group of urban centres. By the time world population crossed three billion in 1960, 25 per cent of humanity was living in cities. The world's urban population rose to 40 per cent by 1980 and is projected to cross 50 per cent by the year 2000.

This radical shift of settlement patterns over the last 200 years was spurred by the onset of the Industrial Revolution and has been fuelled by the continuous emergence of ever more powerful organisations characteristic of the mental stage of social development.

Role of Money in Development

With the rise of large commercial urban centres, the principle instrument for development shifted from physical matter to social institution — from arable land to money. Money has been the single greatest organisational invention of the past five thousand years. The emergence of money as a pre-eminent social institution vividly illustrates the central role of organisation in the process of social development.

The creation of money was made possible and spurred by the generation of food surpluses. One of the earliest forms of money was the receipt issued for grain deposits at government warehouses in ancient Babylon, which gradually became transferable to third parties. The capacity of early farmers to produce more food than was required for consumption by the family naturally prompted them to trade their surplus for other goods or services. As long as these exchanges were conducted by means of barter, they were severely limited both in volume and speed. Barter exchange required the double coincidence of a buyer and seller both wanting what the other possessed in surplus.

It also involved a very complicated form of valuation, since every type of commodity would have a different price depending on the goods or service for which it was to be exchanged. Direct barter involving 1000 different commodities would require 500,000 rates of exchange. Barter transactions worked best within a narrow geographical area due to the physical difficulties of transporting products over long distances. The perishable nature of many products also limited barter exchanges. Producers had no incentive to produce more than they were confident of either consuming or exchanging with other consumers during the period before a product deteriorated.

The use of money spread gradually from one country to another by a process of imitation similar to the manner in which ideas, technologies and other social institutions are transmitted from one place to another and bear fruit wherever the soil is

Money and Economic Development

sufficiently prepared. The adoption of money in place of barter had a tremendously liberating and expansive impact on early society. As urbanisation increased the number, size and speed of transactions by bringing many more people into proximity, money increased the number, size, speed, and efficiency of transactions even over long distances.

The capacity to convert the fruits of one's labour into money meant that those fruits could be stored indefinitely, overcoming the limitations of time and providing an incentive for people to exert themselves much harder and longer than if what they produced must be consumed immediately. The capacity to convert physical goods into portable money overcame the limitations imposed by space. Whereas products could be transported long distances only at considerable cost and difficulty, money could be moved quickly and inexpensively, making possible trade over much larger geographic areas.

Money also provided a common standard for valuation of all products and services, thereby vastly reducing the complexity of exchange rates. By eliminating the necessity of the double coincidence required for barter trade, money made it possible for a much larger number of transactions to be completed. At the same time, its ease of movement and accounting enormously increased the speed of commercial transactions. *The increasing volume and speed of transactions made possible by money combined with the increasing size and density of urban population had an exponential impact on the development of society.*

Money had a transforming effect on society equivalent in magnitude to that brought about by the emergence of urban communities. It helped liberate society from the strict confines of the land and the retarding influences of tradition, spurring the evolution from the physical to the vital stage of social development. Before money, land was the principle productive resource and source of wealth. Those who controlled the land controlled the wealth of society. The hereditary transmission of property rights during the feudal period left little incentive for individual initiative and little room for individual advancement.

During the Middle Ages, European society actually reverted for a time to barter before money returned and gained ascendance. The return of money and the rise of commerce in European society coincided with the demise of the agrarian based feudal system.

Money gradually replaced heredity not only as a source of wealth, but as a source of social power and privilege as well. The moneyed commercial classes became increasingly influential, creating the backdrop for the emergence of democratic values and forms of government a few centuries later. Money freed the individual from servitude to the soil. A person could earn money and use it to purchase whatever was required for personal sustenance and also utilise it as capital to earn a living.

It impersonalised and democratised transactions, empowering the possessor with economic voting power that drastically reduced discrimination based on class and status. Money increased the individual's freedom of choice and gave greater scope for the development of individual talents and potentials.

Social organisations that spur development at one stage tend to ossify and die out later on, as hunting tribes, guilds, East India companies and colonial empires, feudal and monarchical institutions have in the past. Some institutions exhibit the capacity to evolve along with society, adapting and changing to match the character of the times. Money has exhibited this capacity to evolve with the times. Sharing the characteristics of this physical stage of development, early money was itself a physical commodity, grain, gold or silver.

Only gradually did representative forms of money appear, but these too were full-bodied commodity money, convertible at any time into the commodity that they represented. During the vital stage, more symbolic forms of money such as certificates of deposit, bank notes, checks, letters of credit, bonds and other forms of negotiable securities came into prominence. The complete separation of money from its physical roots came at a much later stage of social development with the appearance of fiat money that does not have a commodity value and cannot be redeemed for a commodity.

Organisations of the Mental Stage

Knowledge is the central characteristic of the mental attribute of human consciousness which has assumed an increasingly dominant role during the last few hundreds years. Although we speak of the mental phase as being of very recent origin, it is evident that the mental component has been an active contributor to development since primitive societies developed agriculture and invented the wheel.

What has changed very markedly is the relative contribution of this mental attribute, which is made visibly evident by the increasing speed of development in modern times. The knowledge that the mental component acquires and applies to further human progress has had a profound effect on all aspects of social life ranging from pure mental concepts to practical physical applications.

The action of mind in four specific fields has had an especially powerful influence on the course of global development — political thought, social organisation, education, science and technology.

The development of philosophical thought and values expresses in social life as changing concepts about the purpose of life, the role and nature of human beings, and the relationship between the individual and the collective. This abstract and exalted field of mental speculation appears far removed from practical considerations. Yet it has been the source of the revolutionary thoughts and values that have radically transformed the political and social structure of civilization over the past five centuries, leading to the establishment of democratic principles and forms of governance as a global standard, if not quite yet a global practice.

This movement can be traced back to the revival of humanistic thought, spread of education and secular values that arose during the Renaissance. It gained momentum with the spiritual empowerment of the individual by the Reformation, the birth of modern science, the affirmation of rationalistic ideals during the Enlightenment, and the declaration of human values by the American and French Revolutions. These movements have culminated during this century in the collapse of colonial empires following World War II and the rapid spread of democratic forms of government in Latin America, Eastern Europe and Africa over the past two decades.

The tremendous release of individual energy and collective dynamism that accompanied the practical acceptance of these ideals has provided the impetus for momentous social accomplishments that until recently seemed inconceivable.

Education

This transformation of the political organisation of societies which has extended basic human rights at first to the middle class and eventually to the common man was mirrored by a parallel development of the social organisation for education that was equally far reaching and powerful in its impact. Education is the systematic organisation of the cumulative knowledge and experience of humanity and the transmission of that knowledge to the next generation in a concentrated and abridged form.

It is the central instrument for making the past discoveries and experience of humanity more and more conscious and accessible for application by society to meet the opportunities and challenges of the future.

If the distribution of political power to the entire population was inconceivable to the pre-revolutionary aristocracy and common people of Europe, then the concept and practice of universal education prevalent today would have been absolutely unthinkable.

The Renaissance and Reformation led to a revival of interest in education that, like science and philosophy, had been eclipsed in Europe during the Middle Ages. Prior to 1600, education was confined to a small population consisting mostly of Christian scholars and the nobility. Both Luther and Calvin believed that every individual should read the Bible and urged establishment of state educational systems. In the 17th Century education spread gradually but maintained a strong religious orientation.

Leading thinkers of the Enlightenment stressed the importance of intellectual knowledge to the practical advancement of society and the importance of secular education. During the next century secularism and social progress began to prevail and for the first time advanced scientific and mathematical knowledge became a part of the school and university curriculum in Europe and North America.

The growing recognition of the importance of education for social progress led to the extension of elementary education to the middle classes and prompted more states to assume responsibility for establishing and maintaining national school systems.

Over the last two hundred years, education has become one of the principle organisations in modern society. Since the end of World War II, it has come to be universally recognised as a principle instrument for national development, leading to a worldwide expansion of primary and secondary education along with a multiplication of colleges, universities and professional schools.

At the same time, the breadth of the educational curriculum has been expanded and significantly reoriented to cover a great many areas of applied knowledge such as specialised fields in engineering, physical and biological sciences, business management, economics and most recently computer sciences. Education has awakened the mind of humanity to its innate potentials and to the enormous untapped opportunities in its external environment.

This growing awareness has released infinite energy for mental creativity, social innovation and practical invention. It has raised the aspirations and expectations of people everywhere for the fruits of progress. It has equipped individuals with the mental knowledge and skills to fashion and manage more and more powerful and complex forms of social systems, and to design, manufacture and operate more and more powerful and complex forms of technology. It has created an unprecedented openness and tolerance, which are an essential basis for global development in the coming years.

Technology

Mind applying itself to the field of thought creates new concepts and more powerful ideals. Applying itself to the field of society, it creates new and improved social organisations. Applying itself to the field of matter, it discovers the physical laws of nature and creates new technologies and inventions. The application of mind's creative powers to the field of science, technology and practical invention has had an enormous impact on social progress during the last two centuries.

History reveals a slow and uneven advance in applied scientific knowledge and technology. There have been periods of great inventiveness and great discoveries in the distant past, followed by periods of stagnation. But nothing can equal in sheer numbers and significance the explosion of human invention that has occurred since the onset of the Industrial Revolution. A classic study by Lilly found that the relative rate of inventiveness rose seven-fold between 1700 and 1900 to reach a level at least ten times higher than had been achieved during earlier millennia.

A number of specific factors have contributed to this accelerating rate of inventiveness, but the essential cause has been the emergence of the mental principle as the spearhead of social development. Its energies released by politically awakening and social freedoms, its thought liberated from blind submission to tradition and refined by education, the power of mind has applied itself to transform the social and material life of humanity. Superstitious beliefs and religious dogma characteristic of the physical stage have been powerful deterrents to fresh thinking and innovation during much of human history.

In the Middle Ages in Europe, inventions that seemed a little too clever or unusual were frequently condemned as satanic and their inventors persecuted. Thus, Copernicus' heliocentric theory was rejected as inconsistent with the scriptures and remained unpublished during his lifetime. Churchmen condemned Galileo's refracting telescope as an instrument of the devil. After he openly endorsed Copernicanism, he was sentenced to life imprisonment for 'vehement suspicion of heresy'. The movement of rationalist thought ushered in by the Enlightenment reduced the inhibiting influence of superstition and religious dogma and cleared the way for the emergence of the experimental sciences.

There is a common tendency to view technology as a thing apart and to explain the developmental achievements of the last 200 years exclusively or primarily in technological terms. This view is inadequate because it attempts to isolate advances in technology from the general advance of knowledge and social organisation characteristic of the mental stage of development.

In earlier periods, scientific investigation and technological innovation were carried out as isolated activities without the support of the social organisation. Prior to the 15th Century, there were no reliable mechanisms for the recording, preservation and dissemination of inventions, so most discoveries were applied only locally and a great many were lost altogether.

Individual inventors adapted and improved mechanisms for specific applications, but in most cases their innovations were never transmitted to others or standardised for widespread use. The technological developments of the Industrial Revolution would not have been possible without the organisation of scientific knowledge and the establishment of scientific associations throughout Europe in the 16th and 17th Century.

The publication of scientific journals aided the conservation and organisation of society's technical knowledge. Until legal protection for patents was introduced at the end of the 18th Century, inventors had no way of knowing about similar inventions and no way to stake an economic right to their discoveries, except by keeping them secret. In France exclusive rights to an invention were protected by letters of patent granted only by royal authority and records were kept in a single central location inaccessible to all but a few.

Technology is knowledge of matter organised and applied through a practical organisation. The widespread application of technology during and after the Industrial Revolution depended on the development of several other types of social organisation. The organisation of agriculture by enclosure of common lands in England generated surplus farm incomes, freed people to migrate to the towns, and fuelled rapid population growth, which resulted in an increased market for manufactured goods and made mechanisation feasible.

The organisation of urban commercial centres, transport and foreign trade created demand for larger volumes of production than could be readily produced by human labour. Poor roads in 17th Century Europe retarded industrial invention.

There was little incentive to increase production so long as expansion of the market was severely hindered by poor transportation. The development of sea trade routes during the 18th Century opened a much wider market for manufactured products, stimulating a new outburst of invention.

The organisation of mass production according to the principles of division and specialisation of labour made the adaptation of mechanised technology practical. The organisation of education equipped the society with the skills necessary to design, manufacture and utilise an endless stream of more complex and sophisticated inventions. Technology developed as an integrated part of the evolving fabric of the social organisation.

Internet

We witness today the confluence of factors that characterise the mental stage – unprecedented political freedom, a global affirmation of the individual and the rights of the common man, abundant and overflowing social energy, an irrepressible drive of mental inquisitiveness, the accumulation and codification of knowledge in all fields, the universal aspiration for and spread of education, a worldwide revolution of rising expectations, a veritable explosion of technological inventiveness, and the accelerating pace of organisational creativity and innovation, which is the technology of social development.

These factors coming together in the mental stage have given birth to a new form of organisation whose creativity and potential contribution to social advancement rival in importance the role played by money over the past millennium. The emergence of the Internet as a worldwide system of communication, information exchange, education and commerce is opening up vast opportunities for more rapid development. It is eliminating barriers to communication imposed by space and time, levelling the playing field between rich and poor, and making possible universal access to information and services at very low cost.

We have been tracing the evolution of social institutions that developed by a long, slow unconscious process over centuries or millennia. Now we are confronting a phenomenon that is expanding before our very eyes, proliferating globally with a speed that defies even our most sophisticated capabilities for tracking and measurement. For the first time we have the opportunity to observe the process close up at an accelerated rate that enables us to perceive those conditions that make it possible and to experience first hand as participants the social will that propels this development.

Internet was born and grew up in the USA, a social environment in which political freedom, social self-expression and individual empowerment have been elevated almost to cult status; in which widespread prosperity has distributed material comforts to the majority of people; in which higher education has been extended to more people than anywhere else in the world; in which the discoveries of science generate keen anticipation and excitement; in which the quest for information has become an insatiable thirst; in which the productive value of information has become a self-evident fact of life; and in which new technologies are accepted, assimilated and mastered with greater eagerness and facility than at any other time or place in history.

Viewed in this context it is evident that the development of Internet is neither a fortuitous discovery nor an inevitable evolution of technological trends. It is a natural expression and embodiment of the aspiration of modern society for unlimited and immediate access to information and unlimited means for individual creativity and self-expression. This aspiration has released a colossal energy in society that is by no means restricted to any single country or form of expression, but rather flows and overflows through every conceivable channel that will lend itself as an outlet.

Money and Internet

The evolution of social institutions is the primary engine driving the development of society. Social institutions act as powerful stimuli for development by increasing the frequency, intensity and efficiency of social interactions. This evolution has moved through three successive but overlapping stages of development – physical, vital, and mental – that can be described in terms of the type of organisation predominant during that stage. The paper examines the role of three organisations characteristic of the three stages – urbanisation, money and the Internet.

Early cities were physical organisations where people, activities, fields of life, resources and infrastructure accumulated at high levels of concentration and interacted in complex ways. The growth of population and urban population density increased the intensity of these interactions, creating the critical mass needed for the emergence of markets and generating sufficient demand to spur mechanisation of production during the Industrial Revolution.

Money has played a parallel role at the social level as a medium for urbanisation, multiplying economic activities by several orders of magnitude. Establishment of a money economy freed individuals from dependence on land as an essential resource for production and freed commerce from the double coincidence needed for barter trade. Money increased the frequency and speed of transactions in virtually every field of activity by making it possible for people to convert the fruits of their labour into a common currency that could be exchanged for any products or services. Money provides incentives for people to produce more than they can consume, releasing greater energy and creativity. It serves as a medium for conservation and storage of what each person produces and permits easy transfer over any distance, thereby overcoming limitations imposed by time and space and dramatically increasing the efficiency of transactions.

Internet promises to play a similar role at the mental level of information and knowledge as a medium to organise globalisation. Internet is increasing the frequency, speed and efficiency of information exchange in every field – commercial, industrial, educational, scientific, political, religious, recreational, etc. Internet also overcomes the limits of time and space by enabling instantaneous access to information around the world. It increases enormously the number, intricacy and complexity of interactions made possible between individuals, organisations, facts, activities and fields of knowledge. Internet is an organised medium for bringing all existing social organisations into greater contact to release the maximum energy of society leading to unprecedented levels of social productivity and development.

Summary of the Theory

Development is the upward directional movement of society from lesser to greater levels of energy, efficiency, quality, productivity, complexity, comprehension, creativity, enjoyment and accomplishment. These attributes are both the means for achieving development as well as its most characteristic expressions or results. The factor that they all have in common and which imparts to them their value is *organisation*.

Higher levels of each of these attributes are the resultant expression of higher levels of organisation in society. Organisation is the capacity to mobilise all the available information, knowledge, material resources, technology, infrastructure, and human abilities to meet challenges and take advantage of opportunities. Development is the process of continuously enhancing the capacity of society to respond to opportunities and challenges by increasing its level of organisation. Development is the process of creating newer organisations.

The fabric of society consists of intricate interrelationships and interactions between different activities, systems, organisations, institutions, ideas, beliefs and values. The process of social development occurs by increasing the scope and complexity of the organisation of this fabric. The movement involves a simultaneous development of the social fabric in several dimensions:

- Quantitative expansion in the size and carrying capacity of social activities, systems, organisations and institutions;
- Qualitative increase in the content, productivity and sophistication of the constituent elements of the fabric;
- Geographic or spacial extension of the organised fabric to provide more intensive coverage to larger portions of the population.
- Integration of existing and new organisational elements into an increasingly complex network of interrelationships;

A continuous process of organisational invention and innovation spurs this movement. During each phase new organisations emerge and existing organisations take on new attributes that enable them to act as spearheads of the development process. The contribution of any of these factors may for a time become so significant that we view them as essential causes in their own right.

Actually they are the live evolving ends of the underlying social organisation which fashions them by its excess energy and without which they cannot exist or function.

The accumulated knowledge of the society and its increasing awareness of emerging opportunities and challenges determine the overall direction given to this development process. The energy that drives the process is determined by the intensity of the collective social aspiration for higher levels of accomplishment released by this accumulated knowledge and growing awareness.

These in turn are strongly influenced by the level of organisation of the social collective.

Stated in other words, society becomes increasingly conscious of its inherent capabilities, the opportunities for high achievement and the means to organise itself for that achievement. The more conscious it becomes, the more its energies are released, the clearer the direction given to those energies, the more effective and efficient the organisational arrangements it fashions to support accomplishment, and the greater the magnitude and speed of social progress.

Internet's Four-fold Infrastructure

Like every major social organisation that has come before it, the emergence of the Internet has taken place on the foundations of a four-fold organisational infrastructure. At the physical level, Internet is the product of the creative convergence of two very powerful technology-based systems — computer networks and telecommunications.

The coordination of two or more systems or fields of activity unleashes a tremendous productive power. The linking together of mail order and retailing propelled the growth of Sears to become the largest retailer in the world within quarter of a century. The linking of air transport with a unique system for auctioning flowers has enabled tiny Netherlands to capture 68 per cent of world trade in cut flowers.

The initial infrastructure for Internet was established in 1969 to provide a secure and survivable communications network for organisations engaged in defence-related research. Over the following two decades, it evolved into a fast, convenient, low cost means for universities and research institutions to electronically exchange information and messages.

The spread of personal computers in businesses, government, schools and homes coupled with the growth of local area networks during the 1980s and early 1990s provided a means for million of individual users to link into the system. These developments propelled the growth of the Internet from a thousand or so networks in the mid-1980s to about 60,000 connected networks in mid-1995. By the middle of 1997, the Internet was available to an estimated 100 million register users worldwide.

A huge number of incremental technological advances in computer hardware and software, data transmission and satellite communications contributed to the development of the Internet. Among these, the development of a standardised graphic interface language compatible with a wide range of computing systems formed one of the final links that transformed a text oriented information system into a multimedia system for publishing, broadcasting and transactions — the World Wide Web.

It would be a gross oversimplification and misconception to view the Internet primarily as a technological advancement. All these technologies taken together do not inevitably add up to the Internet. It is possible, perhaps even likely, that had the same technologies been available in an earlier time and under different circumstances, they would not have given rise to a system with the same characteristics. What is new and unique about the Internet, thoroughly in character with the temper of our times, and the source of its unprecedented productive capacities is its organisation. Internet is primarily and pre-eminently a new model and form of social organisation with untold power to transform the way society functions.

Even before Internet emerged as a worldwide phenomenon, the shift in computing from a specialised activity carried out in central data processing departments to an activity performed by millions of individual workers at their own workplaces and the linking of these separate computers into vast networks for exchanging information over long distances changed the way in which work was being carried out in businesses, universities and government.

Even more significant was the organisational model selected by the US Department of Defence. Rather than a hub of computers under centralised control, the system was designed so that every computer on the network could communicate, as a peer, with every other computer on the network. Thus, if part of the network were destroyed, the surviving parts would automatically reroute communications through different pathways. The result was the creation of a vast organisation without central authority or hierarchy.

It is difficult to separate out the mental infrastructure that supported these physical and social components, because it is so closely intertwined with the other elements. Development of scientific and technological capacities and knowledge were obviously central. In addition, the spread of general education, computer literacy and skills have given rise to a society with the mental energy and capacity to readily accept and rapidly adopt this new medium to an infinite variety of uses.

A psychological foundation was also essential. Surely a society that feared technology or a workforce that feared being replaced by computers would not have responded enthusiastically to the creation of an ubiquitous system that lends itself to so many possible applications. In actuality, although the system was developed by government and large organisations, its entry into the mainstream of the national life was almost entirely the result of the public's ready and enthusiastic response and wholesale adoption of the new organisation.

The very rapid development of the Internet in the West has only been possible because these four foundations have been built up and strengthened during the past few decades. The development of these infrastructures required the prior accumulation of huge surpluses of capital, mental energy and leisure time that could be made available by the society and channelled into the new activity. These surpluses are a product of the maturation of the vital stage of development, which generated the enormous growth of economic activity, productivity, capital accumulation, education and leisure in Western society.

Organisational Power of the Internet

From this perspective, the material circumstances and technological developments that made the emergence of this new organisation possible appear less significant than the force that has guided their expression and the organisational structure that makes the Internet unique.

It is impossible to predict the magnitude of the impact and all the ramifications of this new system on social development in the coming decades. But even after discounting the hyperbole generated by marketing firms and media coverage, it is clear that the Internet will and is already exercising a very profound influence on the development of the human community.

- It provides instantaneous access 24 hours a day from anywhere in the world to a growing wealth of information and knowledge that could soon rival that of all but the most sophisticated libraries and may eventually replace the library as a social institution. Immediate access to information will accelerate decision-making and action across a broad spectrum of activities.

- It provides a new medium for commercial transactions that in the USA alone could soon exceed in volume the $50 billion mail order industry. One result will be the weakening of national commercial boundaries and growth of world trade as companies gain easier access to overseas markets. Another will be a reduction in transaction costs by the elimination of some types of intermediate commercial agencies that have been necessary in the past to connect producers from ultimate consumers.

- The very low entry cost for setting up and advertising business activities on the Web helps to level the playing field between large and small firms and opens up a new frontier for entrepreneurship.

- It provides a medium for financial transactions that could radically transform the way securities are marketed.

- It provides a new medium for distance education that will transform the way educational institutions delivery knowledge and instruction, freeing education from the school the way money freed wealth from the land.

- It provides a very rapid, low cost means of personal communication between individuals located anywhere in the world, abridging the psychological distance and perceptual differences between societies.

- It provides a means for special interest groups to form instantaneously around any subject of common interest and act in unison over vast distances. One recent instance is the linking together of hundreds of small, independent speciality retailers and manufacturers in the USA to achieve economies of scale heretofore available only to mega-corporations.

- It offers a low-cost means for any person or group to publish and broadcast views to the world community, providing a practical mechanism for individuals to fully exercise their democratic right of free speech. Internet shifts power to the people.

- It provides a medium to offer the best available knowledge and expertise to everyone. Expert medical information on health problems and remedies can be delivered to millions of people on demand.

- It opens up the prospect that all citizens may soon be able to participate directly in a democratic system that is no longer determined more by the interests of politicians than by the views of the electorate.

Access to and use of the Internet is heavily concentrated in advanced industrial countries and urban centres today. It is primarily geared to provide the types of information and services sought after by the more educated and the wealthy. However, the Internet has the potential to powerfully influence the pace and direction of progress in less developing countries and regions as well.

- It already provides companies in developing countries with immediate access to a wide range of commercial and technical information that is otherwise slow, costly and difficult to obtain.

- These companies also acquire a low cost means to reach potential customers anywhere in the world.

- New industrial products and processes can now be monitored and examined electronically as soon as they are available.

- Reliable information and expert advice can be accessed from outlying areas. Access to the latest scientific information need no longer be restricted by budgetary constraints.

- Scientific knowledge and educational programmes available on the Internet are equally accessible to people all over the globe. The development of the next generation of translation software will reduce language barriers as well.

- The establishment of low orbit satellite links will make it possible for low income countries to establish an alternative delivery system for information, broadcasting, telephone and fax services to vast rural population.

- As the institution of money promoted the development of urban communities, the institution of Internet empowers people everywhere with equal access to information and services and provides a mechanism for maturation of global citizenship and a truly global community.

These are only a few of the most obvious areas in which the Internet will or is already transforming society. But the most profound impact is likely to be in intangible areas that are very difficult to quantify and measure. They can only be vaguely indicated by analogy with the impact of other institutions that have transformed social life, such as language and money.

Language is an organised system of sounds and symbols that enables rapid and accurate communication of thoughts and sensations between people. Before language, the ability of two individuals to communicate was extremely cumbersome and limited. Social life was very primitive. Experience could not be shared with others, recorded or passed on to youth. Organised group activities were severely restricted by the inability to arrive at a common set of objectives, plan of action, division of labour, timeframe and agreed basis for sharing the results. The introduction of language made organised activities possible and with it the birth of developing societies and mature civilizations.

Money has played a similar role as the basis language for commerce. Before money, the ability of two individuals to interact economically was extremely cumbersome and limited. Money provides a common language in which economic goods and services, property and privileges can be expressed, valued and exchanged. The introduction of money has made possible the exponential growth of production, trade and consumption.

Now Internet is establishing a common language and a readily accessible mechanism for the rapid exchange of information and ideas between virtually everyone who has access to the system. *Development is a function of the velocity of social transactions. Money has immensely increased the speed of transactions. Internet is making many transactions instantaneous.* Intellectually, this will exponentially increase the opportunities for exchange and dissemination of ideas and information for business, education, governance and research. The increased velocity and better quality of information, better because more current, will dramatically increase the speed and quality of decision-making. Practically, it will dramatically increase global access to goods and services.

In addition to speed and access, Internet also provides a mechanism for infinitely expanding the interactions between users and for customising services to meet individual needs. Before Internet, the primary delivery systems for information have been one-to-one such as the telephone, fax and post, which like barter are limited by the need for a double coincidence, or one-to-many mass broadcasting systems such as newspapers, radio and television, which cannot discriminate between users or provide customised services. Internet makes many-to-many relationships a reality. By so doing it increases the potential number of interactions and transactions infinitely. It also enables either the source or recipient of information to control content and customise it to meet specific individual needs. As mass production has made more sophisticated products available to more people at lower cost, Internet will make customised and personalised services affordable and accessible.

Money increases energy in society and enables that energy to be utilised more efficiently. Before money, people had little incentive to produce more than they could consume. Money provides a means for individuals to save the fruits of their labour, store them indefinitely, transmute them into any form, transfer them to others or exchange them for any other social commodity. In so doing, money releases people's energy and encourages them to work harder. Similarly, Internet allows the intellectual work of any individual to reach a far wider audience than is otherwise possible and to be more fully utilised by society. It releases mental energy, encourages mental creativity, and makes the results of creativity more widely available.

This new social system derives its unprecedented productive power from the same attributes that have made organisations effective since the dawn of society, but the similarity may not be immediately obvious. Organisations acquire power from their capacity to exercise authority and direct the energies of people. Internet is an organisation without any discernable centre of power or ability to direct anyone or anything. It is the first organisation that anyone can access, but no one can own or control.

Authority exists on the Internet, but it has been impersonalised and internalised. It is impersonalised in the form of strict technical standards, communication rules and language conventions to which all users must conform in order to participate in the organisation. It has been internalised in the sense that usage of the system is strictly voluntary.

The force that drives the growth of the system is the self-directed motivation of individuals and organisations to use it in the absence of any external compulsion. The enthusiastic interest that the Internet has evoked around the world is a measure of the determination of society to fully explore and exploit the potentials of this organisation.

Organisations also derive power from systems, which we term the skills of society. The Internet is a very complex organisation of systems for the generation, transmission, distribution, reception, and cataloguing of information. As the Internet becomes a more common and accepted means of carrying out activities, it will equip society with an entirely new order of skills to raise productivity, increase convenience, improve quality and accelerate actions.

The power of an organisation increases with its complexity, with its ability to coordinate and integrate a wider range of activities. Cities became centres of intense energy and high productivity by maximising physical coordination between different activities concentrated in one location.

Money derives much of its power from its ability to relate to every type of social activity, convert one into the other, and coordinate each with all the others. Internet has a parallel capability to cross-reference any subject and create meaningful linkages between previously unrelated topics. Every new social organisation spreads gradually until it enters into relationship and integrates with every other social organisation.

The development of car travel has supported the growth of fast food, hotels, transport, commerce, industry, education, suburban communities, tourism and recreation. The development of television combines and integrates entertainment, educational programming, news, advertising, direct marketing, politics, sports and public service.

Internet combines and integrates the functions of mail, telephone, fax, motion pictures, television, radio, newspapers, libraries, schools, conferences and discussion groups. It makes it possible to interrelate political, commercial, financial, educational, recreational, scientific, medical, religious, cultural and personal activities, stimulating the growth and increasing the productivity of them all. *It creates the maximum number of potential synaptic connections between different subjects and activities.*

Ultimately organisations derive their power from the values they embody and express. Although some people decry the absence of values on the Internet, by which they mean the lack of control over the suitability of content, the Internet actually embodies high and strong values from which it derives an almost irresistible strength. These include physical values such as speed, timeliness, efficiency and productivity; organisational values such as standardisation, systemisation, coordination, integration and communication; and psychological values such as equality of access, public service and empowerment of the individual.

As money empowers the individual with unlimited access to economic goods, Internet empowers the individual with unlimited access to knowledge. It enables a person to do what previously only an organisation could accomplish. It makes people more competent and less dependent. It increases freedom of choice. It may soon bring a time when no book need ever go out of print and every student can choose his own teacher. Internet reduces the limitations imposed on humanity by space and time. It helps elevate people from the physical to the mental stage. As money has become a symbol of private property, individual acquisition and self-affirmation, the Internet is a symbol of our collective accomplishments, shared inheritance and human unity.

5

Gift Economy

A gift economy (or gift culture) is a society where valuable goods and services are regularly given without any explicit agreement for immediate or future rewards (i.e. no formal *quid pro quo* exists). Ideally, simultaneous or recurring giving serves to circulate and redistribute valuables within the community. The organisation of a gift economy stands in contrast to a barter economy or a market economy.

Informal custom governs exchanges, rather than an explicit exchange of goods or services for money or some other commodity. Various social theories concerning gift economies exist, including some forms of communism and anarchism. Some consider the gifts to be a form of reciprocal altruism. Another interpretation is that social status is awarded in return for the gifts.

The Backdrop

Contrary to popular conception, there is no evidence that societies relied primarily on barter before using money for trade. Instead, non-monetary societies operated largely along the principles of gift economics. When barter did in fact occur, it was usually between either complete strangers or would-be enemies.

Lewis Hyde locates the origin of gift economies in the sharing of food, citing as an example the Trobriand Islander protocol of referring to a gift in the Kula exchange ring as "some food we could not eat," even though the gift is not food, but an ornament purposely made for passing as a gift. The potlatch also originated as a 'big feed'. Hyde argues that this led to a notion in many societies of the gift as something that must "perish".

The anthropologist Marshall Sahlins writes that Stone Age gift economies were, as evidenced by their nature as gift economies, economies of abundance, not scarcity, despite modern readers' typical assumption of objective poverty. Gift economies were replaced by market economies based on commodity money, as the emergence of city states made money a necessity.

The Characteristics

A gift economy normally requires the gift exchange to be more than simply a back-and-forth between two individuals. For example, a Kashmiri tale tells of two Brahmin women who tried to fulfil their obligations for alms-giving simply by giving alms back and forth to one another. On their deaths they were transformed into two poisoned wells from which no one could drink, reflecting the barrenness of this weak simulacrum of giving. This notion of expanding the circle can also be seen in societies where hunters give animals to priests, who sacrifice a portion to a deity (who, in turn, is expected to provide an abundant hunt). The hunters do not directly sacrifice to the deity themselves.

Many societies have strong prohibitions against turning gifts into trade or capital goods. Anthropologist Wendy James writes that among the Uduk people of northeast Africa there is a strong custom that any gift that crosses subclan boundaries must be consumed rather than invested. For example, an animal given as a gift must be eaten, not bred. However, as in the example of the Trobriand armbands and necklaces, this "perishing" may not consist of consumption as such, but of the gift moving on. In other societies, it is a matter of giving some other gift, either directly

Gift Economy

in return or to another party. To keep the gift and not give another in exchange is reprehensible. "In folk tales," Hyde remarks, "the person who tries to hold onto a gift usually dies."

Carol Stack's *All Our Kin* describes both the positive and negative sides of a network of obligation and gratitude effectively constituting a gift economy. Her narrative of The Flats, a poor Chicago neighbourhood, tells in passing the story of two sisters who each came into a small inheritance. One sister hoarded the inheritance and prospered materially for some time, but was alienated from the community. Her marriage ultimately broke up, and she integrated herself back into the community largely by giving gifts. The other sister fulfilled the community's expectations, but within six weeks had nothing material to show for the inheritance but a coat and a pair of shoes.

Social Structures

There are many examples of how a gift economy works in modern culture within a mixed economy, such as marriage, family, friendship, kinship, and social network structures.

Pacific Islanders

Pacific Island societies prior to the nineteenth century were essentially gift economies. This practice still endures in parts of the Pacific today - for example in some outer islands of the Cook Islands. In Tokelau, despite the gradual appearance of a market economy, a form of gift economy remains through the practice of *inati*, the strictly egalitarian sharing of all food resources in each atoll. On Anuta as well, a gift economy called "Aropa" still exists.

There are also a significant number of diasporic Pacific Islander communities in New Zealand, Australia, and the United States that still practice a form of gift economy. Although they have become participants in those countries' market economies, some seek to retain practices linked to an adapted form of gift economy, such as reciprocal gifts of money, or remittances back to their home community. The notion of reciprocal gifts is seen as essential to the *fa'aSamoa* ("Samoan way of life"), the *anga fakatonga*

("Tongan way of life"), and the culture of other diasporic Pacific communities.

Native Americans

Native Americans who lived in the Pacific Northwest (primarily the Kwakiutl), practised the potlatch ritual, where leaders give away large amounts of goods to their followers, strengthening group relations. By sacrificing accumulated wealth, a leader gained a position of honour.

Mexico

In the Sierra Tarahumara of North Western Mexico, a custom exists called kórima. This custom says that it is one's duty to share his wealth with anyone.

Spain

In place of a market, anarcho-communists, such as those who inhabited some Spanish villages in the 1930s, support a currency-less gift economy where goods and services are produced by workers and distributed in community stores where everyone (including the workers who produced them) is essentially entitled to consume whatever they want or need as "payment" for their production of goods and services.

Papua New Guinea

The Kula ring still exists to this day, as do other exchange systems in the region, such as Moka exchange in the Mt. Hagen area, on Papua New Guinea.

Gift Economies

Information is particularly suited to gift economies, as information is a non-rival good and can be gifted at practically no cost.

Science

Traditional scientific research can be thought of as an information gift economy. Scientists produce research papers and

Gift Economy

give them away through journals and conferences. Other scientists freely refer to such papers. All scientists can therefore benefit from the increased pool of knowledge. The original scientists receive no direct benefit from others building on their work, except an increase in their reputation. Failure to cite and give credit to original authors (thus depriving them of reputational effects) is considered improper behaviour.

Filesharing

Markus Giesler, in his ethnography "Consumer Gift Systems" has developed music downloading as a system of social solidarity based on gift transactions.

Open-source Software

In his essay "Homesteading the Noosphere", noted computer programmer Eric S. Raymond opined that open-source software developers have created "a 'gift culture' in which participants compete for prestige by giving time, energy, and creativity away". Members of the Linux community often speak of their community as a gift economy.

Social Theories

Various social theories concerning gift economies exist. Some consider the gifts to be a form of reciprocal altruism. Another interpretation is that social status is awarded in return for the gifts. Consider for example, the sharing of food in some hunter-gatherer societies, where food-sharing is a safeguard against the failure of any individual's daily foraging. This custom may reflect concern for the well-being of others, it may be a form of informal insurance, or may bring with it social status or other benefits.

Hyde

According to Lewis Hyde, a traditional gift economy is based on "the obligation to give, the obligation to accept, and the obligation to reciprocate," and that it is "at once economic, juridical, moral, aesthetic, religious, and mythological." He describes the spirit of a gift economy (and its contrast to a market economy) as:

> The opposite of "Indian giver" would be something like "white man keeper"... Whatever we have been given is supposed to be given away not kept. Or, if it is kept, something of similar value should move in its stead... The gift may be given back to its original donor, but this is not essential... The only essential is this: *the gift must always move.*

Hyde also argues that there is a difference between a "true" gift given out of gratitude and a "false" gift given only out of obligation. In Hyde's view, the "true" gift binds us in a way beyond any commodity transaction, but "we cannot really become bound to those who give us false gifts."

Hyde argues that when a primarily gift-based economy is turned into a commodity-based economy, "the social fabric of the group is invariably destroyed." Much as there are prohibitions against turning gifts into capital, there are prohibitions against treating gift exchange as barter. Among the Trobrianders, for example, treating Kula as barter is considered a disgrace. Hyde writes that commercial goods can generally become gifts, but when gifts become commodities, the gift "...either stops being a gift or else abolishes the boundary... Contracts of the heart lie outside the law and the circle of gifts is narrowed, therefore, whenever such contracts are narrowed to legal relationships."

Mauss

Sociologist Marcel Mauss argues a different position, that gifts entail obligation and are never 'free'. According to Mauss, while it is easy to romanticise a gift economy, humans do not always wish to be enmeshed in a web of obligation. Mauss wrote, "The gift not yet repaid debases the man who accepts it," a lesson certainly not lost on the young person seeking independence who decides not to accept more money or gifts from his or her parents. And as Hyde writes, "There are times when we want to be aliens and strangers." We like to be able to go to the corner store, buy a can of soup, and not have to let the store clerk into our affairs or vice versa. We like to travel on an airplane without worrying about whether we would personally get along with the pilot.

A gift creates a "feeling bond." Commodity exchange does not. The French writer George Bataille in his book *La part Maudite* use Mauss's argument in order to construct a theory of economy: to his point of view the structure of gift forms the presupposition for all possible economy. Particularly interested about the potlatch as described by Mauss, Bataille claims that its antagonistic character obliges the receiver of the gift to confirm a subjection; the structure of the gift can refer thus immediately to a practice that bears out different roles for the parts that undertake an action in it, installing in this act of donating the Hegelian dipole of master and slave.

Kropotkin

Anarchists, particularly anarcho-primitivists and anarcho-communists, believe that variations on a gift economy may be the key to breaking the cycle of poverty. Therefore they often desire to refashion all of society into a gift economy. Anarcho-communists advocate a gift economy as an ideal, with neither money, nor markets, nor central planning. This view traces back at least to Peter Kropotkin, who saw in the hunter-gatherer tribes he had visited the paradigm of "mutual aid".

Peter Kropotkin argues that mutual benefit is a stronger incentive than mutual strife and is eventually more effective collectively in the long run to drive individuals to produce. The reason given is that a gift economy stresses the concept of increasing the other's abilities and means of production, which would then (theoretically) increase the ability of the community to reciprocate to the giving individual. Other solutions to prevent inefficiency in a pure gift economy due to wastage of resources that were not allocated to the most pressing need or want stresses the use of several methods involving collective shunning where collective groups keep track of other individuals' productivity, rather than leaving each individual having to keep track of the rest of society by him or herself.

Bell

The economist Duran Bell postulates that exchanges in a gift economy are different from pure commodity exchange in that they are mainly used to build social relationships. Gifts between individuals or between groups help build a relationship, allowing the people to work together. The generosity of a gift improves a person's prestige and social standing. Differences in social rank are not defined by differences in access to goods, but rather by "his ability to give to others, the desire to accumulate being seen as an indication of weakness."

Burning Man

Burning Man is a week-long annual art and community event held in the Black Rock Desert in northern Nevada, in the United States. The event is described as an experiment in community, radical self-expression, and radical self-reliance. The event outlaws commerce and encourages gifting. Gifting is one the 10 guiding principles, as participants to Burning Man (both the desert festival and the year-round global community) are encouraged to rely on a gift economy. The practice of gifting at Burning Man is also documented by the 2002 documentary film "Gifting It: A Burning Embrace of Gift Economy", as well as by Making Contact's radio show "How We Survive: The Currency of Giving [encore]".

Religious Views

Islam

In Islam, the free gift of alms is a religious requirement, which has made social foundations an important part of Muslim communities.

Judaism

According to the Hebrew Bible, tzedakah is a religious obligation that must be performed regardless of financial standing. It is considered as one of the three main acts that can annul a less than favourable heavenly decree.

Hinduism

Bhiksha is a devotional offering, usually food, presented at a temple or to a swami or a religious Brahmin who in turn provides a religious service (*karmkand*) or instruction.

Buddhism

In South East Asia, Theravada Buddhists continue to sponsor "Feasts of Merit" that are very similar to potlatch. Such feasts usually involve many sponsors and occur mainly before and after the rainy season.

6

Money and Politics

In US, in 1995, an independent study commissioned by the Congress determined that no more B-2 bombers should be built in 1995. At the cost of $493 million per plane, the B-2 bombers were costly. Furthermore, the Pentagon had declared that they did not want any more B-2 bombers. However, one year later, members of the Congress voted to allocate funding to build another B-2 bomber. Why did members of the Congress agree to this needless expenditure?

One Possible Reason

The political action committee (PAC) of Northrup Grumman, the builder of B-2 bombers, donated $320,775 to members of Congress in 1995. This amount was twice the sum given to Congress in 1993 and 1994. In fact, when another bill was proposed to eliminate funding from the B-2 in June 1996, Northrup Grumman gave another $75,200 to finance campaigns of members of the Congress (Beaulieu, 1996, p. 15).

This incident testifies to our politicians' excessive financial dependence on well-endowed donors. More importantly, it demonstrates how these donors have played a significant role in shaping public policy. By paying substantial amounts of money to politicians, corporations and rich individuals have been able to gain direct access to political representatives and lobby effectively for their causes. Concomitantly, low-income and poor people who do not offer financial contributions do not have the opportunity to voice their opinions on behalf of their issues (Beaulieu, 1996, p. 15).

According to Public Campaign (2000), an organisation that is dedicated to the creation of a public financing system, 80 per cent of donors who contributed $200 or more had an annual family income of more than $100,000 a year, with five per cent having an income of $50,000 or less in 1996.

Therefore, even though US household with at total income of $100,000 or more constitute 12 per cent of the total number of households in the US, 80 per cent of these households exert the greatest influence on public policy. The Centre for Responsive Politics also reports that almost 70 per cent of the PAC contributions in the 2000 election stems from business interests, 21 per cent from labour and 11 per cent from other groups (in Public Campaign, 2000, p. 5).

Research studies have also revealed that money donors do not donate large sums of money for altruistic reasons or affirmation of their political beliefs. Based on a survey of donors in the 1996 presidential elections, Francia and others (1999) report that 76 per cent of the respondents stated that their primary reason for donating to political candidates was to shape government policies. A 2000 poll conducted by Lake Snell Perry and Associates involving 1,000 voters and 200 donors also revealed that 54 per cent of the donors spoke directly to a major elected official compared to nine per cent of the voters (Lake and Borosage, 2000).

Therefore, it is evident that money exerts a significant impact in determining which political constituents are heard by their political representatives. These studies demonstrate clearly that the donor class that represents only a minority of the nation has considerably more latitude in influencing government policy than the majority of the population in the nation.

The following section offers a sampling of concrete examples of how the Congress has been influenced by their donors and acted in accordance with their interests.

Automotive Industry: Only after the tragedy involving Firestone tires on Ford Explorers that resulted in the deaths of over 100 people did Congress finally decide to update the 30-year-old standards for tires in October 2000. Auto safety experts believe that the long overdue legislation to improve tire standards is insufficient in providing genuine safety to the public. As Public Citizen President Joan Claybrook puts it, "Congress passed a face-saving bill for industry, not a life-saving bill for the public" (qtd. in Public Campaign, 2000). One of the primary reasons for Congress' protective stance towards the auto industry is that it has contributed over $12 million to political campaigns in 2000, up from nearly $11 million in 1998 (Public Campaign, 2000).

Telecommunications: Passed in 1996, the Telecommunications Act was touted by Congress as a means to increase competition in the industry, decrease prices and improve service for the public. In reality, the new legislation essentially deregulates the industry, thus enabling large telecommunication corporations to merge with one another and increase prices at the expense of the public. Telecommunications corporations contributed $3.5 million to members of the Congress in 1995. The two most enthusiastic supporters of the new legislation, Senate Commerce Committee Chairman Larry Pressler who received $103,165 from telecom PACs and House Telecommunications and Finance Subcommittee Chairman Jack Fields who received $97,500, were the two chief beneficiaries of the corporations' generosity (Beaulieu, 1996).

Ergonomics: In response to rising injuries in work environments because of increasing mechanisation, President Clinton established new workplace safety regulations on ergonomics. However, in March 2001, the new regulations were repealed with voting results that followed the party lines. This reversal of policies can be attributed to campaign contributions. During the 2000 elections, corporations exceeded the contributions of labour leaders by a ratio of 1,000:1 (Public Campaign, 2001).

In spite of the democratic principles of the American political system, politicians cannot be considered to be true representatives of their people. It is little wonder that American voters and donors concur that politicians are not governed by their political beliefs. Rather, their opinions and behaviour are heavily influenced by the vast resources of their political contributors (Lake and Borosage, 2000). Even more significantly, these politicians are not representative of their constituents when they lend their ears solely to those who can pay.

The reduction of federal taxes for corporations from 39 per cent in the 1950s to 17 per cent in the 1980s is symptomatic of the political clout of business interests. Similarly, the failure of Congress to pass a health-care reform bill for many years reflects the capacity of wealthy contributors to sabotage legislations that will genuinely improve the quality of health care for ordinary Americans (Beaulieu, 1996). Unless political reforms occur to sever the connection between politicians and big business interests, Americans will continue to lose their trust and faith in the political system.

Political Reform and Soft Money

There can be no doubt that American politics involves too much money. In the 2000 election cycle, the Democratic Party raised over 520 million dollars. Even this insane figure pales in comparison to the republican's 715 million. Despite these staggering figures, the real issue is not the money itself, but its effect on policy decisions. We've heard about 'soft money' for years, but its impact is rarely discussed.

First of all, soft money allows an individual to donate more than his allotted maximum to a particular candidate by using an organisation - a state party, for example - as a middleman. They donate to the given organisation, and the organisation uses their donation in the campaign of the candidate that the donor supports.

One example of this situation is the oil/energy industry. They support the republican party's stance on the environment, and their donations show this. They attempt to influence the election with money, thereby solidifying their interests.

Election Cycle	Total Contribution	Soft Money Contribution	Donations Democrats	Donations Republicans	% Democrats	% to Republicans
2002 so far	$5,380,345	$2,627,694	$1,017,599	$4,305,246	19%	80%
2000	$33,486,154	$16,024,822	$6,728,672	$26,254,713	20%	78%
1998	$21,677,051	$8,762,013	$4,864,258	$16,732,696	22%	77%
1996	$24,847,230	$9,899,387	$5,533,584	$18,933,949	22%	76%
Total	$85,390,780	$37,313,916	$18,144,113	$66,226,604	26%	73%

Any type of organisation can act as a middleman between large donors and political parties. Political parties, corporations, unions, and special-interest groups all play a role in the soft money loophole. Despite the outrageous amounts of money being spent on election campaigns, the biggest problems with large donations is that they attack the principle of all votes being equal.

Under the current system, individuals are limited to donating a certain dollar amount to parties or candidates. However, the soft money goes into a general party fund and can be raised through such things as dinners with politicians. In the 2002 election cycle, the largest donor to the republican party was the 2001 President's Dinner Committee, which raised a full ten times as much money as the next highest donor. Suppose a politician has one of these $10,000 a plate dinners. Company X pays for twenty people to attend. This leads to certain corporations or industries, making very large donations, and thereby greatly influencing policy decisions.

Some organisations - Microsoft, Citigroup, and SBC Communications, to name a few - donate responsibly. Many groups, however, think otherwise. The Service Employees International Union donated almost all of their 8.5 million dollars to the democrats, while the NRA and Philip Morris each donated over 90 per cent of their 3 million dollars to the republicans.

Politicians know who their biggest supporters are, and make concessions to their wishes. In effect, this can make the votes of twenty people far more important than that those votes of most other citizens.

The problems of the system are obvious, and although this cycle seems impossible to end, several ideas can at least make the system less financially driven, and somewhat equalise the importance of votes. Legislation that effects such change much be passed through congress. In 1986, Bill Bradley proposed a bill to limit campaign contributions and 'pork-barrel legislation.' Before it was passed, however, congress debated it, and changed it such that it not only made the financial situation worse, but also had unnecessary legislation attached to it (2).

Simply put, there is too much money in politics. The votes of large donors are worth more than the votes of average citizens. And even when legislation is introduced that would reform the present state of campaign financing, it often gets modified by congress, and in effect, waters down its impact. The first step towards campaign finance reform is to show politicians that we care about the issue, and then elect people who are willing to tackle the problem.

Political Power through Money

With the recent criminal investigations into the Enron Corporation, our need for campaign finance reform has become even clearer. As the justice department attempts to discover whether or not the company's campaign contributions have influenced the policies of the current white house administration, we must ask ourselves whether this is a common occurrence or an isolated incident.

Without assuming what will come out of the Enron investigations, we can recognise that there are a number of important issues raised: Is it fair that candidates vote according to the wishes of their contributors? Do contributions give such donors more access to politicians?

Money and Politics

The Executive Branch: How the president's donors are paid in full: The president has the ability to draft legislation and then present it to congress for a vote. Most notably, President George W. Bush asked congress to take a look at his Economic Stimulus Plan. He claims that it would give businesses tax breaks and bailouts in order to help them pay off creditors, and prevent them from laying off thousands of workers.

However, under the original draft of the plan that was passed by the House of Representatives, large amounts of money would have ended up in the hands of very few, namely, those who had donated substantial funds to the president and the republican party. For example, Chevron Texaco has given the republican party more than $5.2 million since 1990.

Under Bush' stimulus plan, they stood to receive around $572 million in the form of a retroactive tax cut. Enron has given $5.5 million during the same period, and they stood to receive $254 million. General electric stood to receive over $600 million in return for there contributions of less than $2 million. The list could go on extensively. It seems obvious that the money spent to get a candidate elected is much less than the eventual pay backs.

If this is not bad enough, the package approved by the House also gives a tax break on foreign profits to companies such as Merrill Lynch and Citigroup. Not only is this problematic because of the large returns these companies receive from their investments into certain candidates or political parties, as the Washington Post reported, "it's hard to see how this measure would do anything to stimulate the American economy."

This bill directly demonstrates the powerful impact that can be made by large donations to political parties. Not only will candidates reward their donors with large pay backs, they are even willing to do so at the expense of our nation during its time of need.

Congressional Branch: Where profits meet partisanship: The influence of donors works similarly in congress. Just as the president, a congressman can submit legislation for vote. Also in the same way, the legislation is often based upon the wishes of a congressman's donors. Members of congress can show the influence of their donors by adding various amendments - that may seem totally irrelevant - to legislation that is often urgently needed (disaster relief aid, for example).

This is when the need for campaign finance reform becomes most evident. The aforementioned Economic Stimulus Package was passed by the republican majority in the House of Representatives, most of whom share the same donors as the president. That version of the bill was defeated in the democratic-controlled Senate. When donors exert their influence over the legislative branch, congress becomes full of partisan bickering. The entire process begins to take on the tone of "you scratch my back, I'll scratch yours," until one side ends up ahead. The needs of the people are never placed first.

Again, this is not an isolated incident. After the recent acts of terrorism, it became obvious that our nation was not prepared to deal with such large scale attacks. In response to the threat of bioterrorism, both the Senate and the House drafted legislation to stockpile the nation's supply of vaccines. The sponsors of this bill were Billy Tauzin (R-LA.) and John Dingell (D-MA) in the House, and Bill Frist (R-TN) and Ted Kennedy (D-MA) in the senate. They have all received large contributions from pharmaceutical companies and health care agencies ($35,000; $32,000; $116,000; $75,000 in 2000 respectively).

Obviously, there could be a need for these vaccines. And in such a case, it would be much better to be safe than sorry. But the pharmaceutical companies are using this an excuse to lobby for deregulation of the industry, and this is something that will not affect bioterrorism. This is something driven, not by a desire to help the American people, but by a desire to profit.

In the House Energy Plan, H.R. 4, the controversial measure to open up parts of the Arctic National Wildlife Refuge for oil drilling was included. This measure's passing is largely due to the substantial donations made by the oil industry to the republican controlled house and the president.

Even so, representatives Jan Schakowsky (D-IL), John W. Olver (D- MA) and Wayne T. Gilchrest ® -MD) - none of whom receive much, if any, money from the oil industry - stood against the drilling and gave examples of more profitable, and environmentally sound ways of curbing our nations need for oil.

Their proposals intended to require auto manufactures to make sport utility vehicles and light trucks meet the same fuel efficiency standards as cars by 2007. This plan would significantly reduce carbon dioxide emissions, and would save over a million barrels of oil per day, which is the maximum amount of oil that President Bush thought could be gained from the Arctic drilling.

The one million barrel per day savings does not even take into consideration an additional proposal to increase fuel efficiency in cars. In this situation, it can't be doubted that the big oil companies have the president and the house of representatives firmly clasped in the palm of their hands. There is no way that a government so entrenched in a system of donations and pay backs, and so loyal to the will of an industry, can produce legislation that is drafted in the best interest of the people.

The True Partisan Politics: High speed internet, prescription drugs, and insurance. Under the 1996 telecommunications act, the "Baby Bells" are not allowed to offer high speed internet access (without allowing other companies to use their infrastructure) on the grounds that they own practically all of the phone cable in the United States.

This issue has little or no relation to party politics. Neither democrats nor republicans have taken any stance that is directly for or against this act. However, the Baby Bells have been lobbying extensively to get the act amended to allow them to offer such access without allowing their competitors to use their infrastructure.

Senators Billy Tauzin (R-LA) and John Dingell (D-MI) proposed a deal in which the Bells can offer an exclusive lease to use their cable. The two companies that stand to loose the most are AT&T and AOL/Time Warner: currently the two largest suppliers of broadband internet in the United States.

Not surprisingly, Senator Tauzin had Verizon and SBC Communications as his number one and four contributors during his 2000 election campaign. And this doesn't even include contributions from SBC and Bell South used to pay for Tauzin's half-million dollar Mardi Gras party during the Republican Convention in Philadelphia.

Senator Dingell had these companies - Verizon and SBC — as his number three and four contributors, with Bell South at number seven. Not surprisingly, the opponents of this bill have received large amounts of money from AT&T and AOL/Time Warner. John Conyers Jr., (D-MI) received a total $21,500 from these corporations for his 2000 election, making them his second and fourth largest contributors, respectively.

Despite many politicians' promises for prescription drug coverage, and the belief of many American's that such coverage is necessary, this reform is unlikely to happen as soon as promised. There is nothing close to a consensus on how to reduce the cost of prescription drugs for the American people. Obviously, some debate on a subject is necessary to determine the best possible solution. However, this debate is not about who has the best ideas, but rather, whose donors' have the most clout.

In its two forms, the bill provides for a type of voucher system that senior citizens can use to purchase private health insurance at a lower cost (7). This bill benefits the pharmaceutical industry, as a voucher for health insurance will not actually lower the price — and thereby won't decrease the profits made by manufacturers — of prescription medication.

The supporters of this bill are Bill First (R-TN) and John Breaux (D-LA), who received $120,000 in 2000 and nearly

$70,000 in 1998 from the pharmaceutical industry, respectively. Not surprisingly, neither of them received much, if any, money from insurance companies. Another option, for example, could have been for the government to control the outrageous costs of medication. This approach would benefit insurance companies and lower the profits of the pharmaceutical companies.

These are just a few examples of congressional representatives displaying their loyalty to the wills of their donors, rather than to their constituents or their own personal conscious. We have presented here a limited number of instances; there are many more. Reverting to the Economic Stimulus Plan, we see that even the few members of congress who are opposed to the heavy influence that corporate America exerts upon the legislative process fall prey to the same influences.

More specifically, consider Senator Feingold. Although his statements against the president's Economic Stimulus Plan should be commended, it must be noted that he didn't receive donations from any of the corporations that stood to gain from this particular proposal.

Money Buying Political Power

Stephen Todd: The few members of congress opposed to these blatant abuses and undue influence that corporations put on their colleagues are under the same influences. Although Senator Feingold's statements against the presidents and the house's Economic Stimulus Plan should be commended, it must be noted that none of the corporations that stood to gain donated to his campaign.

His largest contributions came from lawyers and law firms, the retired, and the education sector (University of Wisconsin, for example). So long as campaign financing plays a major role in shaping legislation, one must wonder whether these representatives ever act according to their own personal convictions, or in the best interest of the population that they represent.

When Schakowsky, Olver, and Gilchrest stood out against the president's energy plan, claiming that the outrageous gasoline prices across the Midwest were the result of price gouging by the oil industry, it seemed as though they were simply being sensible. However, after looking at their main contributors, we must wonder if they were working for their constituents or their donors. Olver received the vast majority of his money from various unions, such as the United Auto Workers, the Teamsters Union, the Intl. Brotherhood of Electrical Workers, and the United Transportation Union. Combined, Olver had a large portion of his campaign financed by industrial and transportation unions.

The steel workers of America, on congressional record S11284, stated their opposition to Bush's plan to open up the Arctic wildlife refuge for drilling. Olver was, in fact, saying exactly what his donors wanted him to say. Ms. Schakowsky had similar donors, with the United Auto Workers at the top of her list. In addition, she received almost $17,000 from liberal one-issue and non-profits groups, which included environmental and human rights organisations. Once again, her stance is based those who funded her election as much as those who voted for her.

Mr. Gilchrest received most of his money from the retired community and another sizable percentage from Baltimore Gas and Electric Company. Again, these are groups that would be effected negatively by the president's energy plan. Despite the environmentally conscious position taken by these politicians, the data shows that they may have been more concerned about who paid for their campaigns, and less concerned about the actual issues at hand.

When considering almost any issue, the solution advocated by either congress or the president will not necessarily be in the best interest of the people who these elected officials are supposed to serve. Essentially, everybody will find a solution that is in the best interest of their financial supporters. For example, those politicians who were funded by the airlines, energy companies, and environmental groups would say that the key to dropping

Money and Politics

greenhouse gas emissions would be doing the following: forcing car makers to be more efficient, making SUV's conform to the same emissions standards as cars, or forcing designers to employ new technologies such as the emission recycling engines in the large truck engines made by Caterpillar and Cummins.

Those who received money from the automakers would blame the problem on industrial emissions, or on the transportation sector. Who will come out ahead in the congressional struggles? I would like to believe that those who had the best ideas, the most well-thought-out proposals, would come out ahead. I would like to say that the best leaders, that those who took a stand based on their beliefs - rather than based on the desires of those who finance their campaigns - would emerge on top.

7

Electronic Money

In modern economy, Electronic money (also known as *e*-currency, *e*-money, electronic cash, electronic currency, digital money, digital cash, digital currency, cyber currency) refers to money or scrip which is only exchanged electronically. Typically, this involves the use of computer networks, the internet and digital stored value systems. Electronic Funds Transfer (EFT), direct deposit, digital gold currency and virtual currency are all examples of electronic money. Also, it is a collective term for financial cryptography and technologies enabling it.

While electronic money has been an interesting problem for cryptography, to date, the use of *e*-money has been relatively low-scale. One rare success has been Hong Kong's Octopus card system, which started as a transit payment system and has grown into a widely used electronic money system. London Transport's Oyster card system remains essentially a contactless prepaid travel card. Two other cities have implemented functioning electronic money systems. Very similar to Hong Kong's Octopus card, Singapore has an electronic money programme for its public transportation system (commuter trains, bus, etc.), based on the same type of system.

The Netherlands has also implemented a nationwide electronic money system known as Chipknip for general purpose, as well as OV-Chipkaart for transit fare collection. In Belgium, a payment service company, Proton, owned by 60 Belgian banks issuing stored value cards, was developed in 1995. A number of electronic money systems use contactless payment transfer in order to facilitate easy payment and give the payee more confidence in not letting go of their electronic wallet during the transaction.

Electronic Money Systems

In technical terms, electronic money is an online representation, or a system of debits and credits, used to exchange value within another system, or within itself as a stand alone system. In principle this process could also be done off-line. Occasionally, the term electronic money is also used to refer to the provider itself. A private currency may use gold to provide extra security, such as digital gold currency. Some private organisations, such as the United States armed forces use independent currencies such as Eagle Cash.

Centralised Systems

Many systems—such as PayPal, WebMoney, cashU, and Hub Culture's Ven—will sell their electronic currency directly to the end user, but other systems such as Liberty Reserve only sell through third party digital currency exchangers. In the case of Octopus card in Hong Kong, electronic money deposits work similarly to regular bank deposits. After Octopus Card Limited receives money for deposit from users, the money is deposited into a bank. This is similar to debit-card-issuing banks redepositing money at central banks.

Africa and Afghanistan are seeing prepaid cell phone minutes being used as electronic money using the M-Pesa system. Some community currencies, like some Local Exchange Trading Systems (LETS) and the Community Exchange System, work with electronic transactions.

Decentralised Systems

Decentralised electronic money systems include:

- Ripple monetary system, a monetary system based on trust networks.
- Bitcoin, a peer-to-peer electronic monetary system based on cryptography.

Off-line Anonymous Systems

In the use of off-line electronic money, the merchant does not need to interact with the bank before accepting money from the user. Instead merchants can collect monies *spent* by users and *deposit* them later with the bank.

In principle this could be done off-line, i.e. the merchant could go to the bank with his storage media to exchange *e*-money for cash. Nevertheless the merchant is guaranteed that the user's *e*-money will either be accepted by the bank, or the bank will be able to identify and punish the cheating user. In this way a user is prevented from spending the same funds twice (double-spending). Off-line *e*-money schemes also need to protect against cheating merchants, i.e. merchants that want to deposit money twice (and then blame the user).

Using cryptography, anonymous *e*-cash was introduced by David Chaum. He used blind signatures to achieve unlinkability between withdrawal and spend transactions. In cryptography, *e*-cash usually refers to anonymous *e*-cash. Depending on the properties of the payment transactions, one distinguishes between online and off-line *e*-cash. The first off-line *e*-cash system was proposed by Chaum and Naor. Like the first on-line scheme, it is based on RSA blind signatures.

Hard vs Soft Electronic Currencies

A *hard electronic currency* is one that does not have services to dispute or reverse charges. In other words, it only supports non-reversible transactions. Reversing transactions, even in case of a legitimate error, unauthorised use, or failure of a vendor to supply goods is difficult, if not impossible. The advantage of this arrangement is that the operating costs of the electronic currency system are greatly reduced by not having to resolve payment disputes. Additionally, it allows the electronic currency transactions to clear instantly, making the funds available immediately to the recipient. This means that using hard electronic currency is more akin to a cash transaction. Examples are TokenPay, Pecunix, Liberty Reserve, Western Union, KlickEx and Bitcoin.

A *soft electronic currency* is one that allows for reversal of payments, for example in case of fraud or disputes. Reversible payment methods generally have a "clearing time" of 72 hours or more. Examples are PayPal and credit card. A hard currency can be *softened* by using a trusted third party or an escrow service.

Future Progression

The main focuses of electronic money development are:
- being able to use it through a wider range of hardware such as secured credit cards
- linked bank accounts that would generally be used over an internet means, for exchange with a secure micropayment system such as in large corporations (PayPal, KlickEx).

Mobile medical devices can assist in the medical field in ways of diagnosing patients' illnesses and having mobile monitoring systems with alarms that have remote controlled devices. "Cell phone electronic currency" will also be available in the future. It will not only make paying without paper money, it will also replace bank cards, and life turns out to be "card less". The benefits of that not only make users more convenient, also reduce the cost of exchange system. Electronic currency has been an ongoing event, it is predicted that by the end of 2012, 360 million people will be using this feature worldwide; approximately three billion adult users can trade with electronic currency through mobile network and internet by 2014. Therefore, for those mobile network providers, "cell phone electronic currency" means huge opportunity.

Various Issues

Although electronic money can provide many benefits—such as convenience and privacy, increased efficiency of transactions, lower transaction fees, and new business opportunities with the expansion of economic activities on the Internet—there are many potential issues with the use of e-money. The transfer of digital currencies raises local issues such as how to levy taxes or the possible ease of money laundering. There are also potential macro-economic effects such as exchange rate instabilities and shortage of money supplies (total amount of electronic money versus the total amount of real money available, basically the possibility that digital cash could exceed the real cash available).

8

Cash and Credit Finance

The term credit is upon the lips of everyone. An international scramble for credit supply is in process. Some of the competitors are more favourably placed than others. Eastern Europe appeals to Western Europe for accommoation. Western Europe appeals to England. England placed a few faint hopes upon the United States, but they were rudely dispelled. America is suffering from a credit scarcity, and cannot satisfy her home demands.

The New York merchants, dependent upon their European trade, have sought in vain for sufficient long credits to restore that trade to its pre-war conditions. Money rates have proved prohibitive, and the American bankers dare not tie up their credit facilities for any lengthy period. The demands upon them from the interior of the country are so pressing that a stringency pervades the whole structure. New York money rates in December, 1919, rose to over 20 per cent.

In the absence of credit facilities from America the position of Europe is critical. Loans can only be raised by the various Continental Governments at the unprecedented rate of over 9 per cent. Houses cannot be built. Employment cannot be found. Food supplies are jeopardised. Yet in spite of the gravity of the problem there is no real appreciation of what credit is.

As a preliminary to a correct grasp of the question we must ascertain what is the real essence of cash money. Let us then retrace our steps into an era where we can exercise a less disturbed vision. History tells us that cattle once served as money, and was superseded by the metals, copper, silver, and gold in turn. The modern economist has analysed gold in its economic aspect, and has found that it possesses certain qualities which render it the most suitable commodity to serve as money.

The Qualities

These qualities are variously stated. One of the most brilliant of modern economists lists them as follows: (1) Ease of transport; (2) durability; (3) identity of quality; (4) difficulty of counterfeit; (5) divisibility (including fusibility). The first renders gold capable of being brought to market, the second renders it possible to conserve it for the market, the third renders it easy of valuation, the fourth makes it difficult to deceive the purchaser, the fifth makes it possible to market it in any quantity without altering its value.

It will be observed that cattle possess some of the qualities set out above, though to a less extent than gold, while others, such as divisibility, they cannot be said to possess, without doing violence to the ordinary meaning of language. Yet cattle served as money. Copper again possesses all the above qualities, though to a less degree than gold. In its time copper also served as money. The question naturally arises, What was the essential characteristic of these commodities that determined their use as money, and what cause decided that they should each in turn be superseded?

Reflection will show that all the qualities enumerated above are but separate rays that can be brought to one focus. They each serve to give the commodity embodying them a certain advantage in exchange over all others. In combination they determine that the commodity in question is the most exchangeable commodity. This, then, is the explanation. In any economic society commodity-money will take the guise of that commodity which the society finds to be the most exchangeable one.

Most Exchangeable Commodity

Gold is the most exchangeable commodity. The possessor of gold can always exchange it for goods. The possessor of goods cannot nearly so easily exchange them for gold. Hence gold is the cash money of the community.

We are so used to the existence of gold as the basis of cash money that it appears to have no possible rivals. Yet its present triumph is of quite recent date. In England gold finally superseded silver in 1816, the law, however, simply codifying an already established economic triumph.

Throughout the rest of the world the triumph is within living memory. Portugal adopted gold in 1854, Germany in 1873, Scandinavia in 1875, Roumania in 1890, Austria in 1892, Russia and Japan in 1897, and Peru in 1901.

In the Latin Union (France, Italy, Belgium, Switzerland, Greece) the triumph of gold has not yet met with legal recognition, neither has it entirely in the United States of America, Mexico, Holland, or Spain. In none of these countries, however, has any serious attempt ever been made to restore silver to an equality with gold without disastrous results. In China and India silver is still the most exchangeable commodity, although the trend is undoubtedly towards its supersession by gold.

It should not be supposed, however, that the pre-eminence of gold as commodity-money has not been questioned or that its future is assured. The threat has come not from the dwindling power of its former rival, silver, but from another quarter. Last century Russia made an attempt to introduce a currency of platinum, but failed. The latter metal at that time was closely equal to gold in value, weight for weight, and it had no economic superiority. Its inferiority in use was marked. It was unknown to the mass of the people, and almost its sole use was in the manufacture of scientific apparatus for the chemical laboratory.

The gold has invaded the industrial world. It is used in the making of electric lamps, it enters into the mouths of people in the form of dental fillings. Its increased value has given it an economic advantage over gold, in that its cost of transport is lessened. Moreover, it is superseding gold' as an ornament. Platinum as a setting for diamonds is superior to the yellow metal.. Already in America it is in vogue for engagement rings. Harmony of colour has naturally decided that wedding rings should be made of the same metal. Hence it is possible that platinum will win that place in popular esteem now occupied by its more tawdry rival.

One potent factor is at work. International and interstate balances have grown in volume, and to settle them by the transport of gold is a costly affair. As platinum is some three times more valuable than gold, its use would mean a proportionate saving. It is, however, unwise to hazard too much upon such a point. The source of platinum supply in pre-war days was Russia, now excluded from the world's markets. The supply comes chiefly from Colombia. If Russian industry could re-established platinum would probably decline in value and its rivalry be less dangerous. According to Professor Jevons, money is used- (1) as a commodity; (2) as a store of wealth; (3) as a medium of exchange; (4) as a measure of value. This list is incomplete. Money is also used (5) as a medium of credit and (6) as a basis of credit.

The origin of the cash nexus in economic society lay in the fact that in an exchange both parties were normally the gainers. If a man were a better bootmaker than cloth-weaver, it would pay him to make boots in exchange for cloth, provided that he could find a cloth-weaver who needed boots, or that he could use a mechanism which would enable him ultimately to obtain the cloth that he wanted. That mechanism was cash money. He sold his boots for cash to whoever needed boots, and he waited until he found a weaver who had cloth to sell. By this means he was

Cash and Credit Finance

enabled to devote himself more and more to that occupation which he had made his special branch of industry. In doing so he was promoting to a small degree the system known as the division of labour.

The division of labour proved to be a great industrial advance. By enabling men to specialise on one particular trade it called new industries into being. As the economic machine grew stronger, greater developments could take place. At the same time, it caused an increasing strain upon the cash resources of the community. This vital consideration has not been sufficiently emphasised by economists.

In the feudal days the great bulk of the people were peasants, who grew their own food and made their own rough clothes. Let us picture a typical village of some hundred souls living in cottages grouped round the feudal manor. While the men toiled in the fields, the women spun and wove.

The wool clipped from the sheep was made into rough garments without the intervention of any cash transaction. Money values were less than now. A sheep in the eleventh century cost only 5d. The clothes of the peasant probably closely equalled a sheep in exchange value. The total value of clothing consumed each year in such a community would perhaps not be more than some £2 Now picture the same village at the height of the craft gilds (AD 1300).

The cash nexus has largely diffused through society. The peasant sells his produce at the market town and buys his clothing. The value of an outfit of clothes in the meantime has risen from 5d. to 2s. To buy one outfit of clothing for 100 people per annum would probably need £10 in cash, if all purchases were made at once. But another important factor has to be considered. The clothing industry has been specialised.

The wool must be sold to the carding industry, from there to the spinner, thence to the weaver, and in turn to the fuller and dyer, and finally to the tailor. The woollen clip, instead of being made into clothes without any cash intervention, causes a call upon cash resources some five or six times before it reaches its final destination. If, therefore, the total value of clothes consumed per year in the village be £10, the annual cash demand created in this branch of industrial life alone is some £50.

The figure is somewhat exaggerated, it is true, since carding, spinning, weaving, fulling, dyeing, and tailoring were not so separated as is suggested above. It serves, however, to show how the division of labour caused a strain upon the cash resources. An extension of this line of thought will suggest how important the strain upon cash was bound to become.

Not only did the peasant buy clothes, but he bought implements, boots, building materials. Again the clothing gildsman bought from the other gildsmen. Cash was required after every output of product in order that sale could take place. Specialisation of industry, or division of labour, went on apace, with an increasing call for cash. Some materials were perhaps to pass through the hands of some fifty purchasers before the final product was obtained.

Let us translate the above argument into general terms. A primitive feudal community produced everything for personal consumption. Assuming, as a basis, that the total money value of all the products was £100 a year, nevertheless the cash requirements of such a community were nil. Now, under the influence of the division of labour, a change of system takes place, and each producer produces, not for personal consumption, but to sell.

One result is increased industrial efficiency. The total value of the product is increased, let us assume, to £1,000. The partially manufactured goods must pass from purchaser to purchaser at increasing values before they reach the state of final product. If the number of transfers involved is five on an average, the cash transactions of the community have increased from nil to £5,000 per year. This figure again is an exaggeration, in that it makes no allowance for the fact that the product is enhancing its money value at each transfer. The wool from the sheep's back might, for

Cash and Credit Finance

example, be sold to the carder for £1, by him to the spinner for £2, and, when spun, to the weaver for £3, then to the fuller for £4, to the dyer for £5, to the tailor for £6, and to the final purchaser for £7. A nearer estimate would probably give £2,500 as the total amount of the cash transactions.

The year's cash payments of the community will then have increased from nil to £2,500. But the process still continues. The total produce in another century has increased to a money value of £2,000; the number of independent stages has doubled.

The cash transactions per annum will have quadrupled to £10,000, since the £2,000 worth of goods will have to pass through the hands of ten purchasers at an average price of £1,000. The conclusion is, therefore, that the yearly cash transactions of the community will increase at a much greater rate than the total annual value of the produce.

The way out for the community is either-(1) to increase its cash resources; (2) to speed up the circulation of its stock of money; or (3) to find an effective substitute for cash money. Economic history shows that a progressive community will have recourse to all three methods.

There are, however, serious limitations to the first two of these methods. The increase of the cash store is ultimately limited by the discovery of new mines and by the standard of mining engineering attained. The circulation of cash money depends upon the system of transport, the state of the roads, the custom of paying wages.

The number of times cash can change hands in a year is not capable of indefinite increase. Money must be immobilised for certain purposes. It must be kept back to pay the weekly wage bill. It must be transported from one industrial centre to another. While in transit, it is temporarily unavailable for cash payments. The principal method of meeting the growing demand will therefore be to have recourse to the third method. The need of finding a suitable substitute for cash money to meet growing requirements is the origin of credit.

Socialist Idea

The Economist describes credit as an exchange of present for future wealth. The Socialist regards it as a mere book-keeping transaction. Both are to some extent correct, but both have ignored an essential point. They are describing the ideal, without regard to the real. Credit is indeed largely a book-keeping transaction. The Clearing House enables a large mass of credits on one side to be cancelled against an equal amount on the other. Ideal credit is the exchange of present for future wealth.

The credit extended to the manufacturer is a claim upon the commodities already produced by him and by its use he is enabled to produce further commodities and apply the proceeds from their sale to cancel his obligation.

Underlying the whole superstructure is, however, one point of prime importance, and that is the store of gold. No credit is advanced today that is not directly or indirectly a call upon gold. A banknote is valid because it is a call upon gold on demand. In Europe the call is indirect for the great mass of the people, because the note is practically inconvertible.

But the note can be used to buy American dollar notes, which are convertible, and the value of the European banknote is determined in the last resource by the ease or difficulty of obtaining gold for it from the American Treasury or National banks. The cheque is an evidence either of a deposit or an overdraft, and is a call upon the bank's stock of Treasury or bank-notes. It is therefore an indirect call upon gold. The bill of exchange is not really a credit instrument at all. It is rather collateral security based upon goods, by which the merchant obtains from the broker, either in notes or cheque, a call upon the world's gold store.

When the broken nations of Europe appeal for credit, they are appealing, not for a mere bookkeeping transaction, nor for an exchange of future against present wealth. The book-keeping transactions could be done as competently by them as by anyone else. Their present wealth exists in the form of their railways, their mines, their factories. Their future wealth could be supplied by their own energies but for the one determining fact, which sterilises their action and reduces them to economic impotence. They have lost their call upon the world's gold store.

The credit of the various countries is not related to the fertility of their lands/to the richness of their mines, to the size of their factories, nor to the energies of their people. Their lands may remain untilled, their mines unworked, their factories empty, and their people idle. Their credit is related to the amount of gold available immediately or in the near future to support the vast mass of paper credit in existence.

When industrial society had reached a certain pitch of development, the need for credit emerged. In its earliest form it was merely a desire for security. Cash stores were so great that they could no longer be kept safely in the merchant's shops. The merchants could not always use them immediately in commerce. They deposited them at the goldsmiths'.

Experience showed that cash economy could be effected by the use of merchants' gold-deposit notes instead of actual gold, and further experience proved that greater economy was attainable by use of goldsmiths' notes. The goldsmith's note superseded the merchant's because it was more exchangeable or circulating. The credit of the goldsmith stood higher than that of the merchant; he was in the eyes of his community the more creditable person. The more circulating form of credit ousted the less.

The private banks followed the economical experience of the times. The need was for a circulating form of credit to supplement the cash resources. Experience had shown that in England the most convenient coin was the pound sterling. This was confirmed by the fact that other nations used a coin of somewhat equal value. The private banks therefore wisely issued the £1 note and supplemented it by smaller notes.

The Bank of England was privileged and aristocratic. It preferred rather to teach than to learn. It issued cumbrous notes of £20, which people did not want. Therefore the circulation of the private banks invaded the sphere of influence of the Bank of England.

The flimsy six-partner firms challenged the powerful monopolist. To protect itself the Bank reduced its notes to £5, and forced its rivals to increase theirs in value. World experience rapidly went against it. Other nations successively reduced their notes in value, but the Bank of England remained obstinate. The Great War of 1914 found it in an impossible position, and the State protected the Bank's dignity by issuing £1 and 10s. notes through its agency.

Paper Money

The issue of paper money is an automatic attempt on the part of a community to escape from cash stringency. Metallic money owes its position to the fact that gold is the most exchangeable and, therefore, the most readily circulating commodity. It can only be replaced by an instrument having equal or greater power of circulation. The sovereign circulates because it is of known worth, usable in convenient amounts.

The private notes circulated because they were the closest approximation to the sovereign within the reach of the community. The folly of the State in limiting the issue of such notes to small and obscure firms prevented the notes from having that backing which ordinary economic influences, if allowed to operate, would have produced for them. State wars filched from them, by the drain upon cash, the small backing that they had. The cause was misinterpreted, and legislation was passed to limit any increase of circulating credit.

The Currency School tried to bind the community down to the cash basis. They simply diverted the economic stream from a natural to an unnatural channel. Circulating credit was no longer available, so non-circulating credit had to be used. The whole effort of finance since the passing of Peel's Act has been directed to making credit circulate. The cheque-overdraft system is a personal system, not a circulating one. The Cheque Clearing House has only succeeded in giving it a semi-circulating character. The strain upon the cash and credit resources of the community has been constantly growing. It has only partly been met by gigantic and unnecessary efforts.

Cash and Credit Finance

The deposit system has centralised the cash resources, but has never been broad enough as a base, to allow an overdraft credit system sufficient for the community's needs. The result has been obvious. On every occasion that industry has expanded, the overdraft system has broken down. Expansion of industry means a larger wage-roll, a demand for cash for internal currency. That in turn means a withdrawal of deposits, which causes a restriction of credit. This restriction causes a collapse of industry. Centripetal finance dare not confess its failure, and talks in ponderous terms, but without meaning, of over-speculation.

The civilized world has suffered constantly from a credit stringency. The defect is obvious in an acute form today over Continental Europe. It is less obvious in England, except to the producer, who is being forced to stop production, discharge his workers, and face bankruptcy, because the banks are withdrawing his overdraft.

It is still less obvious in the United States of America, where, however, the Federal Reserve banks are drawing on Europe to counterbalance the demands upon their gold stores caused by the country's internal needs. Statesmen and bankers deliver homilies about the dangers of speculation without apparently realising that there is no hard-and-fast line between speculation and enterprise, and that undue checking of the one means the destruction of the other.

The scarcity of credit, however, is not purely a war phenomenon. It is simply presenting itself in a more acute form now than formerly. The scarcity is artificial. It needs none of the ponderous phrases of the economist to teach the masses the meaning of scarcity.

During the war certain commodities, sugar or matches, for example, were scarce. The result was that the wealthy classes were in a privileged position. They could obtain such commodities when the poor could not. The shopkeepers no longer exerted themselves to find consumers, but waited for the consumers to come to them. Then they parted with the valued commodity only to the privileged few.

Matches could be obtained by old customers, and by new customers who were prepared to bring in business by purchasing quantities of tobacco. The same held with respect to sugar. Precisely this condition has been normal with regard to credit since the strangling of the private banks of issue. The old country banker tried to extend his issue with his clients. He exerted himself to find safe points of issue for his notes.

The cheque-overdraft banker does not do so. He waits for the customers to find him. He treats them cavalierly. He reserves his credit for the favoured few, or extends it exceptionally to a new client who is prepared to bring in big business.

The inability of cheque-overdraft credit to expand proportionately to the needs of the community has had dire results. It starved British and Irish agriculture, and made us dependent upon extraneous sources for food. It ruined our smaller business men, and drove us into the arms of the trusts. It made unemployment a constant aspect of modern life.

The cheque-overdraft system is a failure because it lacks the one fundamental property of economic finance, circulating power. It has only been able to retain a certain degree of that quality by a constant process of withdrawal. It long ago ceased to pretend to finance agriculture.

It has since refused to finance new industries. It has made its commitments of shorter and shorter date. At one time merchants could obtain accommodation for six months, now the period is generally three months, and even the three-month bills which the banks accept from the brokers have partially matured before they are taken up. The Bank of England confines itself practically to seven-day bills. The inevitability of such a withdrawal was clearly foreseen by the old private bankers, but their warnings were not listened to.

The lack of circulating power in the cheque-overdraft system has not only led to a withdrawal of banking credit from agriculture, from new industries in favour of established concerns, but it has led to discrimination with regard to the latter. The banker is

Cash and Credit Finance

harassed by the need for conserving the deposits. The cheques are constantly being presented for redemption. In stable periods they cancel each other mutually in the clearing house, leaving only a small balance to be paid in gold. But stable periods arc becoming less constant in industry.

The slightest instability causes a big demand upon the gold store. Growth of internal trade means a call upon gold for internal currency. Growth of external trade needs a similar call from abroad. Cheques and notes are presented for redemption in gold. If such redemption is prohibited in internal transactions by suspension of cash payments it is accomplished indirectly. Exchange on America is bought. The pound falls and the dollar rises. The dollars so bought are redeemed in gold, and the American call upon the English gold store is increased.

The strain upon the world's gold stores is constantly increasing. It could only be met effectually by permitting the use of a medium of equal or greater circulating power, the private banknote. This is forbidden by law. The remedy has been sought therefore by loaning credit only when collateral security, easily convertible into cash, is offered. The most readily convertible collateral under the present system is not true wealth, not the factories or the products of industry, but artificial claims to dividends, those stocks and shares which enjoy an open market. Hence the banks lend only to persons who can offer gilt-edged security.

What, in effect, is the result of such an operation ? If credit is only extended to those who already possess convertible titles to property the outcome is obvious. The gold-controlling class has a constant advantage over the rest of the community. The owner of dividend-earning bonds is granted further credit. The owner of real, but not readily saleable, wealth is denied it. There is accordingly a constant gravitation of wealth into the possession of the holders of saleable titles to dividends.

Centripetal finance must preserve its call upon gold. It does so by loaning credit to those who possess the call upon gold. The call upon gold necessarily concentrates into fewer and fewer hands. That industry is stifled, that competent producers must remain salaried employees, that the labourer sees no outlet from the drab existence of wage-earning, these facts weigh as nothing compared with the necessity of conserving the soundness of a financial structure which is built upon an unsound basis.

Let us turn to another aspect of the question. Credit should be synonymous with trust. An act of credit means that one person lends to another, with the trust that the loan will be returned. There can be no compulsion in the matter at all. Otherwise the transaction is no longer one of pure credit, but is overlaid with coercion.

The most primitive instinct in man is distrust. Lowly organised communities hoard their savings-hide them away wherever they can find an imagined safe place. Division of labour means trust in someone else, that his labour has produced something which is worth buying. It is interdependent upon the use of money.

Growth of Cash

The growth of cash resources leads the community to the state in which hoarding is no longer secure. Surplus gold must be trusted to other persons to mind. A further step in economic progress shows the best use for saved money is not in giving it to another to hide, but to use in commerce. This marks a tremendous advance.

Distrust has been converted into trust. Socialising forces have been brought into play. But trust in others to use one's savings in commerce has its limitations. The money must be returnable. That can only be secured if the borrower uses it wisely-that is, puts it to productive purposes. For if he squander it in non-productive uses, the lender will not be in a position to obtain repayment.

This conception of credit Is important because all the modern trends of so-called credit are in the opposite direction. Credit is being withdrawn from the directly productive members of society and extended to financial middle-men. Moreover, there has been an increase of so-called public credit. The fact that States and

Cash and Credit Finance

municipalities waste the community's resources is lost to sight. Yet public loans are not pure credit to all. They are only partially voluntary. They are based, not upon productivity, but upon taxation. The credit of a community is thought to be inexhaustible because the power of taxation has not yet been seriously challenged.

The spectacle of the present generation struggling under a growing burden of public debt is a gloomy one, but the prospect of the future is still more hopeless. We are purchasing a temporary relief at the expense of our children's children. Generations are to be born into economic slavery. Yet in spite of intensive taxation in the present and prospective taxation in the future, the capacity of the community voluntarily to create public debt has been exhausted almost the world over.

Increase of such debt threatens to be on a coercive basis. Recourse has been had to forced loans in Continental Europe, the same has been threatened in Australia, while England is faced with the spectre of a huge debt which it cannot succeed in funding. The end is not in sight. The military conflict of 1914-18 is being followed by a financial repercussion throughout the world, with more disastrous results in human misery than the horrors of war.

The situation is the outcome of a refusal to recognise the elementary economic truth that a credit instrument must be free from all constraint. The Kings in early days enforced their own cash currency. Whether good or bad, the King's coin had to be accepted. The result was that the Kings took advantage of their position to cheat their subjects. Slowly they learned that depreciation of cash money led to national disaster. They were obliged to Stop their malpractices. The path uphill proved harder than the path downhill.

When Queen Elizabeth tried to restore the coinage debased by Henry VIII to its old value, it was found that the new coin disappeared from circulation as soon as minted. Sir Thomas Gresham, Master of the Mint, enunciated the so-called Gresham's law that bad money drives out good. Gresham was dealing, be it noted, not with a competitive, but with a State currency. There is no evidence that under open competition bad money would oust good money. If money circulated on its own merits and not under State fiat, the better type would oust the worse, and the debased currency of the Kings would not be accepted by their subjects.

The same law holds with regard to credit money. Under open competition the private banknote, issued by reputable firms and based upon real wealth or constructive ability, has always competed successfully against State paper money, or against the notes of privileged banks, until suppressed by law. Under State control of finance, bad credit money drives out good credit money. It also drives out good cash money.

Evidences of public debt circulate instead of credit instruments representing real wealth. Debased State paper has forced gold out of circulation. No country in Europe dare allow free traffic in gold. If it did so, its gold store would migrate outside its borders and its credit system would utterly break down. The countries of Europe have had to protect their gold stores by prohibiting the export of gold. These measures can have only temporary success, and do not operate with respect to fresh supplies of gold from the mines. The gold that is coming into the open market from the mines at the present time is being bought for the United States.

With the advent of paper money, power passed from the Kings to the politicians. The latter have not yet learned the lesson that the Kings were taught by their experience in debasing the coinage. Statesmen still think that coercive credit is better than free credit, that evidences of public debt are as good as evidences of real wealth or productive ability. They have suppressed the free note in favour of the privileged note. They have even suppressed or limited the privileged note in favour of the State note.

Everywhere the result has been the same. Forced paper currency has always become debased. Whether it be the French assignat, the American green-back, the Soviet rouble, or the Treasury note, its value has fallen. Statesmen have multiplied evidences of public debt so enormously that the community can

Cash and Credit Finance 241

no longer absorb them. The money value of such evidences has everywhere fallen and the interest charges risen.

The banks have been obliged to take up huge proportions of public issues. The pressure exerted upon them by the State's hold on the central gold reserve left them no other course. The National Banks of England, France, Germany, Belgium, the United States of America, were obliged to support their respective States in a destructive war.

The deposit banks were compelled to lend their aid to a vicious system of finance. Otherwise their cash resources would have been drained away as in the Napoleonic wars. The result has been to superimpose upon the circulating medium, the insufficient stock of gold, a huge superstructure of non-circulating or semi-circulating debt evidences which are straining the whole credit resources of the civilized world.

If those gold stores could be maintained intact, industry might stagger fitfully along, as it did in pre-war days. Under the centripetal system of finance, however, there is a constant tendency for the greater gold store to absorb the smaller. Gold in pre-war days had drifted from the local stores to the central national store, and had shown a tendency to drift further to the centre of the centripetal system, the northeastern area of the United States.

That process has been accelerated during the war. The interest due to America on the war debts is a yearly lien upon Europe's gold store. The issue of debased paper in England and on the Continent is a powerful factor which, under Gresham's law, will prevent inflow of gold.

One result of State control of credit can be foreseen. As gold migrates to America, it will become necessary further to restrict English credit, with the result either that English industry must dwindle or must be carried on to an increasing extent by the aid of American credit.

The one-time mistress of the world's industry will find herself reduced to the role of a humble handmaiden, suing for favours from her powerful cousin.

What, then, is the essence of cash and credit finance? Simply this, that under a free system the most circulating form of commodity or credit will serve as money. But free circulation connotes value. A man will only accept freely what he considers to have value, either in itself or in the result.

Free credit means a note issue based on evidence of real wealth or productive ability. Under a coercive system, on the other hand, the worse form of cash money or credit will replace the better. Bad money or credit based upon evidences of public debt will oust value money or credit based on productive capacity.

Usury, an Evil?

In Economics and Commerce, Usury is essentially a term of reproach. The usurer has been anathematised by the Church, punished by the State, denounced by the Moralist. The masses have risen in revolt against him and stoned him to death. Pogroms against usurers, especially when of Jewish blood, have been rife since the cash nexus infused itself into society. The end of the conflict has been extraordinary.

The Church has ceased to curse, and is content to live upon its unearned revenues. The State has abandoned its efforts to punish, and is content to pay away millions of pounds each year to satisfy those who have lent it money. The Moralist is prepared to defend the system he once denounced. To him it is a stabilising and socialising factor. The masses, when not reduced to apathy, make sporadic attempts to burst the spell which binds them.

The change has been wrought by a simple artifice. Usury is a hateful idea. Usurers are rightly objects of moral scorn. But interest is an economic phenomenon and dividend-receivers are high in social esteem. Yet usury and interest are one and the same thing. Usury is payment for the use of some object. Interest is nothing more.

The most pervading factor of modern industrialism is the dividend. Compared to it rent is a minor issue. Society contains more dividend-receivers than rent-lords. The total portion of annual

Cash and Credit Finance 243

produce paid to holders of stocks and shares is greater than that paid to holders of title-deeds. The problem has presented itself under many changing aspects, from the direct loan of gold by a patty moneylender to the formation of huge dividend-making concerns. Astounding as it may seem, the economists, after centuries of study, have produced no adequate explanation of interest.

Different Theories

At least four different theories of interest hold the field. Not one of them commands respect. Let us examine them briefly and then proceed to establish the true explanation.

The first theory is called the 'productivity' theory. Its ablest exponent was Bastiat. Capital helps the labourer to greater production, therefore the man who supplies the capital is entitled to a share of the increased product. To clinch the argument Bastiat presents a concrete case. There are two carpenters, William and James. James makes a plane.

William realises that he could make more planks by the aid of the plane. He therefore tries to borrow it. But, says James, "If I lend my plane I am deprived of its use, and you, who did not make it, will benefit. That is not fair." Obviously James is in the right. Nevertheless James is prepared to lend the plane for a just consideration. In a year it will be worn out, and of course he must receive a new one. Furthermore, he must receive a part of William's increased output-say a plank. So William borrows the plane on the understanding that he shall return at the end of a year a new plane and a plank.

At first sight the argument seems convincing. Reflection will show that it is not a statement of an economic principle at all, but merely a mental trick. Economics is a science of trends, not an exposition of a static fact.

The position indicated above could not perpetuate itself, because it contains the very factors which would eliminate it from economic society. For if William recompense James for his old plane by making him a new one, then William has made a plane.

Therefore there are two producers of planes in this microcosmic society, and only one consumer. The supply of planes will, therefore, outstrip the demand. They will become a 'drug in the market, and interest will not be paid for their use.

On another important point the argument is wrong. It is without foundation in economic history. No period can be shown where payment of interest for planes was made in planks. In more general terms, no period is known where interest on one form of capital was paid in another form. When cattle were money, loans were made in cattle and interest was paid in cattle. When metal was money, loans were made in metal and interest paid in the same.

The second theory is the 'use' theory. A man is prepared to pay rent for the use of a house, he is prepared to pay hire for the use of a horse. Why, then, should he not pay for the use of a capital ? Again a mental trick, a presentation of one side of the shield. If the demand for houses is keen, rent will be paid. Suppose the supply exceeds the demand? Take a proprietor who does not desire to use his manor, and would let it to a tenant, save that no tenant is forthcoming. Then the reverse phenomenon will occur. The proprietor will receive nothing for the use of the house, but will even pay a caretaker to look after it.

If a farmer requires not the services of his horse and everyone in the neighbourhood has sufficient horses, then the former will pay to keep his horse in idleness. He will even lend it gratis to keep it in trim. So it is with money. Economic history teaches us that hoarding precedes lending. A man hoards his money because he has no present use for it. If another borrows it and repays it when the owner requires it, he is doing the owner a service, in that he is saving him the risk and trouble of hoarding it.

Gide's criticism of the 'use' theory of interest is interesting. "As the capital which is the object of a loan is nearly always circulating capital-as a rule, money-it is not a lasting possession like a house, but is destroyed in the very act of production. Coal thrown into the furnace disappears in smoke; raw material is transformed;

money is spent in wages. How, then, can interest pay for the use of a thing, the characteristic of which is that it is consumed at its first use?

"It is easy to reply that the capital lent is neither the coal nor the money, but the value. Now that is permanent, preserving its identity much better than a house, which sooner or later falls into ruins.... The borrower may become the owner of the money and keep it as long as he likes, but he has not become owner of its value, since he must give it back in the form of other money." Gide therefore considers the 'use' theory the best explanation of interest.

This seems a close approach to sophistry. Underlying it, however, there is an economic truth, which Gide does not clearly state. Capital in the form of a house is not the cause of interest value is. But what is the permanence of value to which Gide refers? To speak of value preserving its identity, unless you can identify it, is meaningless. Value is not the value of a house, which may decline. It is not the value of the money, because the actual money lent may be used to buy a worthless house. What, then, is the identity of the value received by the borrower and returnable (with interest) to the lender ? Surely it is none other than the call upon gold. The borrower loans a certain call upon gold, and he expects return in the form of a greater call upon gold.

This point will become clear in dealing with the true cause of interest. The third theory of interest is the 'abstinence' theory, originated by Senior. Before capital can be used it must be saved. The man who saves it is doing a social service. He is abstaining from gratifying an immediate desire for the benefit of society, and his reward takes the shape of interest.

This explanation is entirely unsatisfactory, and has been abandoned. A mere refraining from an act is not a cause. Abstention is not an act of production. As Gide points out, to refrain from eating eggs is not to produce chickens. Moreover, the explanation does not square with economic life as a whole. The Indian ryot hoards without the stimulus of interest. The small dividend-receivers may indeed practise abstinence under the stimulus of gain, but the financial Kings of the world have no need to do so. Their income increases faster than they can consume it. Lassalles' fine wealth of scorn destroyed for ever Senior's ingenious theory. "The profit of capital is the 'wage of abstinence.' Happy, even priceless expression !

The ascetic millionaires of Europe: like Indian penitents or pillar saints they stand, on one leg, each on his column, with straining arm and pendulous body and pallid looks, holding a plate towards the people to collect the wages of their abstinence. In their midst, towering up above his fellows as head penitent and ascetic, the Baron Rothschild! This is the condition of Society ! How could I ever so much misunderstand it!"

The fourth theory is the 'time' theory. It is due to Boehrn-Bawerck. The newest of all four, it is still held in certain respect. Interest is the price of time. Time is a factor in value. A hundred pounds down is worth more than a hundred pounds in the future. A dinner at once, as M. Gide instances, is of more value than one tomorrow. If not, a dinner a hundred or a thousand years hence is as important as one today.

Here again we have only one side of the shield. A dinner today is valueless to a man who has already dined. A dinner tomorrow is an agony to a dyspeptic. Surplus dinners are a debit not an asset to a wise man. Surplus money is a burden. Yet interest originated, in the first place, from the use of surplus money. Money was hoarded because it might be more valuable tomorrow than today, next year than tomorrow. The horse sense of the community is closer to the truth than the erudition of Boehm-Bawerck. Well may a celebrated modern exponent of economic science ask, at the end of all such explanations: "Is not our general preference for cash simply due to the fact that we know we have always the power to invest it at interest, so that we are really reasoning in a circle?"

Let us reason in a straight line instead. Usury or interest, both the Economists and the Socialists assert, is the fruit of capital. The

Cash and Credit Finance 247

system in which capital operates is called capitalism. What, then, is capital?

Immediately we are faced by an astounding fact that there has been a historic change in the definition of capital. In its earliest concept capital meant real wealth used in producing further real wealth. Today it means paper claims (stocks and shares) to real wealth, or to debt, used in manufacturing further paper claims (dividend warrants and bonus shares) to the same. Ricardo is definite. "Capital is that part of the wealth of a country which is employed in production, and consists of food, clothing, tools, raw materials, machinery, etc., necessary to give effect to labour."

John Stuart Mill affirms the same thing. "Whatever things are destined to supply productive labour with the shelter, protection, tools, and material which the work requires, and to feed and otherwise maintain the labourer during the process, are capital." So far there is no doubt about it. Capital is material, the sum of those things which are used to produce further material wealth. Paper claims have not entered into the concept.

Category of Capital

Henry George excludes all paper claims from the category of capital. "Though all capital is wealth, all wealth is not capital." "Many things are commonly spoken of as wealth which... cannot be considered as wealth at all. Such things have an exchange value... but they are not truly wealth, inasmuch as their increase or decrease does not affect the sum of wealth. Such are bonds, mortgages, promissory notes, bank bills, or other stipulations for the transfer of wealth." If paper claims are not wealth, still less are they capital.

Karl Marx makes capital originate with money. "The circulation of commodities is the starting-point of capital...." "If we ... consider only the economic forms produced by this process of circulation we find its final result to be money: this final product of the circulation of commodities is the first form in which capital appears." Real wealth is fading from the concept of capital, and money forms are usurping its place. The capital which acquires interest is no longer real wealth, but a metallic or paper claim to wealth.

Gide says: "The capital which is the object of a loan is nearly always circulating capital-as a rule, money." Later on we find that metallic money drops into the background. The producer of interest is the paper claim.

Gide finds that "in everyday language, capital does not mean the instrument of production, but all wealth which brings in a revenue to its possessor independently of his labour." But the wealth is not real wealth at all, as the writer goes on to state. "Long after the capital lent has been squandered in riotous living, or blown away in smoke on the battlefields, it will still remain as lucrative capital-i.e., as a credit claim in the hands of the moneylender or the fundholder.

The wand of the economist has succeeded in transforming capital by gradual stages from material wealth to paper claims. A wonderful metamorphosis indeed. Is this truth or illusion, the white light of science or the black art of wizardry ? The steam-engine, as capital, can draw a train. As capital, says the economist, the steam-engine can draw interest. The paper bond, under the deft handling of the economist, shares one function of capital, that of drawing interest. What a pity the economists are not clever enough to make it draw a train.

The Socialist school sidesteps the difficulty. It will not commit itself by saying what Capital is, but defines it by what it does. Capital, it says, is that which produces Interest. This is indeed a vicious circle. What is Interest? Interest is the fruit of Capital. What, then, is Capital ? Capital is that which produces Interest. The economists see the absurdity of the Socialist position. Gide says: "It is certain that the role of capital has changed with economic evolution; from a simple instrument of production, it has become an instrument of gain. It is no longer an aid to labour; it commands labour. It is this new social regime which Socialists call Capisalism. The fact that no wealth can be produced without the aid of some other pre-existing wealth, is an economic law the importance of which cannot be exaggerated. . . . We must give some name to this pre-existing wealth. Now the name we give it is Capital. If Socialists will not accept this name, let them propose another."

Capital and Finance

There is another and easier alternative. Let us continue to call Capital by its name-Capital, and let us give the proper name to that which obtains interest. Capital is real wealth used in production of further wealth. Concretely it includes tools, machinery, engineering works, materials of every description.

Finance is the claim or call upon wealth used to exchange present or future wealth. In our present system it includes gold, token claims to gold (i.e., silver, copper, nickel), and paper claims to gold. Paper claims to gold may be of fixed or varying gold values-i.e., bank-notes and cheques, or bonds, stocks, shares, mortgages. Production of wealth is a different thing to exchange of wealth. A machine is capital because it is used to produce. A gold coin is finance because it is used to exchange. The one operates upon commodities, the other upon ownership. A mine shaft is capital, because it aids in raising the ore to the surface. A railway is capital because it brings the produce to the market. The coin, the bill, the note do not operate upon the product in the same way at all. They alter neither its form nor its position. They transfer its ownership.

Capital and Finance are two inseparable factors in an economic society where the consumer of a commodity is not the producer. Though inseparable, they are not identical. The Siamese twins were joined, but they were two identities. The whole of the science of economy has been befogged by the failure to recognise the clear-cut distinction between Capital and Finance. The province of Capital is production, that of Finance is exchange. The simplest tool of the primitive hand-workers is as much capital as the mightiest machine used in industry. The cowrie shell of the Pacific islanders is as much finance as the biggest paper bond of a financial pool. Tools and machines assist labour to alter the form or the position of wealth; they do not change its ownership.

Cowrie shells and bonds do not, and cannot, alter the form or the position of wealth, they but serve to transfer the ownership.

Let us apply this concept to the social problem. The Marxian doctrinaire says that the labourer is exploited by capitalism. He does not define capitalism, because he has no clear idea of what he means by capital. He does not know whether he means the machine or the paper bond. To him it is all capital. One might as well confuse a house with the mortgage on a house, and imagine that the sleeping accommodation of a city could be doubled by mortgaging all the houses!

The Marxian doctrinaire is not incorrect on one point, that the labourer does not get a proper return for his labour. The wealth of the world goes in greater degree to the non-producer than to the producer. Where, then, does the exploitation occur? Does it occur in production or in exchange? Is there some ghoulish property in the machines which the labourers use, that they filch from their users a part of the produce in the making?

If so, Capital can rightly be regarded as an exploiter of the labourer. But economics in that case will have to be written in the language of the Arabian Nights. In addition to the genii of the ring and of the lamp, we must admit those of the hammer and the crane, of the steam-engine and the loom, all evil genii filching a part of the labourer's product.

But there is the simpler explanation that the labourer is exploited, not in production, but in exchange. He works for a wage, for a financial consideration. The value of the financial consideration that he receives for his product is less than the value of his product. The reason is obvious.

To provide capital for the labourer, to build him the factories and the machines which should improve his lot, finance is necessary. The financiers who provide that finance exact an undue toll in the form of dividend. To provide the labourer with his raw material, credit is necessary, and the financiers who provide that credit also exact an undue toll for it in the form of interest. The problem of exploitation can be reduced to a simple equation,, with the minor factors such as rent omitted: Full product of labourer = Finance of shareholder (dividend) + Finance of credit agent (interest) + Finance of labourer (wage).

Having made clear this fundamental distinction between Finance and Capital, let us proceed to ascertain the true cause of interest. Finance is either coin or credit. Credit, in existing society, is the call upon gold. Gold owes its position to the fact that it is the most exchangeable or circulating commodity. In exchange it has an advantage over all other commodities. This advantage is not a transient or accidental one: it is inherent and permanent. Moreover, since the exchange of commodities is an increasing factor in an industrial society, the most exchangeable commodity must obtain an increasing advantage over the less exchangeable ones.

This advantage must find expression in economic relations. How does it do so ? It cannot do so in value or price. The price of a commodity is determined at long last, and ignoring transient fluctuations in supply and demand, by the cost of producing a similar article. Suppose, for example, that 1 oz. of gold costs as much to produce as 10 yards of cloth or I cwt. of mutton. Then these things will normally be equal in exchange and the equation will be: 1 oz. gold=10 yards cloth=1 cwt. mutton.

But the owner of the gold can always buy cloth or mutton. Anyone with coin in his pocket can walk into a shop and get what he wants. This is not erudite economy, but a simple fact of life. On the other hand, the cloth producer cannot always sell, neither can the butcher. The possessor of gold has therefore the advantage over the possessor of goods. He can exchange gold for goods at will, or he can defer his purchase. If, however, all gold possessors deferred their purchases, the butchers, clothiers, bakers, and farmers would be ruined. Some inducement must be offered to the possessor of gold, who is in a position to defer parting with his gold, to part with it temporarily, at any rate, to keep industry going.

This inducement may be in the form of increasing the value of gold. Suppose the clothier and the butcher lower the price of their stocks to one-half. Then the equation is: 1 oz. gold =20 yards cloth =2 cwt. mutton.

Now the possessor of gold can purchase double quantities whenever he likes. But he still has the most exchangeable commodity. Why should he buy? Why not withhold until he really desires the commodities which he can purchase at any time? How, then, can he be induced to part with his gold? Obviously by offering him a consideration for its temporary use. That consideration is interest.

Interest, then, is the economic expression of the superiority of gold in exchange. It follows that interest is not a function of capital at all, but a function of finance. It is a toll levied, not on production, but on exchange.

This may not be in accordance with the teachings of economists, but it is in accord with the facts of economics. Let us follow the question further. If interest is a function of capital, then, by the process of supply and demand, the rate of interest will rise as the demand for capital rises, and will fall as the supply of capital increases. If interest is a function of finance, the rate will rise as the demand for money rises, and fall as the supply of money increases. In the first case the supply of and demand for capital will govern interest, in the second the supply of and demand for money will do so.

If the supply of and demand for money does not reflect itself in the rate of interest, it must do so in prices. This supposition is favoured by the economists, and to support it they have invented the Quantity Theory of Money, according to which price varies directly in proportion to the quantity of money in the market. This, like other economic theories, not being based upon observed fact, but upon preconceived notions, is wrong.

The Californian gold discoveries of 1849 caused a great influx of gold into England. There was no proportional increase of price, but enterprise was greatly stimulated. The American Civil War and the issue of inconvertible paper notes forced gold to England. No increase of prices occurred, but interest fell and industry throve.

Cash and Credit Finance

Circulating medium was plentiful and so commanded a less rate of interest. The tradesmen and the community benefited.

The value of gold, as stated above, is determined, like all values, by the cost of reproducing the commodity. If mining improves, the value of gold will tend to fall, because more gold can be produced per hour. The discovery of the rich Rand mines led to a lowering of gold value, and a consequent increase in prices, because gold, as a commodity, was easier to obtain. On the other hand, the great output led to an increased supply of the circulating medium. Hence the rate of interest fell.

The average yearly gold output between 1870 and 1889 was some Between 1890 and 1902 the average was The result was an immense drop in the rate of interest. Consols at 2 3/4 per cent, were quoted at 97 in 1893 and 114 in 1896. Since that date there has been a growing call upon gold. States and communities have heaped up their public debt. The periodic payment of interest means a periodic call upon gold. Interest rates have risen until States today have to pay 7 to 9 per cent. Still more unfortunately productive concerns have to pay 9 to 10 per cent. Industry is forced to close down, and the spectre of unemployment haunts the world.

The economists tell us that interest is a function of capital. Does that in any way account for the rise in interest rates? The capital of England is in its mines, its plant, its motor transport, its factories. These were increasing prior to the war, and their increase should have meant a reduction in interest. Yet interest rates rose. Consols fell from 114 in 1896 to 91 in 1901. During the recent war Consols have fallen from 75 in 1914 to 45 in 1920. Was capital really destroyed to such an extent as to account for this fall? We started the war with factories, ships, railways, lorries, mines, etc.

Many of the ships were destroyed, but the railways, lorries, mines were not. What was destroyed was the product. Millions of tons of good steel went in shells and tanks, now lumbering the fair face of the world. The capital of England remained almost intact. Indeed, more factories were built, more ships constructed, lorries were completed in thousands. The war and its destruction stopped in 1918, but the bank rate rose to 7 per cent, in 1920. What, then, caused the rise in interest ? Not destruction of capital, but inflation of finance.

Enormous public debts were created which represent claims upon the gold store of the country. Those claims have to be met periodically, and to meet them puts a strain upon our credit resources by increasing the strain on gold. Hence trade credit is restricted, overdrafts are called in, and business men are asked to find employment where there is no prospect of selling their produce. The economists of the world meet in international conferences and speak of the need for further credits, while the bankers, by cutting down overdrafts, prove the need for reduced credits.

What does it mean, in actual fact ? Nothing other than this, that the community is surfeited with bonds and debt-evidences of non-circulating nature, all of which have value ultimately because they represent, not real wealth, but varying calls upon gold. This colossal mass of paper credit has been erected, not upon the capital of the country, but upon a meagre central stock of gold. It may be asked why the superstructure cannot be extended still further. If the various calls upon gold balance themselves automatically, why should not credit be still further extended, since it represents only paper transactions? One answer is not far to seek.

The small trickle of gold from the gold stores of the various countries towards the centre of the system, America, has increased in volume. It has become a stream and threatens to become a flood. Central Europe has been more or less denuded of the precious metal. Whither is it going? Largely, in the first place, to the vaults of the Federal Reserve Banks of the United States. But it does not stop there. The Americans are selling their paper titles to procure gold for their own needs, and the metal is going into the interior. That is one of the chief reasons why the English

Cash and Credit Finance 255

banking system is restricting credit, stifling industry, and increasing unemployment.

Capital, the economists tell us, is the source of interest. If a man makes with his own hands a small machine, that machine is capital. If he operates that machine and increases his product, the increase is the profit derived from capital. If, instead of making the machine, he borrows money to buy it, then the increased produce will be divided. Part will go to the owner of the machine, the capitalist, as profit, and part will go to the lender of the money, the financier, as interest. If the demand for money in the community increase, then the financier's share of the profit will increase. If the money scarcity becomes intense, the capitalist proper will have to part with almost the whole of the surplus produce to the financier. Does this happen ? Let us appeal to economic history.

Limited Liability

The limited liability company has ousted the private financier in almost all economic transactions. The shareholder receives his part of the produce in dividends. Does the dividend represent interest or profit ? The answer is that it combines both these items. One factor has swallowed up two shares of the surplus produce. The financier has obtained not only his own portion, but that of the capitalist. But what has happened to the capitalist ? He has disappeared from the scene. Very few men today manage and control their own machines. The capitalist of two generations ago has been reduced to a salaried manager. Centripetal finance has divorced the worker from his tools, and made him dependent upon a wage. It has divorced the capitalist from his capital and made him dependent upon a salary. The financier gets the reward of the increased productive ability of both classes.

Interest, the economist tells us, is a payment for the use of capital. The statement does not square with the plain facts of economics. Take the case of a capitalist. He owns a workshop, machines, materials, all forms of real capital. His capital is valued at £1,000 on a fair valuation. He has a friend, a financier, who has £1,000 in gold, or in a call upon gold. The equation is, therefore, £1,000 in capital-£1,000 in gold.

Now the capitalist needs help from the financier. He wants credit. He offers to exchange, not capital for gold, but the call upon capital for the call upon gold. He gives the financier a mortgage upon his entire capital, value £1,000.

The financier should give him, in return, a call upon his gold, value £1,000. Neither will realise the call upon the other's stock. The capitalist will draw cheques, and the cheques will be cancelled without the gold in the bank being disturbed. The financier will hold the mortgage and, upon repayment of the loan, will return it for cancellation, without the workshop, machines, etc., being disturbed. But experience shows that the equation is not, £1,000 capital=£1,000 gold.

For the call on £1,000 capital the financier will not lend the call on £1,000 gold. He will only lend the call on £750, if as much, and at a certain rate of interest. The equation is, probably, Call on £1,000 capital plus £50 interest per annum= Call on £750 gold.

In other words, so far from interest being a payment for the use of capital, it is a payment by capital for the use of the call upon gold. Interest may be the fruit of capital, but it is the financier who plucks the fruit. Let us consider another aspect of the case. A community possesses certain cash resources, sufficient to allow its products to be exchanged. Increased industry, clever invention, improved methods, double the output. How is the output to be exchanged ? As already explained, either by increasing the cash resources, or by quickening their circulation, or by finding a substitute for cash. Normally all three ways will be tried.

If the substitute for cash does not possess a great amount of circulating power it will be of little use. The community will, therefore, endeavour to get more cash resources. Failing that, it will accelerate the circulation. Movement, however, cannot be accelerated without stimulus. The stimulus must be found. One such stimulus is found by increasing the rate of interest. If interest rates are raised, endeavours will be made to pay debts more

Cash and Credit Finance 257

quickly. Overdrafts will be cleared more promptly, settlement of accounts pressed for, and cheques encashed sooner.

The whole mechanism of exchange will be speeded up. But there are definite limits to such speeding up. Cheques must reach the clearing house for clearance, and the rate at which they can do so is limited by questions of transport, including postal delays. Equilibrium will in the end be established, but the point of equilibrium will not be the optimum. Those firms that can obtain credit at the higher rates will exchange their products. The others will go out of business. One important feature will be obvious. The financier will obtain a higher share of the profit.

What, then, is interest? It is the toll exacted from society by the holders of gold or the call upon gold, by virtue of the circulating advantage of the latter over all other forms of wealth. The rate of interest varies, not with the capital of society, but with its financial needs and resources, and is one of the factors which determines the speed at which the call on gold circulates.

Analogies are, necessarily, imperfect. The following may serve to present the above idea concretely. Picture a country separated into two parts by an innavigable river. To the south of the river the ground is fertile and crops can be grown in plenty. To the north the ground is well mineralised and favourable for industry. The community is progressing. In time a bridge is thrown over the river. Interchange between the north and south banks leads to specialisation. Industries spring up in the north, agriculture develops in the south. The traffic over the bridge increases in volume.

The owners levy a moderate toll upon it. In time the volume of traffic so grows that it congests the bridge. Industries are checked owing to inability to market the produce. The traffic over the bridge must be speeded up. The owners increase the toll and make it dependent upon the time the traffic takes to cross the bridge. Slow traffic must pay more than fast.

The result is that the vehicles become faster and faster. The owners widen the bridge as much as possible so that it can take a greater volume. The excessive speed of vehicles causes a collision. Traffic is suspended, and both portions of the community are deprived of their necessaries. Slowly the wreckage is cleared, and the traffic gradually gets into its stride again.

The above account gives a representation of modern economic society. The bridge is the gold basis upon which exchange is conducted. The toll for passage over the bridge is the interest paid by society for the call upon gold.

Its rate varies with the speed of circulation. The breakdown is the financial crisis from which industry slowly recovers and speeds up until the inevitable breakdown again happens.

9

Purchasing Power

Monetary Systems and Purchasing Power

Gresham's Law

There are influences that determine the purchasing power of money, when the money in circulation is all of one kind. The money mechanism operates when a single metal is used. We have now to consider the monetary systems in which more than one kind of money is used. One of the first difficulties in the early history of money was that of keeping two (or more) metals in circulation. One of the two would become cheaper than the other, and the cheaper would drive out the dearer.

This tendency was observed by Nicolas Oresme, afterwards Count Bishop of Lisieux, in a report to Charles V of France, about 1366, and by Copernicus about 1526 in a report or treatise written for Sigismund I, King of Poland. Macleod in his Elements of Political Economy, published in 1857,2 before he had become aware of the earlier formulations of Oresme and Copernicus, gave the name 'Gresham's Law' to this tendency, in honour of Sir Thomas Gresham, who stated the principle in the middle of the sixteenth century. The tendency seems in fact, to have been recognised even among the ancient Greeks, being mentioned in the 'Frogs' of Aristophanes:

> "For your old and standard pieces valued and approved and tried, Here among the Grecian nations and in all the world beside, Recognised in every realm for trusty stamp and pure assay, Are rejected and abandoned for the trash of yesterday, For a vile, adulterate issue, drossy, counterfeit, and base Which the traffic of the City passes current in their place."

Gresham's or Oresme's Law is ordinarily stated in the form, "Bad money drives out good money," for it was usually observed that the badly worn, defaced, lightweight, 'clipped,' 'sweated,' and otherwise deteriorated money tended to drive out the full-weight, freshly minted coins. This formulation, however, is not accurate. It is not true that 'bad' coins, e.g. worn, bent, defaced, or even clipped coins, will drive out other money just because of their worn, bent, defaced, or clipped condition. Accurately stated, the Law is simply this: Cheap money will drive out dear money. The reason the cheaper of two moneys always prevails is that the choice of the use of money rests chiefly with the man who gives it in exchange, not with the man who receives it. When any one has the choice of paying his debts in either of two moneys, motives of economy will prompt him to use the cheaper, If the initiative and choice lay principally with the person who receives, instead of the person who pays the money, the opposite would hold true. The dearer or 'good' money would then drive out the cheaper or 'bad' money.

What then becomes of the dearer money? It may be hoarded, or go into the melting pot, or go abroad, - hoarded and melted from motives of economy, and sent abroad because, where foreign trade is involved, it is the foreigner who receives the money, rather than ourselves who give it, who dictates what kind of money shall be accepted. He will take only the best, because our legal-tender laws do not bind him.

The better money might conceivably be used in exchange at a premium, i.e. at its bullion value; but the difficulties of arranging payments in it, which would be satisfactory to both parties, are such that in practice it is never so used in large quantities. In fact, the force of Gresham's Law is so great that it will even sacrifice the convenience of a whole nation. For instance, in Italy fifteen years ago the overissue of paper money drove not only gold across the Alps, but also silver and copper.

These could circulate in Southern France at a par with corresponding coins there because France and Italy belonged to the Latin Union. Consequently, for a time there was very little small change left, below the denomination of 5 lire notes. Customers at retail stores often found it impossible to make their purchases because they lacked the small denominations necessary, and because the storekeeper lacked the same small denominations, and could not make change. To meet the difficulty, 30,000,000 of 1 lire notes were issued, and these were so much in demand that dealers paid a premium for them.

Gresham's Law applies not only to two rival moneys of the same metal; it applies to all moneys that circulate concurrently. Until 'milling' the edges of coins was invented and a 'limit of tolerance' of the mint (deviation from the standard weight) was adopted, much embarrassment was felt in commerce from the fact that the clipping and debasing of coin was a common practice. Nowadays, however, any coin which has been so 'sweated' or clipped as to reduce its weight appreciably ceases to be legal tender, and being commonly rejected by those to whom it is offered ceases to be money. Within the customary or legal limits of tolerance, however - that is, as long as the cheaper money retains the 'money' power - it will drive out the dearer.

Gold Exchange Standard

Bimetallism is today a subject of historical interest only. It is no longer practised; but its former prevalence has left behind it in many countries, including France and the United States, a monetary system which is sometimes called the 'limping' standard. Such a system comes about when, in a system of bimetallism, before either metal can wholly expel the other, the mint is closed to the cheaper of them, but the coinage that has been accomplished up to date is not recalled.

Suppose silver to be the metal thus excluded, as in France and the United States. Any money already coined in that metal and in circulation is kept in circulation at par with gold. This parity may continue even if limited additional amounts of silver be coined from time to time. There will then result a difference in value between silver bullion and silver coin, the silver coin being overvalued.

This situation is represented in figure. Here the pipe connection between the money reservoir and the silver-bullion reservoir has been, as it were, cut off, or, let us say, stopped by a valve which refuses passage of silver from the bullion reservoir to the money reservoir but not the reverse (for no law ever can prevent the melting down of silver coins into bullion). Newly mined silver cannot now become money, and thus lower the purchasing power of the money.

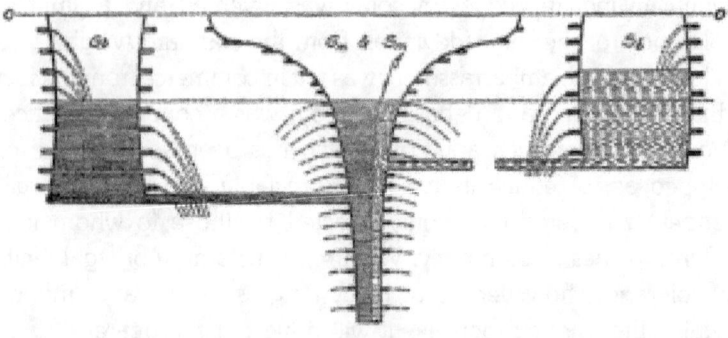

Figure

On the other hand, new supplies of gold continue to affect the value of currency, as before-the value, not only of the gold, but also of the concurrently circulating overvalued silver. If more gold should flow into the money reservoir, it would raise the currency level. Should this level ever become higher than the level of the silver bullion reservoir, silver would flow from the money reservoir into the bullion reservoir; for the passage in that direction (i.e. melting) is still free. So long, however, as the currency level is below the silver level, i.e. so long as the coined silver is worth more than the uncoined, there will be no flow of silver in either direction. The legal prohibition prevents the flow in one direction, and the laws of relative levels prevent its flow in the other.

In the case just discussed, the value of the coined silver will be equal to the value of gold at the legal ratio. Precisely the same principle applies in the case of any money, the coined value of which is greater than the value of its constituent material. Take the case, for instance, of paper money.

So long as it has the distinctive characteristic of money,- general acceptability at its legal value, - and is limited in quantity, its value will ordinarily be equal to that of its legal equivalent in gold. If its quantity increases indefinitely, it will gradually push out all the gold and entirely fill the money reservoir, just as silver would do under bimetallism if produced in sufficiently large amounts. Likewise, credit money and credit in the form of bank deposits would have this effect. To the extent that they are used, they lessen the demand for gold, decrease its value as money, and cause more of it to go into the arts or to other countries.

So long as the quantity of silver or other token money, e.g. paper money, is too small to displace gold completely, gold will continue in circulation. The value of the other money in this case cannot fall below that of gold. For if it should, it would, by Gresham's Law, displace gold, which we have supposed it is not of sufficient quantity to do. The parity between silver coin and gold under the 'limping' standard is, therefore, not necessarily dependent on any redeemability in gold, but may result merely from limitation in the amount of silver coin. Such limitation is usually sufficient to maintain parity despite irredeemability.

This is not always true, however; for if the people should lose confidence in some form of irredeemable paper or token money, even though it were not overissued, it would depreciate and be nearly as cheap in money form as it is in the raw state. A man is willing to accept money at its face value so long as he has confidence that every one else is ready to do the same. But it is possible, for instance, for a mere fear of overissue to destroy this confidence.

The payee, who, under ordinary circumstances, submits patiently to whatever money is customary or legal tender, may then take a hand and insist on 'contracting out' of the offending standard. That is, he may insist on making all his future contracts in terms of the better metal, gold, for instance, and thus contribute to the further downfall of the depreciated paper.

Irredeemable paper money, then, like our irredeemable silver dollars, may circulate at par with other money, if limited in quantity and not too unpopular. If it is gradually increased in amount, such irredeemable money may expel all metallic money and be left in undisputed possession of the field. But though such a result - a condition of irredeemable paper money as the sole currency - is possible, it has seldom if ever proved desirable.

Unless safeguarded, irredeemability is a constant temptation to abuse, and this fact alone causes business distrust and discourages longtime contracts and enterprises. Irredeemable paper money has almost invariably proved a curse to the country employing it. While, therefore, redeemability is not absolutely essential to produce parity of value with the primary money, practically it is a wise precaution.

The lack of redeemability of silver dollars in the United States is one of the chief defects in our unsatisfactory monetary system, and a continuing danger. It is possible to have various degrees of redeemability. One of the most interesting systems of partial redeemability is the system now known as the gold-exchange standard, by which countries, not themselves on a strict gold basis, nevertheless maintain substantial parity with gold through the foreign exchanges. By this system the government or its agent, while not redeeming its currency in gold, redeems it in orders on gold abroad. That is, the government sells bills of exchange on London or New York at a stated price. The currency which it thus receives, and in a sense redeems, it keeps out of circulation until the price of foreign exchange falls (i.e. until the demand for redemption ceases).

The gold-exchange standard may be regarded as a kind of limping standard with the added feature of partial redemption.

This added feature, however, greatly modifies the nature of the limping standard. The limping standard without the gold-exchange attachment may at any time break down, if the silver (or whatever else the overvalued money may be) should become so redundant, relatively to trade, as completely to displace gold. As soon as all gold is driven abroad, parity with gold ceases.

But with the gold-exchange system this catastrophe is avoided. In fact, with this system it is not necessary to have gold in circulation at any time. The willingness of the government to sell foreign exchange at a fixed price, and to lock up the silver it receives thereby, takes that much currency out of circulation just as effectively as though the equivalent of gold had been exported. So long as the government is willing and able to maintain the price of bills of exchange with a gold country, it, *ipso facto*, maintains approximate parity with gold.

Deposit Currency and Purchasing Power

Mystery of Circulating Credit

Here, we explain the nature of bank deposit currency, or circulating credit. Credit, in general, is the claim of a creditor against a debtor. Bank deposits subject to check are the claims of the creditors of a bank against the bank, by virtue of which they may, on demand, draw by check specified sums of money from the bank. Since no other kind of bank deposits will be considered by us, we shall usually refer to 'bank deposits subject to check' simply as 'bank deposits.' They are also called 'circulating credit.' Bank checks, as we have seen, are merely certificates of rights to draw, i.e. to transfer bank deposits. The checks themselves are not the currency; the bank deposits which they represent are the currency.

It is in the connection with the transfer of bank deposits that there arises that so-called 'mystery of banking' called 'circulating credit.' Many persons, including some economists, have supposed that credit is a special form of wealth which may be created out of whole cloth, as it were, by a bank. Others have maintained that credit has no foundation in actual wealth at all, but is a kind of unreal and inflated bubble with a precarious, if not wholly illegitimate, existence. As a matter of fact, bank deposits are as easy to under stand as bank notes, and what is said of bank deposits may in substance be taken as true also of bank notes. The chief difference is a formal one, the notes circulating from hand to hand, while the deposit currency circulates only by means of special orders called 'checks.'

To understand the real nature of bank deposits, let us imagine a hypothetical institution, a kind of primitive bank existing mainly for the sake of deposits and the safe keeping of actual money. The original bank of Amsterdam was somewhat like the bank we are now imagining. In such a bank a number of people deposit $100,000 in gold, each accepting a receipt for the amount of his deposit. If this bank should issue a 'capital account,' or statement, it would show $100,000 in its vaults and $100,000 owed to depositors, as follows:

Assets	Liabilities
Gold .. $100,000	Due depositors .. $100,000

The right-hand side of the statement is, of course, made up of smaller amounts owed to individual depositors. Assuming that there is owed to A, $10,000, to B, $10,000, and to all others $80,000, we may write the bank statement as follows:

Assets		Liabilities	
Gold	$100,000	Due depositor A ..	$10,000
		Due depositor B ..	10,000
		Due other depositors	80,000
	$100,000		$100,000

Purchasing Power

Now assume that A wishes to pay B $1000. A could go to the bank with B, present certificates or checks for $1000, obtain the gold, and hand it over to B, who might then redeposit it in the same bank, merely handing it back through the cashier's window and taking a new certificate in his own name. Instead, however, of both A and B visiting the bank and handling the money, A might simply give B a check for $1000. The transfer in either case would mean that A's holding in the bank was reduced from $10,000 to $9000, and that B's was increased from $10,000 to $11,000. The statement would then read: -

Assets		Liabilities	
Gold	$100,000	Due depositor A	$ 9,000
		Due depositor B	11,000
		Due other depositors	80,000
	$100,000		$100,000

Thus the certificates, or checks, would circulate in place of cash among the various depositors in the bank. What really changes ownership, or 'circulates,' in such cases is the right to draw money. The check is merely the evidence of this right and of the transfer of this right from one person to another.

In the case under consideration, the bank would be conducted at a loss. It would be giving the time and labour of its clerical force for the accommodation of its depositors, without getting anything in return. But such a hypothetical bank would soon find - much as did the bank of Amsterdam-that it could 'make money' by lending at interest some of the gold on deposit. This could not offend the depositors; for they do not expect or desire to get back the identical gold they deposited.

What they want is simply to be able at any time to obtain the same amount of gold. Since, then, their arrangement with the bank calls for the payment, not of any particular gold, but merely of a definite amount, and that but occasionally, the bank finds itself free to lend out part of the gold that otherwise would lie idle in its vaults. To keep it idle would be a great and needless waste of opportunity.

Let us suppose, then, that the bank decides to loan out half its cash. This is usually done in exchange for promissory notes of the borrowers. Now a loan is really an exchange of money for a promissory note which the lender - in this case the bank - receives in place of the gold. Let us suppose that so-called borrowers actually draw out $50,000 of gold. The bank thereby exchanges money for promises, and its books will then read:

Assets		Liabilities	
Gold reserve	$50,000	Due depositor A	$9,000
Promissory notes	50,000	Due depositor B	11,000
		Due other depositors	80,000
	$100,000		$100,000

It will be noted that now the gold in the bank is only $50,000, while the total deposits are still $100,000. In other words, the depositors now have more 'money on deposit' than the bank has in its vaults! But, as will be shown, this form of expression involves a popular fallacy in the word 'money.' Something good is behind each loan, but not necessarily money. Suppose that the borrowers become, in a sense, depositors also, by redepositing the $50,000 of cash which they borrowed, in return for the right to draw out the same sum on demand. In other words, suppose that after borrowing $50,000 from the bank, they lend it back to the bank. The bank's assets will thus be enlarged by $50,000, and its obligations (or credit extended) will be equally enlarged; and the balance sheet will become:

Assets		Liabilities	
Gold reserve	$100,000	Due depositor A	$9,000
Promissory notes	50,000	Due depositor B	11,000
		Due old depositors	80,000
		Due new depositors, i.e. the borrowers	50,000
	$150,000		$150,000

What happened in this case was the following: Gold was borrowed in exchange for a promissory note and then handed

Purchasing Power

back in exchange for a right to draw. Thus the gold really did not budge; but the bank received a promissory note and the depositor a right to draw.

Evidently, therefore, the same result would have followed if each borrower had merely handed in his promissory note and received, in exchange, a right to draw. As this operation most frequently puzzles the beginner in the study of banking, we repeat the tables representing the conditions before and after these 'loans,' i.e. these exchanges of promissory notes for present rights to draw.

Before the Loans

Assets		Liabilities	
Gold reserve . . .	$100,000	Due depositors . .	$100,000

After the Loans

Gold reserve. . . .	$100,000	Due depositors . .	$150,000
Promissory notes . .	.50,000		

Clearly, therefore, the intermediation of the money in this case is a needless complication, though it may help to a theoretical understanding of the resultant shifting of rights and liabilities. Thus the bank may receive deposits of gold or deposits of promises. In exchange for the promises it may give, or lend, either a right to draw, or gold, - the same that was deposited by another customer. Even when the borrower has only a promise, by fiction he is still held to have deposited money; and like the original cash depositors, he is given the right to make out checks.

The total value of rights to draw, in whichever way arising, is termed 'deposits.' Banks more often lend rights to draw (or deposit rights) than actual cash, partly because of the greater convenience to borrowers, and partly because the banks wish to keep their cash reserves large, in order to meet large or unexpected demands. It is true that if a bank loans money, part of the money so loaned will be redeposited by the persons to whom the borrowers pay it in the course of business; but it will not necessarily be redeposited in the same bank. Hence the average banker prefers that the borrower should not withdraw actual cash.

Besides lending deposit rights, banks may also lend their own notes, called 'bank notes.' And the principle governing bank notes is the same as the principle governing deposit rights. The holder simply gets a pocketful of bank notes instead of a bank account. In either case the bank must be always ready to pay the holder - to 'redeem its notes' - as well as pay its depositors, on demand, and in either case the bank exchanges a promise for a promise. In the case of the note, the bank has exchanged its bank note for a customer's promissory note. The bank note carries no interest, but is payable on demand. The customer's note bears interest, but is payable only at a definite date. Assuming that the bank issues $50,000 of notes, the balance sheet will now become:

Assets		Liabilities	
Gold reserve	$100,000	Due depositors	$150,000
Loans	100,000	Due note holders	50,000
	$200,000		$200,000

We repeat that by means of credit the deposits (and notes) of a bank may exceed its cash. There would be nothing mysterious or obscure about this fact, nor about credit in general, if people could be induced not to think of banking operations as money operations. To so represent them is metaphorical and misleading. They are no more money operations than they are real estate transactions. A bank depositor, A, has not ordinarily 'deposited money'; and whether he has or not, he certainly cannot properly say that he 'has money in the bank.' What he does have is the bank's promise to pay money on demand. The bank owes him money. When a private person owes money, the creditor never thinks of saying that he has it on deposit in the debtor's pocket.

Proportioned Deposit Currency

With the extension of the equation of monetary circulation to include deposit circulation, the influence exerted by the quantity of money on general prices becomes less direct; and the process of tracing this influence becomes more difficult and complicated. It has even been argued that this interposition of circulating credit breaks whatever connection there may be between prices and the quantity of money. This would be true if circulating credit were independent of money. But the fact is that the quantity of circulating credit, M', tends to hold a definite relation to M, the quantity of money in circulation; that is, deposits are normally a more or less definite multiple of money.

Two facts normally give deposits a more or less definite ratio to money. The first has been already explained, viz. that bank reserves are kept in a more or less definite ratio to bank deposits. The second is that individuals, firms, and corporations preserve more or less definite ratios between their cash transactions and their check transactions, and also between their money and deposit balances. These ratios are determined by motives of individual convenience and habit. In general, business firms use money for wage payments, and for small miscellaneous transactions included under the term 'petty cash'; while for settlements with each other they usually prefer checks. These preferences are so strong that we could not imagine them overridden except temporarily and to a small degree.

A business firm would hardly pay car fares with checks and liquidate its large liabilities with cash. Each person strikes an equilibrium between his use of the two methods of payment, and does not greatly disturb it except for short periods of time. He keeps his stock of money or his bank balance in constant adjustment to the payments he makes in money or by check. Whenever his stock of money becomes relatively small and his bank balance relatively large, he cashes a check. In the opposite event, he deposits cash. In this way he is constantly converting one of the two media of exchange into the other. A private individual usually feeds his purse from his bank account; a retail commercial firm usually feeds its bank account from its till. The bank acts as intermediary for both.

In a given community the quantitative relation of deposit currency to money is determined by several considerations of convenience. In the first place, the more highly developed the business of a community, the more prevalent the use of checks.

Where business is conducted on a large scale, merchants habitually transact their larger operations with each other by means of checks, and their smaller ones by means of cash. Again, the more concentrated the population, the more prevalent the use of checks.

In cities it is more convenient both for the payer and the payee to make large payments by check whereas, in the country, trips to a bank are too expensive in time and effort to be convenient, and therefore more money is used in proportion to the amount of business done. Again, the wealthier the members of the community, the more largely will they use checks. Labourers seldom use them; but capitalists, professional and salaried men use them habitually, for personal as well as business transactions.

There is, then, a relation of convenience and custom between check and cash circulation, and a more or less stable ratio between the deposit balance of the average man or corporation and the stock of money kept in pocket or till. This fact, as applied to the country as a whole, means that by convenience a rough ratio is fixed between M and M'. If that ratio is disturbed temporarily, there will come into play a tendency to restore it. Individuals will deposit surplus cash, or they will cash surplus deposits. Hence, both money in circulation (as shown above) and money in reserve (as shown previously) tend to keep in a fixed ratio to deposits. It follows that the two must be in a fixed ratio to each other.

It further follows that any change in M, the quantity of money in circulation, requiring as it normally does a proportional change in M', the volume of bank deposits subject to check, will result in an exactly proportional change in the general level of prices except, of course, so far as this effect be interfered with by concomitant changes in the V's or the Q's. The truth of this proposition is evident from the equation $MV + M'V' = 2pQ$; for if, say, M and M' are doubled, while V and V' remain the same, the left side of the equation is doubled and therefore the right side must be doubled also. But if the Q's remain unchanged, then evidently all the p's must be doubled, or else if some are less than doubled, others must be enough more than doubled to compensate.

Purchasing Power

Disturbance of Equation and of Purchasing Power

Tardiness of Interest Adjustment to Price Movements

The quantity of bank deposits normally maintains a definite ratio to the quantity of money in circulation and to the amount of bank reserves. As long as this normal relation holds, the existence of bank deposits merely magnifies the effect on the level of prices produced by the quantity of money in circulation and does not in the least distort that effect.

Moreover, changes in velocity or trade will have the same effect on prices, whether bank deposits are included or not. But during periods of transition this relation between money (M) and deposits (M') is by no means rigid.

Here, we study these periods of transition. The change which constitutes a transition may be a change in the quantity of money, or in any other factor of the equation of exchange, or in all. Usually all are involved, but the chief factor which we shall select for study (together with its effect on the other factors) is quantity of money. If the quantity of money were suddenly doubled, the effect of the change would not be the same at first as later.

The ultimate effect is, to double prices; but before this happens, the prices oscillate up and down. The temporary effects during the period of transition separately from the permanent or ultimate effects which were considered. These permanent or ultimate effects follow after a new equilibrium is established, - if, indeed, such a condition as equilibrium may be said ever to be established. What we are concerned the temporary effects, i.e. those in the transition period.

The transition periods may be characterised either by rising prices or by falling prices. Rising prices must be clearly distinguished from high prices, and falling from low. With stationary levels, high or low. Our concern is with rising or falling prices. Rising prices mark the transition between a low and a high level of prices, just as a hill marks the transition between flat lowlands and flat highlands.

Since the study of these acclivities and declivities is bound up with that of the adjustment of interest rates, our first task is to present a brief statement regarding the effects of rising and falling prices on the rate of interest Indeed, the chief object to show that the peculiar behaviour of the rate of interest during transition periods is largely responsible for the crises and depressions in which price movements end.

It must be borne in mind that although business loans are made in the form of money, yet whenever a man borrows money, he does not do this in order to hoard the money, but to purchase goods with it. To all intents and purposes, therefore, when A borrows one dollars from B in order to purchase, say, one hundred units of a given commodity at one dollar per unit, it may be said that B is virtually lending A one hundred units of that commodity. And if at the end of a year A returns one hundred dollars to B, but the price of the commodity has meanwhile advanced, then B has lost a fraction of the purchasing power originally loaned to A. For even though A should happen to return to B the identical coins in which the loan was made, these coins represent somewhat less than the original quantity of purchasable commodities.

Bearing this in mind in our investigation of interest rates, let us suppose that prices are rising at the rate of 3 per cent each year. It is plain that the man who lends $100 at the beginning of the year must, in order to get 5 per cent interest in purchasing power, receive back both $103 (then the equivalent of the $100 lent) plus 5 per cent of this, or a total of $108.15. That is, in order to get 5 per cent interest in actual purchasing power, he must receive a little more than 8 per cent interest in money. The 3 per cent rise of prices thus ought to add approximately 3 per cent to the rate of interest. Rising prices, therefore, in order that the relations between creditor and debtor shall be the same during the rise as before and after, require higher money interest than stationary prices require.

Not only will lenders require, but borrowers can afford to pay higher interest in terms of money; and to some extent competition will gradually force them to do so. Yet we are so accustomed in our business dealings to consider money as the one thing stable, - to think of a 'dollar as a dollar' regardless of the passage of time, that we reluctantly yield to this process of readjustment, thus rendering it very slow and imperfect.

When prices are rising at the rate of 3 per cent a year, and the normal rate of interest-i.e. the rate which would exist were prices stationary - is 5 per cent, the actual rate, though it ought (in order to make up for the rising prices) to be 8.15 per cent, will not ordinarily reach that figure; but it may reach, say, 6 per cent, and later, 7 per cent. This inadequacy and tardiness of adjustment are fostered, moreover, by law and custom, which arbitrarily tend to keep down the rate of interest.

A similar inadequacy of adjustment is observed when prices are falling. Suppose that, by the end of a year, $97 will buy as much as $100 at the beginning. In that case the lender, in order to get back a purchasing power equivalent to his principal and 5 per cent interest, should get, not $105, but only $97 + 5 per cent of $97 or $101.85.

Thus the rate of interest in money should in this case be 1.85 per cent, or less than 2 per cent, instead of the original 5 per cent. In other words, the 3 per cent fall of prices should reduce the rate of interest by approximately 3 per cent. But as a matter of fact, such a perfect adjustment is seldom reached, and money interest keeps far above 2 per cent for a considerable time.

How a Rise of Prices Generates a Further Rise?

We are now ready to study temporary or transitional changes in the factors of our equation of exchange. Let us begin by assuming a slight initial disturbance, such as would be produced, for instance, by an increase in the quantity of gold. This, through the equation of exchange, will cause a rise in prices. As prices rise, profits of business men, measured in money, will rise also, even if the costs of business were to rise in the same proportion. Thus, if a man who sold $10,000 of goods at a cost of $6000, thus clearing $4000, could get double prices at double cost, his profit would be double also, being $20,000 - $12,000, which is $8000. Of course such a rise of prices would be purely nominal, as it would merely keep pace with the rise in price level.

The business man would gain no advantage, for his larger money profits would buy no more than his former smaller money profits bought before. But, as a matter of fact, the business man's profits will rise more than this because the rate of interest he has to pay will not adjust itself immediately. Among his costs is interest, and this cost will not, at first, rise.

Thus the profits will rise faster than prices. Consequently, he will find himself making greater profits than usual, and be encouraged to expand his business by increasing his borrowings. These borrowings are mostly in the form of short-time loans from banks; and, as we have seen, short-time loans engender deposits. As is well known, the correspondence between loans and deposits is remarkably exact.

Therefore, deposit currency (AT) will increase, but this extension of deposit currency tends further to raise the general level of prices, just as the increase of gold raised it in the first place. Hence prices, which were already outstripping the rate of interest, tend to outstrip it still further, enabling borrowers, who were already increasing their profits, to increase them still further.

More loans are demanded, and although nominal interest may be forced up somewhat, still it keeps lagging below the normal level. Yet nominally the rate of interest has increased; and hence the lenders, too, including banks, are led to become more enterprising. Beguiled by the higher nominal rates into the belief that fairly high interest is being realised, they extend their loans, and with the resulting expansion of bank loans, deposit currency (M'), already expanded, expands still more. Also, if prices are rising, the money value of collateral may be greater, making it easier for borrowers to get large credit. Hence prices rise still further. This sequence of events may be briefly stated as follows:

- Prices rise (whatever the first cause may be; but we have chosen for illustration an increase in the amount of gold).

Purchasing Power

- The rate of interest rises, but not sufficiently,
- Enterprisers (to use Professor Fetter's term), encouraged by large profits, expand their loans.
- Deposit currency (M') expands relatively to money (M).
- Prices continue to rise, that is, phenomenon No. 1 is repeated. Then No. 2 is repeated, and so on.

In other words, a slight initial rise of prices sets in motion a train of events which tends to repeat itself. Rise of prices generates rise of prices, and continues to do so as long as the interest rate lags behind its normal figure.

Extent of Disturbances in Equation

The expansion of deposit currency indicated in this cumulative movement abnormally increases the ratio of M' to M. This is evident if the rise of prices begins in a change in some element or elements in the equation other than the quantity of money; for if M remains constant and M' increases, the ratio M' to M must increase also. If M increases in any ratio, M' will increase in a greater ratio. If it increased only in the same ratio, prices would increase in that ratio (assuming velocities and quantities unchanged); and if prices increased in that ratio, loans (which being made to buy goods must be adjusted to the prices of goods) would have to be increased in that ratio in order to secure merely the same goods as before. But enterprisers, wishing to profit by the lag in interest, would extend the loans beyond this old or original point. Therefore, deposits based on loans would increase in a greater ratio. That is, the ratio M' to M would increase. In other words, during the period while M is increasing, M' increases still faster, thus disturbing the normal ratio between these two forms of currency.

This, however, is not the only disturbance caused by the increase in M. There are disturbances in the Q's (or in other words T) in F, and in V' These will be taken up in order. Trade (the Q's) will be stimulated by the easy terms for loans. This effect is always observed during rising prices, and people note approvingly that 'business is good' and 'times are booming.' Such statements represent the point of view of the ordinary business man who is an 'enterpriser-borrower.' They do not represent the sentiments of the creditor, the salaried man, or the labourer, most of whom are silent but long-suffering, paying higher prices, but not getting proportionally higher incomes.

The first cause of the unhealthy increase in trade lies in the fact that prices, like interest, lag behind their full adjustment and have to be pushed up, so to speak, by increased purchases. This is especially true in cases where the original impetus came from an increase in money. The surplus money is first expended at nearly the old price level, but its continued expenditure gradually raises prices. In the meantime the volume of purchases will be somewhat greater than it would have been had prices risen more promptly. In fact, from the point of view of those who are selling goods, it is the possibility of a greater volume of sales at the old prices which gives encouragement to an increase of prices. Seeing that they can find purchasers for more goods than before at the previously prevailing prices, or for as many goods as before at higher prices, they will charge these higher prices.

But the amount of trade is dependent, almost entirely, on other things than the quantity of currency, so that an increase of currency cannot, even temporarily, very greatly increase trade. In ordinarily good times practically the whole community is engaged in labour, producing, transporting, and exchanging goods. The increase of currency of a 'boom' period cannot, of itself, increase the population, extend invention, or increase the efficiency of labour.

These factors pretty definitely limit the amount of trade which can be reasonably carried on. So, although the gains of the enterpriser-borrower may exert a psychological stimulus on trade, though a few unemployed may be employed, and some others in a few lines induced to work overtime, and although there may be some additional buying and selling which is speculative, yet almost the entire effect of an increase of deposits must be seen in a change of prices. Normally the entire effect would so express itself, but transitionally there will be also some increase in the Q's.

Here, we observe that the rise in prices - fall in the purchasing power of money - will accelerate the circulation of money. We all hasten to get rid of any commodity which, like ripe fruit, is spoiling on our hands. Money is no exception; when it is depreciating, holders will get rid of it as fast as possible. As they view it, their motive is to buy goods which appreciate in terms of money in order to profit by the rise in their value. The inevitable result is that these goods rise in price still further. The series of changes, then, initiated by rising prices, expressed more fully than before, is as follows:

- Prices rise.
- Velocities of circulation (V and V') increase; the rate of interest rises, but not sufficiently.
- Profits increase, loans expand, and the Q's in crease.
- Deposit currency (M') expands relatively to money (M).
- Prices continue to rise; that is, phenomenon No. 1 is repeated. Then No. 2 is repeated, and so on.

It will be noticed that these changes now involve all the magnitudes in the equation of exchange. They are temporary changes, pertaining only to the transition period. They are like temporary increases in power and readjustments in an automobile climbing a hill.

How a Rise of Prices Culminates in a Crisis?

Evidently the expansion coming from this cycle of causes cannot proceed forever. It must ultimately spend itself. The check upon its continued operation lies in the rate of interest. It was the tardiness of the rise in interest that was responsible for the abnormal condition. But the rise in interest, though belated, is progressive, and, as soon as it overtakes the rate of rise in prices, the whole situation is changed. If prices are rising at the rate of 2 per cent per annum, the boom will continue only until interest becomes

2 per cent higher. It then offsets the rate of rise in prices. The banks are forced in self-defence to raise interest because they cannot stand so abnormal an expansion of loans relatively to reserves. As soon as the interest rate becomes adjusted, borrowers can no longer hope to make great profits, and the demand for loans ceases to expand.

There are also other forces placing a limitation on further expansion of deposit currency and introducing a tendency to contraction. Not only is the amount of deposit currency limited both by law and by prudence to a certain maximum multiple of the amount of bank reserves; but bank reserves are themselves limited by the amount of money available for use as reserves. Further, with the rise of interest, the value of certain collateral securities, such as bonds, on the basis of which loans are made, begins to fall.

Such securities, being worth the discounted value of, fixed sums, fall as interest rises; and therefore they cannot be used as collateral for loans as large as before. This check to loans is, as previously explained, a check to deposits also.

With the rise of interest, those who have counted on renewing their loans at the former rates and for the former amounts are unable to do so. It follows that some of them are destined to fail. The failure (or prospect of failure) of firms that have borrowed heavily from banks induces fear on the part of many depositors that the banks will not be able to realise on these loans.

Hence the banks themselves fall under suspicion, and for this reason depositors demand cash. Then occur 'runs on the banks,' which deplete the bank reserves at the very moment they are most needed. Being short of reserves, the banks have to curtail their loans. It is then that the rate of interest rises to a panic figure. Those enterprisers who are caught must have currency to liquidate their obligations, and to get it are willing to pay high interest. Some of them are destined to become bankrupt, and, with their failure, the demand for loans is correspondingly reduced. This culmination of an upward price movement is what is called a crisis,- a condition characterised by bankruptcies, and the bankruptcies being due to a lack of cash when it is most needed.

It is generally recognised that the collapse of bank credit brought about by loss of confidence is the essential fact of every crisis, be the cause of the loss of confidence what it may. What is not generally recognised, and what it is desired to emphasise, is that this loss of confidence (in the typical commercial crisis here described) is a consequence of a belated adjustment in the interest rate.

It is not our purpose here to discuss non-monetary causes of crises, further than to say that the monetary causes are the most important when taken in connection with the maladjustments in the rate of interest The other factors often emphasised are merely effects of this maladjustment. 'Overconsumption' and 'overinvestment' are cases in point.

The reason many people spend more than they can afford is that they are relying on the dollar as a stable unit when as a matter of fact its purchasing power is rapidly falling. The bondholder, for instance, is beguiled into trenching on his capital He never dreams that he ought to lay by a sinking fund because the decrease in purchasing power of money is reducing the real value of his principal.

Again, the stockholder and enterpriser generally are beguiled by a vain reliance on the stability of the rate of interest, and so they overinvest. It is true that for a time they are gaining what the bondholder is losing and are therefore justified in both spending and investing more than if prices were not rising; and at first they prosper. But sooner or later the rate of interest rises above what they had reckoned on, and they awake to the fact that they have embarked on enterprises which cannot pay these high rates. Then a curious thing happens: borrowers, unable to get easy loans, blame the high rate of interest for conditions which were really due to the fact that the previous rate of interest was not high enough. Had the previous rate been high enough, the borrowers never would have overinvested.

Completion of the Credit Cycle

The contraction of loans and deposits is accompanied by a decrease in velocities, and these conspire to prevent a further rise of prices and tend towards a fall. The crest of the wave is reached and a reaction sets in. Since prices have stopped rising, the rate of interest, which has risen to compensate the rise of prices, should fall again. But just as at first it was slow to rise, so now it is slow to fall. In fact, it tends for a time to rise still further.

The mistakes of the past of overborrowing compel the unfortunate victims of these mistakes to borrow still further to protect their solvency. It is this special abnormality which marks the period as a 'crisis.' Loans are wanted to continue old debts or to pay these debts by creating new ones.

They are not wanted because of new investments but because of obligations connected with old (and ill-fated) investments. The problem is how to get extricated from the meshes of past commitments. It is the problem of liquidation, Even when interest begins to fall, it falls slowly, and failures continue to occur. Borrowers now find that interest, though nominally low, is still hard to meet. Especially do they find this true in the case of contracts made just before prices ceased rising or just before they began to fall. The rate of interest in these cases is agreed upon before the change in conditions takes place.

There will, In consequence, be little if any adjustment in lowering nominal interest. Because interest is hard to pay, failures continue to occur. There comes to be a greater hesitation in lending on any but the best security, and a hesitation to borrow save when the prospects of success are the greatest. Bank loans tend to be low, and consequently deposits (M') are reduced. The contraction of deposit currency makes prices fall still more. Those who have borrowed for the purpose of buying stocks of goods now find they cannot sell them for enough even to pay back what they have borrowed. Owing to this tardiness of the interest rate in falling to a lower and a normal level, the sequence of events is now the opposite of what it was before:

- Prices fall.
- The rate of interest falls, but not sufficiently.
- Enterpriser-borrowers, discouraged by small profits, contract their borrowings.
- Deposit currency (M') contracts relatively to money (M).
- Prices continue to fall; that is, phenomenon No. 1 is repeated. Then No. 2 is repeated, and so on.

Thus a fall of prices generates a further fall of prices. The cycle evidently repeats itself as long as the rate of interest lags behind. The man who loses most is the business man in debt. He is the typical business man, and he now complains that 'business is bad.' There is a 'depression of trade.'

During this depression, velocities (V and V) are abnormally low. People are less hasty to spend money or checks when the dollars they represent are rising in purchasing power. The Q's (or quantities in trade) decline because (1) the initiators, of trade - the enterpriser-borrowers-are discouraged; (2) the inertia of high prices can be overcome only by a falling off of expenditures; (3) trade against money which alone the Q's represent gives way somewhat to barter. For a time there is not enough money to do the business which has to be done at existing prices, for these prices are still high and will not immediately adjust themselves to the sudden contraction. When such a 'money famine' exists, there is no way of doing all the business except by eking out money transactions with barter. But while recourse to barter eases the first fall of prices, the inconvenience of barter immediately begins to operate as an additional force tending to reduce prices by inducing sellers to sell at a sacrifice if only money can be secured and barter avoided; although this effect is partly neutralised for a time by a decrease in the amount of business which people will attempt under such adverse conditions. A statement including these factors is:

- Prices fall.
- Velocities of circulation (F and V) fall; the rate of interest falls, but not sufficiently.

- Profits decrease; loans and the Q's decrease.
- Deposit currency (M') contracts relatively to money (M).

Prices continue to fall; that is, phenomenon No. 1 is repeated. Then No. 2 is repeated, and so on. The contraction brought about by this cycle of causes becomes self-limiting as soon as the rate of interest overtakes the rate of fall in prices. After a time, normal conditions begin to return. The weakest producers have been forced out, or have at least been prevented from expanding their business by increased loans.

The strongest firms are left to build up a new credit structure. The continuous fall of prices has made it impossible for most borrowers to pay the old high rates of interest; the demand for loans diminishes, and interest falls to a point such that borrowers can at last pay it. Borrowers again become willing to take ventures; failures decrease in number; bank loans cease to decrease; prices cease to fall; borrowing and carrying on business become profitable; loans are again demanded; prices again begin to rise, and there occurs a repetition of the upward movement already described.

We have considered the rise, culmination, fall, and recovery of prices. These changes are abnormal oscillations, due to some initial disturbance. The upward and downward movements taken together constitute a complete credit cycle, which resembles the forward and backward movements of a pendulum. In most cases the time occupied by the swing of the commercial pendulum to and fro is about ten years.

While the pendulum is continually seeking a stable position, practically there is almost always some occurrence to prevent perfect equilibrium. Oscillations are set up which, though tending to be self-corrective, are continually perpetuated by fresh disturbances. Any cause which disturbs equilibrium will suffice to set up oscillations. One of the most common of such causes is an increase in the quantity of money. Another is a shock to business confidence (affecting enterprise, loans, and deposits). A third is short crops, affecting the Q's. A fourth is invention.

The factors in the equation of exchange are therefore continually seeking normal adjustment. A ship in a calm sea will 'pitch' only a few times before coming to rest, but in a high sea the pitching never ceases. While continually seeking equilibrium, the ship continually encounters causes which accentuate the oscillation.

The factors seeking mutual adjustment are money in circulation, deposits, their velocities, the Q's and the p's. These magnitudes must always be linked together by the equation $MV + M'V' = 2pQ$, This represents the mechanism of exchange. But in order to conform to such a relation the displacement of any one part of the mechanism spreads its effects during the transition period over all parts. Since periods of transition are the rule and those of equilibrium the exception, the mechanism of exchange is almost always in a dynamic rather than a static condition.

It must not be assumed that every credit cycle is so marked as to produce artificially excessive business activity at one time and 'hard times' at another. The rhythm may be more or less extreme in the width of its fluctuations. If banks are conservative in making loans during the periods of rising prices, and the expansion of credit currency is therefore limited, the rise of prices is likewise limited, and the succeeding fall is apt to be less and to take place more gradually. If there were a better appreciation of the meaning of changes in the price level and an endeavour to balance these changes by adjustment in the rate of interest, the oscillations might be very greatly mitigated.

It is the lagging behind of the rate of interest which allows the oscillations to reach so great proportions. On this point Marshall well says: "The cause of alternating periods of inflation and depression of commercial activity . . . is intimately connected with those variations in the real rate of interest which are caused by changes in the purchasing power of money. For when prices are likely to rise, people rush to borrow money and buy goods, and thus help prices to rise; business is inflated, and is managed recklessly and wastefully; those working on borrowed capital pay back less real value than they borrowed, and enrich themselves at the expense of the community.

When afterwards credit is shaken and prices begin to fall, every one wants to get rid of commodities which are falling in value and to get hold of money which is rapidly rising; this makes prices fall all the faster, and the further fall makes credit shrink even more, and thus for a long time prices fall because prices have fallen."

A somewhat different sort of cycle is the seasonal fluctuation which occurs annually. Such fluctuations, for the most part, are due, not to the departure from a state of equilibrium, but rather to a continuous adjustment to conditions, which, though changing, are normal and expected. As the autumn periods of harvesting and crop moving approach, there is a tendency towards a lower level of prices, followed after the passing of this period and the approach of winter by a rise of prices.

We have analysed the phenomena characteristic of periods of transition. We have found that one such 'boom' period leads to a reaction, and that the action and reaction complete a cycle of 'prosperity' and 'depression.' It has been seen that rising prices tend towards a higher nominal interest, and falling prices tend towards a lower, but that in general the adjustment is incomplete. With any initial rise of prices comes an expansion of loans, owing to the fact that interest does not at once adjust itself. This produces profits for the enterpriser-borrower, and his demand for loans further extends deposit currency.

This extension still further raises prices, a result accentuated by a rise in velocities though somewhat mitigated by an increase in trade. When interest has become adjusted to rising prices, and loans and deposits have reached the limit set for them by the bank reserves and other conditions, the fact that prices no longer are rising necessitates a new adjustment. Those whose business has been unduly extended now find the high rates of interest oppressive. Failures result, constituting a commercial crisis. A reaction sets in;

a reverse movement is initiated. A fall of prices, once begun, tends to be accelerated for reasons exactly corresponding to those which operate in the opposite situation.

Making Purchasing Power More Stable

Problem of Monetary Reforms

The purchasing power of money (or its reciprocal, the level of prices) depends exclusively on five factors, viz.: the quantity of money in circulation, its velocity of circulation, the quantity of deposits subject to check, its velocity, and the volume of trade. Each of these five magnitudes depends on numerous antecedent causes, but they do not depend on each other except that:

- Deposits subject to check depend on money in circulation, the two normally varying in unison.

- The velocities of circulation of money and deposits tend to increase with an increase in the volume of trade.

- Any two or more of the five factors may be in directly related by virtue of being dependent on a common cause or causes. Thus, the same invention may cause an increase in both velocities, or in both money and trade, or in both deposits and their velocity. To take an historical case, we know that the growing density of population has operated to increase all of the five factors.

- During transition periods certain temporary disturbances or oscillations occur in all six magnitudes, the extremes of which are crises and depressions. Normally, the price level is an effect and not a cause in the equation of exchange; but during such transition periods its fluctuations temporarily react on the other five factors, and especially on deposits. A rise will thus temporarily generate a further rise, while a fall temporarily operates in the opposite direction.

The price level, then, is the result of the five great causes mentioned, normally varying directly with the quantity of money (and with deposits which normally vary in unison with the quantity of money), provided that the velocities of circulation and the volume of trade remain unchanged, and that there be a given state of development of deposit banking. This is one of the chief propositions concerning the level of prices or its reciprocal, the purchasing power of money. It constitutes the so-called quantity theory of money.

The qualifying adverb 'normally' is inserted in the formulation in order to provide for the transitional periods or credit cycles. Practically, this proposition is an exact law of proportion, as exact and as fundamental in economic science as the exact law of proportion between pressure and density of gases in physics, assuming temperature to remain the same.

It is, of course, true that, in practice, velocities and trade seldom remain unchanged, just as it seldom happens that temperature remains unchanged. But the tendency represented in the quantity theory remains true, whatever happens to the other elements involved, just as the tendency represented in the density theory remains true whatever happens to temperature.

Only those who fail to grasp the significance of what a scientific law really is can fail to see the significance and importance of the quantitative law of money. A scientific law is not a formulation of statistics or of history. It is a formulation of what holds true under given conditions. Statistics and history can be used to illustrate and verify laws only by making suitable allowances for changed conditions. It is by making such allowances that we have pursued our study of the last ten centuries in the rough and of the last decade and a half in detail. In each case we found the facts in accord with the principles previously formulated.

From a practical point of view the most serious problem revealed by this historical and statistical study is the problem of stability and dependability in the purchasing power of money. We find that this purchasing power is subject to wide variations in two ways: (1) It oscillates up and down with the transitional periods constituting credit cycles; and (2) it is likely to suffer secular variations in either direction according to the incidents of industrial changes. The first transition is connected with the banking system; the second depends largely upon the money metal.

One method of mitigating both of these evils is the increase of knowledge as to prospective price levels. As we have seen, the real evils of changing price levels do not lie in these changes per se, but in the fact that they usually take us unawares. It has been shown that to be forewarned is to be forearmed, and that a foreknown change in price levels might be so taken into account in the rate of interest as to neutralise its evils. While we cannot expect our knowledge of the future ever to become so perfect as to reach this ideal, viz. compensations for every price fluctuation by corresponding adjustments in the rate of interest - nevertheless every increase in our knowledge carries us a little nearer that remote ideal.

Fortunately, such increase in knowledge is now going on rapidly. The editors of trade journals scan the economic horizon as weather predictors scan the physical horizon; and every indication of a change in the economic weather is noted and commented upon. Within the past year a certain firm has instituted a statistical service to supply bankers, brokers, and merchants with records, or 'business barometers,' and forecasts based thereon, with the avowed object of preventing panics. Yet it is probably in regard to the fundamental mechanism by which such forecasts are based that there is the greatest need of a wider diffusion of knowledge.

The range of the ordinary business man's theoretical knowledge is extremely narrow. He is even apt to be suspicious of such knowledge, if not to hold it in contempt. The consequences of this narrowness are often disastrous, as, for instance, when, in pursuance of the advice of New York business men, Secretary Chase issued the greenbacks, or when the ill-advised legislation to close the Gold Room was enacted. And it is not altogether in unusual predicaments such as those brought by the Civil War that the business man's limitations in knowledge react injuriously upon him. Every day he is hampered by a lack of understanding of the principles regulating the purchasing power of money; and in proportion as he fails to understand these principles he is apt to fail in predictions.

The prejudice of business men against the variability of, and especially against a rise of the rate of interest, probably stands in the way of prompt adjustment in that rate and helps to aggravate the far more harmful variability in the level of prices and its reciprocal, the purchasing power of money. The business man has, in fact, never regarded it as a part of the preparation for his work to understand the broad principles affecting money and interest. He has rather assumed that his province was confined to accumulating a technical acquaintance with the nature of the goods he handles. The sugar merchant informs himself as to sugar, the grain merchant as to grain, the real estate trader as to real estate. It scarcely occurs to any of them that he needs a knowledge as to gold; yet every bargain into which he enters depends for one of its two terms on gold. One cannot but believe that the diffusion among business men of the fuller knowledge of the equation of exchange, of the relation of money to deposits, of credit cycles and of interest, which the future is sure to bring, will pay rich returns in mitigating the evils of crises and depressions which now take them so often unawares.

Bimetallism

But while there is much to be hoped for from a greater foreknowledge of price changes, a lessening of the price changes themselves would be still more desirable. Various preventives of price changes have been proposed. We shall first consider those which are more particularly applicable to secular price changes, and afterwards consider those more particularly applicable to the price changes involved in credit cycles. The secular price changes are, as we have seen, chiefly due to changes in money and in trade.

There has been for centuries, and promises to be for centuries to come, a race between money and trade. On the results of that race depends to some extent the fate of every business man. The commercial world has become more and more committed to the gold standard through a series of historical events having little if any connection with the fitness of that or any other metal to serve as a stable standard.

So far as the question of monetary stability is concerned, it is not too much to say that we have hit upon the gold standard by accident just as we hit on the present railway gauge by the accident of previous custom as to road carriages; and just as we hit upon the decimal notation by the accident of having had ten fingers, and quite without reference to the question of numerical convenience in which other systems of numeration would be superior.

We have adopted a gold standard, it is almost as difficult to substitute another as it would be to establish the Russian railway gauge or the duodecimal system of numeration. And the fact that the question of a monetary standard is today so much an international question makes it all the more difficult. Yet, as Professor Shaler, the geologist, has said, "It seems likely that we shall, within a few decades, contrive some other means of measuring values than by the ancient device of balancing them against a substance of which the supply is excessive."

There is no immediate solution of this great world problem of finding a substitute for gold. Before a substitute for gold can be found, there must be much investigation and education of the public. The object here is to call attention to the necessity for this investigation and education, to examine such solutions as have been already proposed and, very tentatively, to make a suggestion which may possibly be acted upon at some future time, when, through the diffusion of knowledge, better statistics, and better government, the time shall become ripe.

One suggestion has been to readopt bimetallism. However, chiefly with the "mechanics of bimetallism" and not its influence on price levels. We have now to note the claim of advocates of a bimetallic standard that such a standard would tend to steady prices. As we have seen, by connecting the currencies of both gold and silver countries, bimetallism, as long as it continues in working order, has the effect of spreading any variation of one particular metal over the combined area of gold, silver, and bimetallic countries.

If variations occur simultaneously in both metals, they may be in opposite directions, and neutralise each other more or less completely; while, even if they happen to be in the same direction, the combined effect on the whole world united under bimetallism would be no greater than on the two halves of the world under silver and gold monometallism respectively.

Even if bimetallism did not enlarge the monetary area, it might reduce monetary fluctuations. Thus a world-wide gold standard might prove more variable than bimetallism. But if the amount of one metal used in coinage increases faster or more slowly than business, while the amount of the other maintains a constant ratio to business, then the use of the two metals results in less steadiness than would result from the less variable of the two, though in somewhat more steadiness than would result from the use of the more variable.

Two variable metals joined through bimetallism may be likened to two tipsy men locking arms. Together they walk somewhat more steadily than apart, although if one happens to be much more sober than the other, his own gait may be made worse by the union. In the seventeenth and nineteenth centuries the two metals were about equally unsteady. In the eighteenth century gold was the more steady. During the first half of the nineteenth century silver was the more steady, while for 1851-1890 gold was the more steady. Since then, silver has been the more steady. On the whole, there is not much to choose between the behaviours of the two.

Bimetallism, then, even could it be maintained, would offer but an indifferent remedy for the variations in the price level, and, moreover, there is always the objection previously noted that the system may break down. We then saw that whatever the ratio at which both metals are to circulate, one metal is likely, sometime, to be produced in such abundance as completely to fill the money reservoir, driving the other metal altogether out of circulation.

Such a result may be long in coming, but eventually it is practically sure to come.

A more important objection remains to be noted. Since bimetallism, as usually proposed, would greatly overvalue one of the two metals, the first great effect of its adoption might be not to steady prices but to disrupt them and upset the relation of debtor and creditor. While the great overvaluation of one metal is not a necessary feature of bimetallism, it has always been the feature which has made it politically popular.

Thus, the bimetallism advocated in the United States during the last twenty or thirty years has been a bimetallism which would grossly overvalue silver. It proposed that 16 ounces of silver should circulate as the equivalent of an ounce of gold, when during much of this time it really required 30 or 35 ounces of silver to be equivalent to one of gold.

Such an overvaluation of silver would mean that silver would be imported from Mexico, India, China, and other silver countries, as well as mined in larger quantities and coined in the United States, thus depreciating the currency both greatly and suddenly. The proposal was well satirised by a cartoon in the 'free silver' campaign of 1898 representing the United States as a ship sailing over Niagara Falls in order to reach smooth sailing below the falls,- if only it survive the shock of the fall!

Bimetallism is the only scheme of steadying the monetary standard which has ever secured political momentum; and even its popularity lay far less in its potency for ultimately steadying than in its potency for immediately unsteadying the standard. We now pass on to consider schemes which have never reached the stage of practical proposals, but are still wholly academic.

The first is polymetallism, a generalisation of bimetallism- The theory of bimetallism contemplates the circulation side by side of two metals; that of polymetallism looks to the contemporaneous circulation of more than two. So long as several metals could be maintained in circulation together, the price level might fluctuate less than if one metal only were used. But all of the theoretical objections against bimetallism apply also against polymetallism. One metal would eventually drive all the others out of a country, or,- if polymetallism were international, - into the arts.

Proposed Solution

Recognising the force of the arguments against bimetallism (and polymetallism), Professor Marshall has suggested as a substitute a system which has been called symmetallism. Under this scheme - symmetallism- two (or more) metals would be joined together physically in the same coin or in 'linked bars.' Evidently any ratio could be used, and neither metal could push the other out of circulation. The value of the composite coin would be the sum of the values of its two constituents, and the fluctuations in its value would be the mean of the fluctuations of its constituents.

Many other schemes for combining metals have been suggested. Among them are the 'joint-metallisms' of Stokes and Hertzka, which are kinds of bimetallism at a variable instead of at a fixed ratio. Another, advocated by Walras, is the gold standard with a 'silver regulator,' which is simply the limping standard such as now prevails in the United States, France, or India except that the quantity of silver in circulation, instead of being fixed, would be systematically manipulated by the government in such a manner as to keep prices steady. But these, like symmetallism and bimetallism, offer a remedy which at best is only partial.

In Walras's scheme, in order to maintain prices, the amount of silver might need to be reduced to zero - after which no further regulation would be possible; or it might need to be increased so far as to expel all gold, after which the system would be no longer a gold standard, but would become an inconvertible silver standard. Worst of all, every one of these proposed remedies would be subject to the danger of unwise or dishonest political manipulation.

It is true that the level of prices might be kept almost absolutely stable merely by honest government regulation of the money supply with that specific purpose in view. One seemingly simple way by which this might be attempted would be by the issue of inconvertible paper money in quantities so proportioned to increase of business that the total amount of currency in circulation, multiplied by its rapidity, would have the same relation to the total business at one time as at any other time.

If the confidence of citizens were preserved, and this relation were kept, the problem would need no further solution. But sad experience teaches that irredeemable paper money, while theoretically capable of steadying prices, is apt in practice to be so manipulated as to produce instability.

In nearly every country there exists a party, consisting of debtors and debtor-like classes, which favours depreciation. A movement is therefore at any time possible, tending to pervert any scheme for maintaining stability into a scheme for simple inflation. As soon as any particular government controls a paper currency bearing no relation to gold or silver, excuses for its over-issue are to be feared.

Even if, in times of peace, these persistent pleas for inflation could be resisted, it is doubtful if they could be resisted in time of war. In time of war many plausible defences can be given, notably the need of government supplies. The history of our own country in this respect is not reassuring. It is natural, therefore, that such schemes should have gotten in bad order. Indeed, their order has been so bad that many have impulsively concluded that the 'quantity theory' which has been appealed to as making possible government manipulation of prices must be fundamentally unsound. Experience has shown, however, that the evil feared need not always be realised.

Another method by means of which government could theoretically keep the price level more stable is by confining the primary money to a precious metal, say gold, and regulating the quantity of this metal in the currency by means of a system of seigniorage. Thus, as the supply of gold from the mines increased, and gold tended to depreciate in value, the value of gold coin could be kept up by making a continuously higher charge for coinage, in the shape of seigniorage.

This charge would become higher as gold bullion became cheaper, in such proportion as to keep the currency in the same relation with the volume of business, and thus to keep the level of prices stable. If, later, the annual production of gold should become very small, and gold, in consequence, should begin to appreciate in value, stability might be maintained by a reversal of this policy, i.e. by gradually reducing the seigniorage so as to prevent appreciation of the currency. There would, however, be a limit to the power to regulate in this direction similar to the limit we noted in the case of Walras's scheme. The seigniorage could never be reduced to less than zero. Money can never be materially cheaper than the metal composing it, since the slightest tendency in this direction will result in coin being exported or melted into bullion. In a period of rising prices, regulation would be easy; in a period of falling prices, regulation might be quite impossible.

Another plan is a convertible paper currency, the paper to be redeemable on demand, - not in any required weight or coin of gold, but in a required purchasing power thereof. Under such a plan, the paper money would be redeemed by as much gold as would have the required purchasing power. Thus, the amount of gold obtainable for a paper dollar would vary inversely with its purchasing power per ounce as compared with commodities, the total purchasing power of the dollar being always the same. The fact that a paper dollar would always be redeemable in terms of purchasing power would theoretically keep the level of prices invariable.

The supply of money in circulation would regulate itself automatically. Should money tend to increase fast enough to impair its purchasing power, the notes would be presented for redemption in gold; for under the arrangement assumed, the gold which would be given would always have the same purchasing power. Should the money tend to become scarce and thus to appreciate, the amount of gold having unchanged purchasing power would be exchanged for the notes.

It is true that this scheme, like a simple paper-money scheme, would be liable to abuse, - but it would have two practical advantages. Having a metallic basis, it would inspire more confidence than a pure paper-money plan, while it would offer less excuse for abuse and less chance to delude the public. Every change in the weight of the gold dollar would be definitely measurable, and would have to be justified to the public. A reduction in weight not fully explained by a fall in prices would be a clear confession of depreciation.

Tabular Standard

The next plan to be considered is that advocated by Professor Marshall and the Committee of the British Association. It is, in essence, the revival of the tabular standard proposed and discussed by Lowe, Scrope, Jevons, and others; a standard which is relatively independent of special legislation. This involves the passing of a law - first merely permissive - by which contracts could be expressed in terms of an index number. Such a law would not be necessary, but it might serve to draw attention to the index method. The money of the country would continue to be used as a medium of exchange and as a measure of value, but not as a standard for all deferred payments.

The standard of deferred payments, when advantage was taken of the law, would be the index number of general prices; and contracts involving deferred payment could, when desired, call for the exchange of a given purchasing power, or of an amount of money varying directly with the index number. To facilitate such a change, it might be well for the government to inaugurate an authorised system of index numbers, but government action would not have to go farther than this, or indeed, necessarily, so far. The aim would no longer be to keep the level of prices absolutely stable. Gold or silver or both would furnish the primary money, and their value would consequently fluctuate with that of the constituent metal or metals. But the contracts based on index numbers would not be affected because made in terms of the index number.

Doubtless the plan would encounter much opposition, but it would appeal strongly to certain classes. For instance, those 'living on their incomes' would like to be guaranteed a stable purchasing power. A widow, or a trustee, or other longtime investor, would prefer to buy bonds which guaranteed a regular yearly purchasing power over subsistence, rather than those which merely promised a given sum of money of uncertain value. A few precedents already exist, suggestive, at least, of what the new system would be. In England, the 'tithe averages' have been made to vary with the value of grain, so that the tithe was in effect so much grain, not so much money; also the Scotch fair prices have existed for more than two centuries for similar purposes, establishing the price of grain on the basis of which rents contracted in grain should be paid in money.

As has been already indicated, government action looking to this result need not necessarily be taken. The beginnings of such a plan for 'a tabular standard of value' could be made at any time by private contracting parties, some index number already in vogue, such as Sauerbeck's or the Bureau of Labour's, being used as a standard. Should the results of such experiments, on the whole, satisfy the contracting parties, others might follow their lead. At first contracts would be interpreted as having been made in terms of money except when otherwise provided. A specific proviso would therefore be required in contracts made in terms of the index number. If the latter form of contract should become more general, however, legislation could be passed, making the index number the standard in all cases, except where specifically provided that payment should be based on a different standard.

It is to be noted that such a custom, however general it might become, would not do away with the desirability of having an elastic currency to respond to seasonal variations of business. Seasonable readjustments of wages, for instance, and of many other prices, are difficult. Custom tends to establish standards holding through successive seasons. Since there is more business at some seasons than others, there will be an element of strain unless there is also an expansion of credit. An elastic banking system, facilitating credit-expansion, would, therefore, remain a desideratum.

Purchasing Power

The system of making contracts in terms of the price level is not intended directly to prevent fluctuations in price level. Its purpose is rather to prevent these fluctuations from introducing a speculative element into business. But an incidental result of the system would be that fluctuations in the level of prices would be less than before, because credit cycles would no longer be stimulated. The alternate abnormal encouragement and discouragement of loans would cease. Hence, credit fluctuations would become less, and the level of prices would be comparatively unaffected by them.

Even if panics should occur, accompanied by sharp falls of prices, they would not be as severe as now. At present, loans must be liquidated in terms of a given amount of money, though that money may buy more (or less) at the time of liquidation than when the loan was contracted, and though the borrower must dispose of more (or less) commodities to raise the given amount. He is compelled to pay, when prices have fallen, on the same basis in terms of money, and a much higher value in terms of goods, than when prices ranged higher. Hence failure often results, credit currency contracts still further because of the general distrust, and depression becomes more severe. With payment in terms of purchasing power, the situation would be altogether different. Falling prices would neither injure borrowers nor benefit lenders.

On the whole, the 'tabular standard' seems to have real merit. Certainly there could be no material harm in trying a 'permissive' law. But the tabular standard is subject to serious if not fatal objections: One is the fact that it would involve the trouble of translating money into the tabular standard and would therefore fail to attract the public sufficiently to warrant its complete adoption by any government. Another objection is that its halfway adoption would really aggravate many of the evils it sought to correct, and therefore discourage, rather than encourage, its further extension.

Even were the system adopted in its complete form for any one country, it would have the disadvantage of isolating that country commercially, and thus reintroducing the inconveniences of an uncertain rate of international exchange. An analogous inconvenience would arise by its partial adoption in any one country. Business men naturally and properly prefer a uniform system of accounts to two systems warring with each other. They would complain of such a double system of accounts in exactly the same way, and on exactly the same grounds, as they have always complained of the double system of accounts involved in international trade between gold and silver countries.

A business man's profits constitute a narrow margin between receipts and expenses. If receipts and expenses could both be reckoned in the tabular standard, his profits would be more stable than if both were reckoned in money. But if he should pay some of his expenses, such as interest and wages, on a tabular basis, while his receipts remained on the gold basis, his profits would fluctuate far more than if both sides, or all items of the accounts, were in gold.

In fact, Ms expected profits would often turn into losses by a slight deviation between the two standards, in precisely the same way as the importer or exporter of goods between China and the United States may have his profits wiped out by a slight variation in the exchange. In either ease, he would prefer to have the same standard on both sides of the account, even if this standard fluctuated, rather than have two standards, only one of which fluctuated; for his profits depend more on the parallelism between the two sides of his account than on the stability of either. It was to escape the evils from having two standards that, after lengthy debate and experiment, the gold-exchange standard was adopted.

Bibliography

Abel, Andrew; Bernanke, Ben: *Macroeconomics*, Pearson. 2005.

Annonymous: The Utility of Country Banks Considered, London, 1802.

Appleby, J. O.: *Economic Thought and Ideology in Seventeenth-Century England*, Princeton University Press, Princeton, 1978.

Barbon, N.: *Discourse Concerning Coining the New Money Lighter*, Pickering & Chatto, London, 1999.

Baumol, W. J., and A. S. Blinder: *Economics: Principles & Policy*, South- Western Cengage Learning, Mason, 2009.

Benston, G. J.: *Regulating Financial Markets: A Critique and Some Proposals*, American Enterprise Institute, Washington, 1999.

Bernstein, Peter: *A Primer on Money and Banking, and Gold*, Wiley, 2008.

Binney, J.E.D.: *British Finance and Public Administration, 1774-1792*, Clarendon Press, Oxford, 1958.

Bodin, J.: *Six Books of the Commonwealth*, Basil Blackwell, Oxford, 1955.

Bowen, H. V.: *The Bank of England: Money, Power and Influence 1694-1994*, Oxford University Press, Oxford, 1995.

Boyle, David: *The Little Money Book*, The Disinformation Company, 2006.

Brantlinger, P.: *Fictions of State: Culture and Credit in Britain, 1694-1994,* Cornell University Press, Ithaca, 1996.

Brewer, J.: *Sinews of Power: War, Money and the English State, 1688-1783,* Alfred A. Knopf, New York, 1989.

Briscoe, J.: *A Discourse of Money: Being an Essay on that Subject, Historically and Politically Handled, with Reflections on the Present Evil State of the Coin of this Kingdom, and Proposals of a Method for the Remedy, in a Letter to a Nobleman* in *Historical and Political Essays or Discourses on Several Subjects.* London, 1698.

Canney, M. and D. Knott: *Catalogue of the Goldsmith's Library of Economic Literature,* Cambridge University Press, Cambridge, 1995.

Carswell, J.: *The South Sea Bubble,* Cresset Press, London, 1960.

Caruthers, B.: *City of Capital: Politics and Markets in the English Financial Revolution,* Princeton University Press, Princeton, 1996.

Clapham, J. H.: *The Bank of England: A History,* The University Press, Cambridge, 1944.

D'Eprio, Peter & Pinkowish, Mary Desmond: *What Are The Seven Wonders Of The World?* First Anchor Books, 1998.

David Laidler: *Money and Macroeconomics: The Selected Essays of David Laidler (Economists of the Twentieth Century),* Edward Elgar Publishing, 1997.

Deardorff, Prof. Alan V.: *"Deardorff's Glossary of International Economics",* Department of Economics, University of Michigan, 2008.

Dickson, P. G. M.: *The Financial Revolution in England: A Study in the Development of Public Credit, 1688-1756,* St. Martins Press, Cambridge, 1967.

Dome, T.: *The Political Economy of Public Finance in Britain, 1767-1873,* Routledge, London, 2004.

Downie, J. A.: *Telling People What to Think: Early Eighteenth Century Periodicals from The Review to The Rambler,* Frank Cass, London, 1993.

Faure, E.: *Le Banqueroute de Law, 17 Juillet 1720,* Gallimard, Paris, 1977.

Feavearyear, A. E.: *The Pound Sterling: A History of English Money,* Oxford University Press, Oxford, 1931.

Finkelstein, A: *Harmony and the Balance: An Intellectual History of Seventeenth-Century English Economic Thought,* University of Michigan Press, Ann Arbor, 2000.

Furbank, P. N. and W. R. Owens: *The Canonisation of Daniel Defoe,* New Haven: Yale University Press, 1988.

Giuseppi, J.: *The Bank of England: A History from its Foundation in 1694,* Evans Brothers, London, 1966.

Goldin, H. E.: *Mishnah: A Digest of the Basic Principles of the Early Jewish Jurisprudence,* G. P. Putnams, New York, 1913.

Goux, J.J.: *Symbolic Economies: After Marx and Freud,* Cornell University Press, Ithaca, 1990.

Greenbaum, S. I., and A. V. Thakor: *Contemporary Financial Intermediation,* Elsevier, Burlington, 2007.

Hargreaves, E.L.: *The National Debt,* Edward Arnold, London, 1930.

Harris, E.: *The Reception of Locke's Politics,* Pickering & Chatto, London, 1999.

Harris, M.: *London Newspapers in the Age of Walpole: A Study of the Origins of the Modern English Press,* Associated University Presses, London, 1987.

Harrison, J.: *The Library of Isaac Newton,* Cambridge University Press, Cambridge, 1978.

Hartley, D.: *Considerations on the Proposed Renewal of the Bank Charter,* London, 1781.

Hodges, J.: *The Present State of England, as to Coin and Publick Charges,* London, 1697.

Hollis, C.: *The Two Nations: A Financial Study of English History,* Routledge, London, 2006.

Hoppit, J.: *The Political Economy of British Historical Experience, 1688-1914,* Oxford University Press/British Academy, Oxford, 2002.

Horsefield, J. K.: *British Monetary Experiments, 1650-1710,* Cambridge University Press, Cambridge, 1960.

Hoxby, B.: *Mammon's Music: Literature and Economics in the Age of Milton.* New Haven: Yale University Press, 2002.

Hutchinson, T.: *Before Adam Smith: The Emergence of Political Economy, 1662-1776.* Oxford: Basil Blackwell, 1988.

Ingrassia, C.: *Authorship, Commerce and Gender in Early Eighteenth Century England: A Culture of Paper Credit,* Cambridge University Press, Cambridge, 1998.

Jevons, William Stanley: "XVI: Representative Money".*Money and the Mechanism of Exchange.* 1875.

Jones, C.: *The Great Nation: France from Louis XV to Napoleon,* Penguin, London, 2003.

Keirn, T.: *Early Modern Conceptions of Property,* Routledge, London, 1995.

Kelly, P. H.: *Introduction to Locke on Money,* Clarendon Press, Oxford, 1991.

Kramnick, I.: *Bolingbroke and His Circle: The Politics of Nostalgia in the Age of Walpole,* Harvard University Press, Cambridge, 1968.

Krugman, Paul & Wells, Robin: *Economics,* Worth Publishers, New York, 2006.

Latouche, R.: *The Birth of Western Economy: Economic Aspects of the Dark Ages,* Methuen, London, 1961.

Law, J.: *Money and Trade Considered with a Proposal for Supplying the Nation with Money,* Edinburgh, 1705.

Lawson, W. J.: *The History of Banking.* London, 1855.

Levenson, T.: *Newton and the Counterfeiter: The Unknown Detective Career of the World's Greatest Scientist,* Houghton Mifflin Harcourt, Boston, 2009.

Locke, J.: *Locke on Money,* Clarendon Press, Oxford, 1991.

Lowndes, W.: *A Report Containing an Essay for the Amendment of the Silver Coins,* London, 1695.

Macaulay, T. B.: *The History of England, from the Accession of James the Second,* London, 1855.

Mankiw, G.: *Principles of Economics,* South-Western Cengage Learning, Mason, 2008.

Mankiw, N. Gregory: *Macroeconomics,* Worth Publishers, New York, 2007.

Martin, J. B.: *'The Grasshopper' in Lombard Street,* London, 1892.

Milton Friedman, Anna Jacobson Schwartz: *Monetary History of the United States, 1867–1960,* Princeton University Press, N.J., 1971.

Mishkin, Frederic S.: *The Economics of Money, Banking, and Financial Markets,* Addison Wesley. Boston, 2009.

Murphy, A. E.: *John Law: Economic Theorist and Policy Maker,* Oxford University Press, Oxford, 1997.

Nicholson, C.: *Writing and the Rise of Finance: Capital Satires of the Early Eighteenth Century.* Cambridge: Cambridge University Press, 1994.

North, D.: *Discourses upon Trade; Principally Directed to the Cases of the Interest, Coyning, Clipping, Increase of Money,* London, 1691.

Roll, E.: *A History of Economic Thought,* Faber and Faber, London, 1992.

Rothbard, M.: *In Search of a Monetary Constitution*, Harvard University Press, Cambridge, 1962.

Schabas, M.: *The Natural Origins of Economics*. University of Chicago Press, Chicago, 2005.

Schumpeter, J.: *History of Economic Analysis*, Allen and Unwin, London, 1954.

Spaulding, W. F.: *The London Money Market*, Sir Isaac Pitman & Sons, London, 1922.

Sullivan, Arthur; Steven M. Sheffrin: *Economics: Principles in action*, Pearson Prentice Hall, New Jersey, 2003.

T.H. Greco: *Money: Understanding and Creating Alternatives to Legal Tender*, Chelsea Green Publishing, White River Junction, 2001.

Thompson, J.: *Models of Value: Eighteenth-Century Political Economy and the Novel*, Duke University Press, Durham, 1996.

Woodmansee, M. and M. Osteen: *The New Economic Criticism: Studies at the Intersection of Literature and Economics*, Routledge, London, 1999.

Zwicker, S. N.: *Lines of Authority: Politics and English Literary Culture, 1649-1689*, Cornell University Press, Ithaca, 1993.

Index

A

American Paper Money, 106.

B

Bad Money, 239, 240, 242, 260.

Bank, 1, 7, 9, 10, 11, 12, 16, 24, 27, 28, 50, 51, 52, 53, 54, 55, 56, 57, 58, 59, 61, 62, 63, 65, 66, 67, 68, 69, 70, 71, 72, 73, 74, 75, 76, 77, 78, 79, 80, 81, 82, 84, 88, 94, 95, 101, 103, 104, 106, 108, 114, 115, 116, 117, 120, 122, 123, 124, 130, 146, 156, 160, 161, 162, 163, 166, 174, 220, 221, 222, 232, 233, 234, 236, 247, 249, 254, 256, 263, 265, 266, 267, 268, 269, 270, 271, 272, 273, 276, 280, 281, 282, 284, 287.

Bank Account, 146, 270, 271.

Bank Deposits, 9, 101, 114, 120, 122, 123, 124, 163, 220, 263, 265, 266, 271, 272, 273.

Bank Money, 1, 10, 161.

Bank Notes, 27, 28, 94, 106, 123, 130, 174, 266, 270.

Barter, 3, 5, 7, 8, 12, 19, 21, 32, 75, 102, 108, 124, 127, 128, 129, 157, 159, 172, 173, 174, 183, 192, 195, 200, 283.

Bell, 59, 202, 214.

Bimetallism, 96, 97, 99, 261, 262, 263, 290, 292, 293, 294.

Buddhism, 203.

Business Loans, 274.

C

Capital, 12, 18, 53, 58, 77, 129, 133, 159, 162, 164, 170, 174, 187, 188, 196, 200, 243, 244, 245, 246, 247, 248, 249, 250, 251, 252, 253, 254, 255, 256, 257, 266, 281, 286.

Cash Nexus, 31, 32, 36, 38, 40, 41, 44, 45, 47, 50, 55, 228, 229, 242.

Centralised Systems, 220.

Circulating Media, 99, 100, 101, 109, 120, 122, 124.

Commodity Money, 1, 3, 7, 8, 9, 10, 20, 21, 22, 30, 129, 138, 174, 196.

Communist System, 146.

Confederate Paper Money, 112.

Credit Cycle, 117, 282, 284, 285.

Credit Finance, 225, 242.

Credit Restriction, 50, 71.

Crises, 84, 113, 114, 115, 116, 117, 119, 120, 274, 281, 287, 290.

Currency, 1, 3, 4, 6, 7, 9, 10, 11, 12, 21, 22, 23, 28, 29, 30, 31, 32, 48, 54, 55, 57, 68, 69, 76, 94, 95, 101, 103, 105, 106, 108, 109, 110, 111, 112, 113, 114, 116, 117, 118, 119, 122, 139, 147, 161, 163, 183, 198, 202, 219, 220, 221, 222, 223, 227, 234, 235, 237, 239, 240, 262, 263, 264, 265, 266, 270, 271, 276, 277, 278, 279, 280, 281, 283, 284, 285, 286, 293, 295, 296, 299.

D

Decision-maker, 145.

Demand, 6, 7, 10, 13, 21, 27, 29, 46, 53, 54, 69, 76, 78, 87, 114, 123, 133, 158, 162, 166, 180, 182, 189, 230, 231, 232, 235, 237, 244, 251, 252, 255, 261, 263, 265, 268, 270, 280, 281, 284, 286, 296.

Demand Deposits, 6, 7, 10, 27, 29.

Deposit Currency, 94, 113, 114, 117, 118, 119, 265, 266, 270, 271,

Index

276, 277, 279, 280, 283, 284, 286.

Disturbance of Equation, 273.

E

e-Money, 219, 221, 223.

Economy, 1, 3, 6, 7, 11, 12, 19, 20, 51, 63, 73, 75, 126, 130, 137, 144, 146, 147, 153, 154, 156, 158, 159, 160, 161, 164, 165, 166, 171, 183, 195, 196, 197, 198, 199, 200, 201, 202, 211, 219, 233, 249, 251, 259, 260.

Education, 131, 133, 134, 135, 139, 140, 167, 170, 175, 176, 177, 178, 180, 181, 187, 188, 189, 191, 193, 215, 291.

Electronic Money Systems, 219, 220, 221.

Exchange, 1, 3, 4, 5, 6, 8, 9, 12, 13, 14, 16, 17, 18, 19, 20, 22, 24, 25, 26, 29, 32, 33, 56, 66, 83, 85, 87, 99, 102, 103, 106, 110, 111, 119, 120, 121, 122, 123, 124, 127, 128, 130, 132, 137, 139, 141, 142, 147, 149, 154, 155, 156, 157, 158, 159, 160, 162, 163, 165, 166, 170, 172, 173, 181, 183, 186, 191, 192, 195, 196, 197, 198, 200, 201, 202, 220, 221, 222, 223, 226, 227, 228, 229, 232, 237, 247, 249, 250, 251, 252, 256, 257, 258, 260, 261, 264, 265, 268, 269, 271, 273, 275, 279, 285, 288, 290, 297, 298, 300.

F

Fiat Money, 1, 7, 9, 10, 11, 30, 31, 130, 175.

Finance, 41, 50, 69, 76, 79, 80, 81, 82, 83, 84, 89, 159, 162, 164, 205, 207, 210, 212, 217, 225, 234, 235, 236, 237, 240, 241, 242, 249, 250, 251, 252, 254, 255.

Financial Thraldom, 71.

Funny Money, 160.

G

Gift Economy, 20, 195, 196, 197, 198, 199, 200, 201, 202.

Gold Exchange Standard, 261.
Gold-backed Banknotes, 28.
Goldsmith Bankers, 26.
Greenbacks, 108, 109, 110, 111, 112, 124, 290.
Gresham's Law, 239, 241, 261, 263.

H

Helicopter Money, 164.
Hierarchical Society, 145.
Hinduism, 203.
Hyde, 196, 197, 199, 200, 201.

I

Interest Rate, 12, 143, 144, 148, 156, 277, 280, 281, 283.
Internet, 147, 168, 180, 181, 182, 183, 185, 186, 187, 188, 189, 190, 191, 192, 193, 194, 213, 214, 219, 222, 223.
Islam, 202.

J

Judaism, 202.

K

Kropotkin, 201.

L

Limited Liability, 71, 77, 78, 79, 255.

M

Making Purchasing Power, 287.
Market Liquidity, 7.
Mexico, 90, 96, 100, 121, 198, 227, 293.
Monetary Policy, 11, 12, 154.
Monetary Systems, 7, 11, 259.
Money, 1, 2, 3, 4, 5, 6, 7, 8, 9, 10, 11, 12, 13, 14, 16, 17, 18, 20, 21, 22, 23, 24, 25, 26, 27, 28, 30, 31, 32, 33, 36, 37, 45, 46, 47, 48, 49, 50, 51, 52, 53, 54, 55, 85, 90, 91, 92, 95, 97, 98, 100, 102, 106, 107, 108, 109, 110, 111, 112, 113, 114, 115, 116, 117, 118, 119, 121, 123, 124, 125, 126, 127, 128, 129, 130, 131, 132, 133, 134, 136, 137, 138, 139, 140, 141, 142, 143, 144, 145, 146, 147, 148, 149, 150, 151, 153, 154, 155, 156, 157,

Index 311

158, 159, 160, 161, 162, 163, 164, 165, 166, 167, 168, 171, 172, 173, 174, 175, 181, 182, 183, 189, 194, 195, 196, 197, 200, 201, 205, 206, 208, 209, 210, 211, 213, 214, 215, 216, 217, 219, 220, 221, 222, 223, 225, 226, 227, 228, 229, 230, 231, 234, 238, 239, 240, 241, 242, 244, 245, 246, 247, 248, 252, 255, 259, 260, 261, 262, 263, 264, 265, 266, 267, 268, 269, 270, 271, 272, 273, 274, 275, 276, 277, 278, 279, 280, 281, 283, 284, 285, 286, 287, 288, 289, 290, 291, 293, 296, 297, 298, 299, 300.

Money Mechanism, 259.

Money on Demand, 270.

Money Reservoir, 262, 263, 293.

Money Rule, 2.

Money Supply, 1, 6, 7, 9, 10, 11, 12, 31, 119, 160, 161, 162, 163, 164, 165, 295.

Money Systems, 1, 10, 219, 220, 221.

Most Exchangeable Commodity, 227, 251, 252.

N

Native Americans, 198.

O

Off-line Anonymous Systems, 221.

Open-source Software, 199.

Organisation, 37, 40, 127, 131, 132, 133, 134, 136, 137, 138, 139, 140, 141, 144, 145, 167, 168, 169, 170, 171, 172, 175, 176, 179, 180, 181, 182, 184, 185, 186, 187, 188, 192, 193, 194, 195, 206, 208, 209.

P

Pacific Islanders, 197, 249.

Paper Money, 3, 11, 28, 101, 102, 103, 104, 106, 107, 108, 110, 111, 112, 113, 120, 124, 222, 234, 240, 261, 263, 264, 295, 296.

Papua New Guinea, 198.

Particular Crisis, 115.

Political Reform, 208.

Population Growth, 168, 169, 180.

Possible Reason, 205.

Practical Life, 125.

Purchasing Power, 7, 110, 118, 120, 124, 158, 160, 259, 262, 265, 273, 274, 275, 279, 281, 283, 286, 287, 288, 289, 290, 296, 297, 298, 299.

Q

Quantity of Money, 90, 93, 111, 119, 120, 124, 163, 252, 270, 271, 272, 273, 277, 285, 287, 288.

R

Representative Money, 3, 8, 28, 30.

S

Shadow Money, 162, 163, 164, 165.

Soft Electronic Currencies, 221.

Soft Money, 208, 209.

Standard of Deferred Payment, 1, 4, 5, 6.

Standardised Coinage, 22.

Statistical Verification, 90.

Store Value, 6.

T

Tabular Standard, 297, 298, 300.

Technology, 134, 138, 164, 175, 178, 179, 180, 181, 184, 185, 187.

Trade Bills of Exchange, 24.

U

Unit of Account, 1, 4, 5, 8, 137.

Urbanisation, 128, 168, 171, 173, 182, 183.

V

Velocity of Deposits, 117.

W

Weakness of Money, 148.

❑❑❑

www.ingramcontent.com/pod-product-compliance
Lightning Source LLC
Chambersburg PA
CBHW050838230426
43667CB00012B/2051